YEAR

OF

WONDER

About the Author

Clemency Burton-Hill was born in London. An author, broadcaster and journalist, she presents the *Breakfast* show on BBC Radio 3 as well as the Proms, BBC Young Musician and New Generation Artists. She has hosted numerous television and radio programmes, including Radio 4's *Front Row*, BBC 2's *The Culture Show* and BBC 4's *The Review Show*, and across the Atlantic has also worked as a journalist and broadcaster for New York's WQXR and the *Wall Street Journal*. She has authored documentaries on women's rights, music, technology and creativity, and regularly hosts live events and interviews from leading arts venues and festivals around the world.

Clemency is the music columnist for BBC Culture and has written on a range of subjects, from the arts to artificial intelligence, for the *Economist*, *FT Weekend* magazine, the *Telegraph*, *Guardian*, *Observer* and *Independent*. She is the author of two novels published by Headline Review: *The Other Side of the Stars* (2009) and *All the Things You Are* (2013).

An award-winning violinist, Clemency has performed as a soloist, chamber musician and orchestral player in some of the world's greatest concert halls, including Milan's La Scala and Vienna's Musikverein, under conductors including Daniel Barenboim.

She lives in north-west London with her family.

About the Music

Discover and Share the Year of Wonder Playlists on Apple Music:
www.applemusic.com/yearofwonder

CLASSICAL MUSIC TO ENJOY
DAY BY DAY

—

YEAR

OF

WONDER

—

CLEMENCY BURTON-HILL

HARPER

An Imprint of HarperCollins*Publishers*

For James, with love

HarperCollins books may be purchased for educational, business, or sales promotional use. For information, please email the Special Markets Department at SPsales@harpercollins.com.

First published in Great Britain in 2017 by Headline Home, an imprint of Headline Publishing Group.

FIRST U.S. EDITION

All chapter openers: manuscript score of the violoncello part of the B-Minor Mass by J. S. Bach. Dresden, Sächsische Landesbibliothek – Staats und Universitäts-bibliothek, D-Dl Mus.2405-D-21. Photo: Alfredo Dagli Orti/REX/Shutterstock.

Library of Congress Cataloging-in-Publication Data has been applied for.

ISBN: 978-0-06-285620-3

19 20 21 22 23 LSC 10 9 8 7 6 5 4 3

Contents

Introduction

We are a music-making species – always have been, always will be – and music's capacity to explore, express and address what it is to be human remains one of our greatest communal gifts. We are also a music-exchanging species: people have used music to communicate and connect with one another since the beginning of time. I'm lucky enough to have had classical music in my life since I was little, and now, as an adult, I have the good fortune of doing a job that involves sharing it with others. One of the many joys of presenting the BBC Radio 3 *Breakfast* show is hearing how the music we play enriches people's daily lives. I can't tell you how cheering it is when a listener gets in touch to say something along the lines of, 'Wow, that piece has really set me up for my day.' And it works both ways: I feel equally grateful when a listener recommends something wonderful that I've never previously heard. (Gratitude that's often accompanied by mild outrage that I've existed so many years without it; like meeting your best friend late in life.) This form of cultural exchange goes back millennia: as human beings we evolved by coming together around the fire every night, singing songs and telling stories – invariably, telling stories *through* singing songs. That's what our ancestors did; that's how they made sense of the world and each other; that's how they learned how to be.

It is an impulse that is still fundamental to who we are. Yet our own modern lives are frazzled and fragmented to an unprecedented degree; most of us probably feel a million miles away from that quotidian fireside jam session. Who, seriously, has the luxury of taking time out each day to listen to *music*? What about the piles of undone laundry, the inboxes of unanswered emails, the dishwashers of unloaded plates? Seriously? Perhaps, though, we have never needed it more, this space to think and reflect and connect and just *be*. This book is in part about exploring what happens when we open up our lives to let such music in. Scientific research is increasingly proving that regular acts of 'self-care' (stay with me!) can have untold benefits on our mental health and spiritual well-being; and while personally I've never been able to get the hang of, say, regular meditation or yoga, I hear others extol the virtues of these daily rituals and I realize they echo my belief about the way music can work on us. How it can act as a powerful mental tonic that can inexplicably but undeniably set you on the path to a better day or night. How a daily dose of such music can be a form of sonic soul maintenance.

'Daily dose', though. 'Virtues', though . . . I am wary of the sense of obligation these words conjure. I don't believe we 'should' listen to certain things just because someone has told us we 'should'. We live in times whereby on the one hand, classical music is being ever more marginalized by mainstream culture, yet on the other, there exists this vague cultural awareness that we 'should' listen to it because it will somehow make us more intelligent, more refined, more civilized. This is not helpful. Nor is the cause of classical music served by those who assume that it is 'superior' to other types of music – which is just plain wrong – or those who, deep down, believe it must remain the preserve of people with certain backgrounds, educations or skin colours – which is opportunity-hoarding at its most lazy and repellent. Amid these conflicting messages, which are connected to even bigger questions around class, education policy and our ever-shifting media landscape, we have somehow lost sight of what's at the centre of it: the music itself. Music that is full of things that may dazzle or move or energize or calm you; music that may make you cry or think or laugh or gasp; music that may teach you things, make you question things, make you wonder. Music that is now available to ever more of us, in vast quantities and for the first time in history, at the click of a button – but which may still remain off-limits to all but a handful of the ultra-initiated.

So, know this: what lies ahead is not some white girl with a posh name telling you that you 'should' listen to classical music every day in order to somehow become a better, smarter or more classy person. I have no interest in making you feel ashamed because you have never heard of some of these composers or their music – why on earth *should* you have done? Nor am I trying to stealthily replace your *Real House-wives* or *Love Island* habit, or whatever else you might be into, with this stuff. You do you: there is no reason why classical music can't happily coexist in a mixed cultural diet.

What I *am* determined to do, though, is to extend a hand to those who feel that the world of classical music is a party to which they haven't been invited. I want to open up this vast treasury of musical riches by suggesting a single piece to listen to every day of the year: by giving it some context, telling some stories about the people behind it, and reminding you that it was created by a real person – probably someone who shared many of the same concerns as you, who wished to express themselves and happened to do so through this particular sequence of musical notes. It's really important to remember that music does not exist in a vacuum: it requires listeners, audiences, witnesses in order to come alive; to be heard, to be felt. *And that's you!*

Classical composers are no different from other writers of music, or any creative artist: all they are doing, in their own way, is seeking to get down on paper something they think and feel – which in turn makes others think and feel. It's an exercise in human connection – and generosity – that might seem complex on the page when you look at all those black notes, but comes down to something exquisitely simple. Nobody sets out to write music that's unintelligible or inaccessible; nobody writes music with the intention that it will never get off the page, or hopes that it will alienate all but the tiniest coterie of dedicated experts. Music's very *raison d'être* is to be brought to life,

3

to be experienced in time, to be *listened to*. In other words, these composers want to talk to you. And whatever your immediate emotional response is to what they say, that is valid, irrespective of whether you've ever had a piano lesson or know your 'portamento' from your 'obbligato' (exactly). As intellectually stimulating as it is for some listeners and experts to dig deeper and learn more about a work or a composer or a style or a technique, there is no such thing as 'getting classical music wrong'. You're human? You have ears? It's yours. It's there for the taking. Welcome.

My objective is to empower you to know that this music, so often kept behind seemingly insuperable barriers by those who wish to protect it for the exclusive pleasure of a tiny minority, is yours to engage with and respond to on your own terms – just as you would any other genre.

Music, which extends across cultures and boundaries, which requires no translation to be understood, is the most uniting language we have. I have witnessed this first hand, working with musicians in the Middle East, Africa, Asia, Latin America and Europe and have been repeatedly awed by the ability that music has to bring disparate, 'different' people together. Just as people are people, made of the same essential stuff, all music is created with the same sonic DNA, the same tonal building blocks, those miraculous vibrations of air that can be shaped in myriad ways to become a Bach cantata here, a Beyoncé chart-topper there.

This is why the labels that are ascribed to music are so unhelpful. 'Popular' music is surely just music that lots of people like to listen to; there is no reason why so-called 'classical' music shouldn't fit into that category too.

∾·

Year of Wonder expands on ideas and passions that have been building inside me for decades, but it finally came into being because I was losing track of the number of friends, family members and even

4

complete strangers who were asking, often sheepishly, if I might be able to make them a classical playlist. Sometimes it was a specific request: music to study to, perhaps, or to work to; music to soothe their newborn babies or fall asleep to or to impress their new partner's parents with; music to exercise to; to unwind to; to garden, commute or throw a dinner party to. The guy who runs my local coffee shop asked me to curate him a classical soundtrack for the late-afternoon/ early-evening shift. My teenage niece was after something to help her through her exam revision. And so on. Most often, what I heard from these playlist-hunters was something along the lines of: 'I heard a piece of what I *think* might be classical music on a TV programme/ film/radio show/online/advert, and I loved it. I don't know anything about classical music, but I'd like to hear some more *and I have no idea where to start . . .*'

I am all about people being able to hear more, but that question of 'where to start' is critical. Technology has opened up this world as never before: what many of us have at our digital fingertips, at least in developed societies, would have been unimaginable to humans before us; for most of history the only way to experience music was to somehow find a way to hear it performed live and get yourself there in person. As we'll see in the book, that might mean walking 250 miles, uphill, in the snow, in winter. (Hats off, J. S. Bach.) As with practically every other industry you could care to name, technology has disrupted the music world in both positive and negative ways. It's true that the decimation of traditional financial models is generally leaving artists and labels less well off than they were in the golden age of the record industry, when even classical stars such as Leonard Bernstein or Yehudi Menuhin, Luciano Pavarotti or Maria Callas could command eye-watering amounts per album and expect to shift millions of physical units. But on another level, the technological revolution of the past decade and in particular the emergence of legal music-streaming platforms has blown open the door to that previously exclusive party in a thrilling and democratizing way. Now anyone with a half-decent internet connection can delve into a world that was previously restricted to those who already knew what they were looking for and had the resources to pay for it.

But the sheer volume of what is now available for free at the click of a button can be daunting, if not paralyzing. That's where this book and its accompanying digital playlists come in. *Year of Wonder* is not in any way intended to be an exhaustive encyclopedia of the classical canon: there are plenty of famous composers who haven't made it in. Nor is it a 'guide' in any technical or musicological sense. I hope you'll emerge with a pretty good idea of how the forms and preoccupations of classical music evolved through the Medieval, Renaissance, Baroque, Classical, Romantic and Modernist eras. I also hope you'll have a sense of some of the connections that can be made across space and time: the history of classical music, like other arts, is one of imitation and emulation and adoration, so I've tried to illuminate hands outstretched across generations and genres; a sonic wink here, a wave there. I sincerely hope to demystify both the music itself and the context in which it was written. But I'm afraid you won't come out the other end knowing how to figure a bass, say, or compose a fugue. (Sorry-not-sorry.)

Instead, this is very much a hand-curated treasury of music that I dearly love and which I hope will enhance your daily life as it has mine. I've deep-dived a thousand years of classical music and come up with 366 works by more than 240 composers, from the medievalist Hildegard of Bingen, a badass-sounding twelfth-century philosopher, scientist, writer and musical mystic, to the millennial Alissa Firsova, who was born in 1986 and writes beautiful music that reflects her concerns as a politically engaged young woman in the twenty-first century. As well as over forty women, so often written out of the history of classical music, you'll meet composers of colour, gay and transgender composers, and differently abled composers (Beethoven, after all, wrote some of his most magnificent works when fully deaf). And although classical music is often perceived as a creaky old museum of dead white European males, you'll meet dozens of contemporary composers, from octogenarians to millennials. I hope you'll come away from this collection believing, as I do, that classical music is very much a living, breathing, diverse, vibrant and defiantly global art form. Truly all of human life is here.

Without wanting to sound crazy, I believe that music holds the mystery of being alive. These pieces, some of which are just a few minutes long, can do so much with so little. They become friends, they become teachers, they become magic carpets. I feel, in the company of the greatest music, recognized, seen, held. Engines of empathy, they allow us to travel without moving into other lives, other ages, other souls.

And – speaking of souls – throughout history, many of our finest classical composers were employed first and foremost by the church; many composed specifically to the glory of God. As such, you'll find a lot of sacred music here. As someone who identifies as a confused agnostic at best, I have occasionally battled with my intensely emotional (even physiological) reaction to such music, especially that of Bach, when I can't justify it on grounds of faith. I have been fortunate to be able to have conversations with many who are deeply engaged with these questions and who have helped me to reconcile my position. Our own interpretations of such music – music which often seems to throw open a window to the divine – are valid. We all have our spiritual touchstones: to be human is to be awe-inspirable. We do not remain indifferent to certain experiences – watching a child be born, a parent die, an ocean at night, a sky full of stars. We all have a need for enchantment, a capacity for awe, a hunger for wonder. For people of all faiths or none, this music can contain all of that and more.

And so: our *Year of Wonder* begins with some liturgical Bach on 1 January and ends with some Straussian champagne on 31 December. I hope you will treat the book as a sort of sonic field guide through your year (any year), dipping in every day, but it goes without saying that these pieces can be enjoyed at any time, on any date, over and over again. And I hope you won't feel obliged, just because it's 'classical music', to listen in some sort of overly reverent setting: lights down, hushed silence, wearing your Sunday best. By all means create your own active listening ritual if you find that enhances your experience of the piece of the day, but trust me, these works are robust: in many cases they've lasted hundreds of years; they can handle you multitasking all around them, fitting them into your real life. So download them onto your phone and listen on your commute; take them with you to the gym; stick them on in the background while you hustle your kids' breakfast before school; make them your soundtrack to fixing dinner, pouring a drink, putting your feet up, or indeed doing the washing, ironing, or catching up with emails; whatever it is you need to do at the moment where you finally get to press play. I believe there is very little in life that this music can't beautifully complement. And I hope, above all, that you will make these pieces yours. For know this: whoever you are, wherever you come from and however you got here, they belong to you.

JANUARY

1 January

Mass in B minor, BWV 232
3: Sanctus
by Johann Sebastian Bach (1685–1750)

We may as well start the year as we mean to go on.

The music of Johann Sebastian Bach is going to feature a lot over the next twelve months. That's because he is arguably the most important figure in not just classical but *all* music: his influence is as keenly felt in music today as it ever was.

Bach's brain was clearly some kind of supercomputer: he wrote at least three thousand pieces whilst holding down a number of jobs, a couple of wives and twenty children. Curious about the music coming out of Italy and France as well as his native Germany, he was able to absorb everything, synthesize the most interesting bits and then – crucially – add his own secret sauce. The essence of what makes Bach the greatest eludes words, but it lies, I think, in the way he combines technical precision with socking great emotion. People often describe Bach as 'mathematical' because of the complex, intricate patterns in his music. But he is not clinical or scientific: as a human being he knew intense joy but also wild grief, and there's never been a composer or songwriter more attuned to the vagaries of the human heart.

Bach was the daddy: without him there'd be no jazz, funk or hip-hop; no techno, no house, no grime. He basically wrote the blueprint for everything that was to come. His stuff is wise and witty and capacious enough to contain more than just multitudes: it contains all of everything.

And so on this first day of a new adventure, let us begin with a great big drumbeat and a choir singing their hearts out. Irrespective of your religious leanings, whoever you are, wherever you come from, this is five or so minutes of music to gladden the heart and lift the soul and say: 'Come on then, new year, let's be having you.'

2 January

Étude in C major, op. 10 no. 1
by Frédéric Chopin (1810–1849)

The Warsaw-born, Paris-based pianist and composer Frédéric Chopin was one of classical music's early superstars and a phenomenally original music thinker, especially when it came to his own instrument. In over 230 surviving works, all of which involve the piano, he expanded the range and the repertoire of what the keyboard could do and devised many new musical forms.

This glittering little study was supposed to be a means of developing the technique of piano students: the music demands outlandishly wide stretches (especially for the right hand) that would have been considered extremely daring in the early nineteenth century. But it's so much more than a glorified homework exercise. Chopin revered the music of Bach and Mozart, and in this mini-masterwork of melodic inventiveness and harmonic richness he shows his debt to both.

It can be a funny old day, 2 January, and sometimes a bit anti-climactic, but this two-minute piece seems to me to encapsulate all the promise of a new year – with its attendant hopes and dreams, discoveries, resolutions and potential revolutions . . .

3 January

O virtus sapientiae
by Hildegard of Bingen (c. 1098–1179)

Women have been multitasking since at least the medieval era. One of the first identifiable composers in Western music, Hildegard of Bingen was a nun, a writer, a scientist, a philosopher, a prophet and a Christian visionary. She founded and led two monasteries. Her prolific texts range from the theological to the botanical, and she was also considered an expert in medicinal cures. (Many years later, early feminists used her reputation as a health writer and healer to argue for the right of women to attend medical schools.) In her day, the polymathic Hildegard was a well-respected public preacher, touring Europe, and a wordmonger extraordinaire. She wrote some four hundred surviving letters as well as songs, poems and plays, including *Ordo virtutum*, probably the world's earliest morality play. In her spare time, Hildegard supervised the creation of illuminated manuscripts, made up a new alphabet and language known as the *Lingua Ignota* – which scholars believe was intended to increase solidarity among her nuns – and became regarded as the founder of scientific history in Germany.

Somehow, this remarkable human also found the time to compose at least seventy pieces of music, most with their own original poetic texts. Writing in a 'monophonic' style – we'll come to 'polyphony' soon – she creates these soaring melodies for her nuns to sing that rise heavenward out of a spare, single line. Her music must have been particularly consoling to sing given the violence and uncertainty of the medieval era.

Perhaps that's why it still feels so resonant. This would be vibrant and unusual music if it were written in any era; that it was written almost a thousand years ago, and by a very busy nun, only heightens the wonder.

4 January

String Quartet no. 13 in B flat major, op. 130
5: Cavatina: Adagio molto espressivo
by Ludwig van Beethoven (1770–1827)

One of classical music's most complex minds, Beethoven bequeathed us symphonies, choral works, instrumental concertos, chamber music and sonatas that rank among the very finest ever written. And then, towards the end of a sometimes troubled life, he wrote a group of string quartets (for two violins, viola and cello) that took this genre of 'chamber music' – indeed *all* music – into a new realm. With their form, their ideas and the heady sound world they weave, these pieces sent musicians and audiences into rhapsodies. Nothing had ever been heard like this before. Beethoven was coming up with music, as the Romantic composer Robert Schumann would later put it, that contains '*a grandeur which no words can express ... [standing] on the extreme boundary of all that has hitherto been attained by human art and imagination*'.

It seems fitting, then, that this movement was included as the final piece on the Voyager Golden Record, the phonograph that was sent into outer space in 1977 to provide a representative range of the sounds, languages and music of planet Earth in case of any meaningful future encounter with extra-terrestrial life. (The Voyager 1 probe entered interstellar space in 2012; Voyager 2 is expected to do so around 2019 or 2020.)

Beethoven's ethereally expressive Cavatina already feels like music that gets to the places other works could never reach. Beethoven was fully deaf by now and seems to be pushing at the boundaries of what can be expressed through music – what can be *heard*. To my mind, the Cavatina explores in a little over six short minutes the profoundest rhetorical questions about human frailty and folly, life and love. In seeking these answers, it reaches a sort of exalted transcendence.

I sure hope the aliens have a decent record player.

5 January

Crucifixus
by Antonio Lotti (c. 1667–1740)

Speaking of transcendence . . .

Antonio Lotti, who was born and died on this day, was a contemporary of J. S. Bach, but curiously his music sounds as though he was writing for a bygone age; it feels closer in spirit to the Renaissance. His setting here of these lines from the Crucifixus – '*He was crucified also for us under Pontius Pilate. He suffered and was buried*' – is an outstanding example of what is known as 'polyphony', meaning a musical texture of two or more independent melodic voices. It's incredibly atmospheric and dramatic: the bass voices enter out of nowhere, really mysteriously, with these long, suspended, oozing vocal lines; and then, as the other voice parts join the party, Lotti throws in all these crunchy, pungent dissonances, keeping us hanging on and hanging on before – ahhhh – gloriously resolving them. These sorts of 'suspensions' are a device that creates tension and release, tension and release (because our ears can't help but long for musical resolution) and have been used by every decent pop songwriter ever since.

I find this music radiant, moving, magnificent. If you can take three and a half minutes to stop whatever you're doing and just let it wash over you, do it.

6 January

Violin Concerto no. 1 in G minor, op. 26
1: Allegro moderato
by Max Bruch (1838–1920)

Max Bruch was an immensely gifted composer from the Romantic era who wrote his first symphony at the age of fourteen and went on to produce more than two hundred pieces of music. And yet, in the classical canon, he's become something of a one-hit wonder: of all of those works it's this seductively sonorous violin concerto that really stands out, and for which he's most celebrated.

Bruch was surprisingly insecure about the piece, which he started at the age of twenty-six. It took him over eighteen months to write and he revised it repeatedly on the advice of his great friend, the virtuoso violinist Joseph Joachim. Yet it was an immediate hit. Ironically, its huge popularity, which even at the time overshadowed everything else he wrote, plunged Bruch into despair. (Although to be fair, his frustration may well have been exacerbated by his having sold all the rights to a publisher, meaning he never made another penny from it.) Bruch's son recalls how, upon receiving yet another invitation to have it performed, the composer exclaimed: *'The G minor Concerto again! I couldn't bear to hear it even once more! My friends, play the Second Concerto, or the Scottish Fantasia for once!'*

Those pieces are pretty great too, but it's this violin concerto that is iconic. Beloved of audiences and performers alike, it's a piece that endures across the generations and somehow does not tarnish with use.

7 January

'Les chemins de l'amour' – 'The Paths of Love'
by Francis Poulenc (1899–1963)

Francis Poulenc, born on this day, was the youngest member of a group of composers known as 'Les Six' which took Paris by storm in the 1920s. His music is by turns witty and melancholy, acerbic and heartbreaking.

In the early part of his career, Poulenc – who was openly gay – had a reputation for being something of a hedonistic *bon vivant*. But the death of a close friend in 1936 and his experiences during the French Resistance in World War Two took his later music in a more spiritual and profound direction.

He was always an outstanding songwriter, whether dealing with parody or tragedy. *'You will find sobriety and dolour in French music just as in German or Russian'*, he wrote in 1950, *'but the French have a keener sense of proportion. We realize that sombreness and good humour are not mutually exclusive. Our composers too write profound music, but when they do, it is leavened with that lightness of spirit without which life would be unendurable.'*

In this cabaret classic Poulenc blends the evocative vibe of the popular Parisian boulevardier with the sort of *valse chantée* by which he'd been bewitched since his youth. It was composed as part of the incidental music for a production of a Jean Anouilh play called *Léocadia*, written in 1940, the year German tanks rolled into Paris. It is tinged with a bittersweet poignancy, the lilting charms of its melody undercut by a sense of impending loss.

In 1941 Poulenc wrote to a friend that composing the song had lifted his spirits from the *'menace of the occupation which weighs on my house – what a sad epoch is ours, and when and how will it all finish up . . .'*

I hope it lifts yours.

8 January

Concerto Grosso in D major, op. 6 no. 1
2: Largo
by Arcangelo Corelli (1653–1713)

Arcangelo Corelli, who died on this day, is considered a genius of the early Baroque era, but he didn't actually write much music. His fame rests on his contribution to a musical form known as the 'concerto grosso': multimovement pieces that bring together a small ensemble of instrumentalists to play in equal roles (rather than a regular 'concerto' whereby a soloist is pitted against an entire orchestra). Corelli, who was by all accounts a bit of a perfectionist, obsessively reworked his collections of concerti grossi, but refused to have them published. The pieces were finally brought out a year after he died – and the Baroque world promptly went mad for them. Other leading composers of the day, including George Frideric Handel, immediately started producing their own versions.

It's not surprising that Corelli's concerti grossi made such an impact. They are a delight to listen to: endlessly inventive, supple, polished. I love how he manages to tease out the expressive capability of each instrument in the group – they are also brilliant fun to play – and how, although they are structured with an almost architectural elegance, he allows plenty of places for improvisation within these boundaries; sort of like a very early version of jazz.

I find them an immensely clarifying listen; sonic balm for the chaos of daily life.

9 January

Requiem Mass
3: Offertorio: Domine Jesu Christe
by Giuseppe Verdi (1813–1901)

Here's a story about the power of music.

It's January 1942. A single score of Verdi's *Requiem* has been smuggled into the Nazi concentration camp Theresienstadt (Terezín) in what is now the Czech Republic. Against impossible odds, a group of defiant Jewish prisoners, led by the former conductor and composer Rafael Schächter, decide to mount a performance of this timeless work in an act that survivors will later describe as an act of spiritual resistance.

Inside the camp, 150 prisoners come together, working with that single tattered score, to sing this timeless masterpiece. Prisoner Edgar Krasa, who survived, will later recall that the performance of the Verdi *Requiem* in Theresienstadt allowed the performers to *'immerse themselves in a world of art and happiness, forget the reality of ghetto life and deportations, and gather strength to better cope with the loss of freedom'*.

Verdi's *Requiem* was performed in the camp no fewer than sixteen times. But as increasing numbers of prisoners began to be deported to Auschwitz and its gas chambers, the camp choir's numbers began to drop – and drop – until eventually there remained just a handful of prisoners singing the Verdi *Requiem* to one another.

But still, they sang.

'*We will sing to the Nazis*', says Schächter, who died in Auschwitz in 1945, '*what we cannot say.*'

10 January

~~~~~~

Toccata arpeggiata
by Giovanni Girolamo Kapsberger (c. 1580–1651)

I'm a big believer that music is music.

This sounds blindingly obvious, but by this I mean that, just as all human beings are created from the same essential building blocks, so is every piece of music that has ever been or ever will yet be written.

This is worth pointing out because so often people feel that so-called 'classical' music is something 'other'; something different from the kind of music they like; something they need to 'know' something about before they can let themselves enjoy it. It's not – it all comes from the same source. And when I chance upon a piece like this one, this hypnotic little charmer from the very earliest years of the seventeenth century, it makes me very happy, for in it I can hear so much of what will manifest in later centuries in all sorts of music. It's like a little wink across the centuries from Kapsberger – a composer largely unknown outside of niche lute circles – that reminds me how intimately we are all connected, whether we realize it or not.

It's an ingenious piece, the 'toccata' bit designating that the performer can play fast and loose with rhythm and tempo and the 'arpeggiata' bit indicating it should be played on a plucked-string instrument (*'arpa'* being the Italian for 'harp'). Kapsberger writes a simple succession of broken chords around which the player can improvise – and they're the same ones you might find in a song by the Beatles, by the Divine Comedy, by Adele . . .

11 January

'Ubi caritas et amor'
from *Four Gregorian Motets*
by Maurice Duruflé (1902–1986)

Duruflé, who was born on this day, is a bit of an enigma. His was a twentieth-century life: he came of age in a Paris that was undergoing seismic change in the arts and music, and witnessed at close hand the developments of cubism, Modernism, atonality, jazz. And yet he was uninterested in following new directions or embracing change. He apparently had no taste for provoking or shocking audiences, unlike so many of his contemporaries (see, for example, 29 May); indeed he looked back to the very distant past for much of his musical inspiration.

Duruflé wrote music that is highly distinctive. His work has a crystalline clarity, no doubt because he wrote very little and chiselled away at each piece for years. As a boy chorister he had apparently loved singing the music of Bach, Haydn, Mozart and his own countryman Gabriel Fauré, but he fell particularly hard for the purity and grace of Gregorian chant, the traditional unaccompanied song of the Western Roman Catholic church which dates from the ninth century. He would later incorporate aspects of chant and 'plainsong' into his own musical palette, especially in the magnificently moving Requiem that he wrote after his father died. Those melodies, he admitted, were *'based exclusively on themes from the Gregorian funeral mass. Sometimes I adopted the music exactly, leaving the orchestra to support or comment, in other passages [it] served merely as a stimulus'.*

Gregorian chant is also the basis for this luminous setting of the Latin motet 'Ubi caritas':

Ubi caritas et amor, Deus ibi est.   *Where charity and love are,*
                                     there God is.

12 January

Octet in E flat major, op. 20
1: Allegro moderato ma con fuoco
by Felix Mendelssohn (1809–1847)

As birthday presents go, this has to rank as one of the all-time greats.

Felix Mendelssohn wrote this exuberant piece of chamber music as a birthday gift for his great friend and violin teacher, Edward Rietz. He was sixteen years old.

It would have been an astonishing accomplishment for anybody, let alone a teenager. Although previous octets did exist, it was still a bold and ambitious choice for Mendelssohn to decide to write for eight equal string players. And what he does with it is so inventive: envisaging the work as a mini-symphony, he writes music that allows the eight instrumentalists to merge into one glorious whole whilst still retaining their own identity.

Mendelssohn always loved this piece – '*I had a most wonderful time in the writing of it,*' he later admitted – and what I particularly love is that, unlike some works of music in which you're somehow made aware of the process by which it is wrought, you can hear that enjoyment in every note.

13 January

Three Romances, op. 22
1: Andante molto
by Clara Schumann (1819–1896)

'Composing gives me great pleasure', Clara Schumann once wrote. *'There is nothing that surpasses the joy of creation, if only because through it one wins hours of self-forgetfulness, when one lives in a world of sound.'*

'Self-forgetfulness', 'self-care', 'time to herself', 'me-time'. Call it what you will, this lady must have needed it. Clara Schumann, née Wieck, was an awe-inspiring talent. One of the most distinguished pianists of the nineteenth century, she blazed a trail by being one of the first notable concert artists to regularly perform music by memory – which later became standard practice – and was revered by some of the leading musical figures of the day, including Liszt, Chopin and Brahms. One critic who was present at a series of recitals she gave in Vienna at the age of eighteen remarked: *'The appearance of this artist can be regarded as epoch-making . . . In her creative hands, the most ordinary passage, the most routine motive acquires a significant meaning, a colour, which only those with the most consummate artistry can give.'*

This consummate and epoch-making artist was also a mother of eight. By all accounts, Clara ran the Schumann household almost single-handedly: she was the chief breadwinner; she looked after her grandchildren after her son Felix died; she had to deal with multiple cases of mental illness in her family; she was a busy and committed teacher, and muse to a number of composers. On top of all that she composed some wonderful music – twenty solo piano works, dozens of songs, chamber and instrumental works – of which this tender and ardent romance came towards the very end.

(Speaking of romance, Clara was married to a man called Robert who also wrote music. More on him later.)

14 January

'E lucevan le stelle' – 'And the stars were shining'
from *Tosca*
by Giacomo Puccini (1858–1924)

Opera has a reputation, sometimes justified, for overblown storylines and high drama. Puccini's *Tosca*, which was premiered in Rome on this day in 1900, is no exception, but it also contains moments of searing emotional truth (and fabulous music throughout). At the moment in Act 3 when this aria occurs, the painter Mario Cavaradossi, who's in love with the singer Floria Tosca and has been caught up in a complex plot (lust, betrayal, the usual operatic fare), is awaiting execution. He has just been told he has a single hour to live.

Svanì per sempre il sogno mio d'amore.	*My dream of love has vanished for ever,*
L'ora è fuggita, e muoio disperato! E muoio disperato!	*That moment has vanished, and I die in despair. I die in despair!*
E non ho amato mai tanto la vita, tanto la vita!	*And never before have I loved life so much, Loved life so much!*

From the moment the solo clarinet enters with its mournful refrain I'm gone. Puccini, by the way, was a bit of a hit factory, writing what we might think of as the pop songs of his day. His influence goes far beyond the operatic world. In 1920, 'the world's greatest entertainer' Al Jolson wrote a song called 'Avalon'. He was promptly sued by Giulio Ricordi, Puccini's publisher, who pointed out that the melody had been lifted straight from 'E lucevan le stelle'. Awkward. Puccini's team was awarded $25,000 in damages and all future royalties for the song . . .

15 January

Quatuor pour la fin du temps – Quartet for the End of Time
5: *Louange à l'éternité de Jesus*
by Olivier Messiaen (1908–1992)

Here's another example of music as a form of spiritual resistance so moving it stops me in my tracks. The French composer Olivier Messiaen was thirty-one and a prisoner of war when he wrote this. When France fell in 1940 he had been rounded up and deported to a German camp located some seventy miles east of Dresden. Among his fellow prisoners in Stalag VIII-A were a clarinettist, Henri Akoka; a violinist, Jean le Boulaire; and a cellist, Étienne Pasquier. Messiaen managed to procure some paper and a small pencil from a sympathetic German guard named Karl-Erich Brüll and in circumstances it's impossible to comprehend, put together the work that many consider to be his masterpiece.

It is an unusual combination – clarinet, violin, piano, cello – and not without its challenges when it comes to both textural blend and sound balance. But those were the instruments at Messiaen's disposal in the camp. Playing battered, makeshift and out-of-tune instruments, the musicians premiered the work on the evening of 15 January 1941, outdoors. There was rain falling and snow on the ground. Reports vary on how many fellow prisoners of war were in the audience in Hut 27 that evening but it seems somewhere between 150 and 400: French, German, Polish and Czech men from all strata of society, huddled together in their threadbare uniforms, on which was stitched 'K. G.' or '*Kriegsgefangene*', meaning prisoner of war. One audience member later recalled: '*We were all brothers.*'

Messiaen was a composer whose religious faith never left him, and the work is laced with the language and spirit of redemption. I've chosen this cello and piano movement, 'Praise to the eternity of Jesus', as a place to start.

16 January

Étude in C sharp minor, op. 2 no. 1
by Alexander Scriabin (1872–1915)

Look, sometimes what we just really need in the middle of January is music that feels like a large glass of red wine.*

You're welcome.

---

* With sincere apologies to non-drinkers or those attempting a Dry January.

17 January

Oboe Concerto in D minor, op. 9 no. 2
2: Adagio
by Tomaso Albinoni (1671–1751)

The oboe occupies a privileged position in the orchestral gang: before the start of any performance the principal oboist will sound a perfect 'A', and it's this note that the rest of the musicians use to tune their own instruments. There's nothing like the sweet, sweet sound of an oboe for a captivating combination of purity and emotional heft.

Oboes are descended from the sorts of pipes that have been used by shepherds for centuries, and their distinctive sound – produced by blowing air through a double reed – can evoke nostalgia as well as something more emotionally raw. The modern instrument that we know was a relatively new phenomenon in the early eighteenth century, and the Italian composer Tomaso Albinoni was one of the first to recognize its potential as a solo instrument. Having written the first ever concerto for solo oboe that survives, he went on to write at least seven more, and was greatly admired by the likes of J. S. Bach, who also wrote fabulously for the instrument.

This one is about as gorgeous an example as it gets.

18 January

〜

'Dirait-on' – 'Should We Say'
from *Les chansons des roses*
by Morten Lauridsen (b. 1943)

Music and poetry – they often go hand in hand, don't they, and I'm fascinated by the ways in which classical composers approach the setting of text. We're going to be hearing a lot of poetry throughout this year, including works by John Donne, Friedrich Schiller, Johann Wolfgang von Goethe, Paul Verlaine, Wilfred Owen, William Shakespeare, and one of my very favourite poets, Rainer Maria Rilke, of whom one of his translators observed, *'roses climb his life as if he were their trellis'*.

When I discovered that the contemporary American composer Morten Lauridsen was a fellow Rilke fan, I was keen to hear how he'd bring the German poet's luminous verse to life in music.

Lauridsen says he was immensely moved by the words of this poem from *Songs of the Roses* and in particular Rilke's expression of *'the state of giving love and not receiving it back'*.

Sweet without being saccharine, Lauridsen's intimate, glowing treatment of the verse only enhances – as the very best musical word-settings do – its gentle power.

19 January

Electric Counterpoint
1: Fast
by Steve Reich (b. 1936)

We come now to one of the towering figures in modern music.

Some composers write music for music's sake – works that may take us in all sorts of emotional or intellectual directions, but which are not 'intended' to have any purpose beyond themselves. Steve Reich – who, as I write, is a peppy octogenarian still composing away, accepting international commissions, nipping across the Atlantic to give premieres, exploring new sonic possibilities, subverting expectations – has been creating inventive and groundbreaking music since the 1960s that invariably offers a degree of social commentary on our times. His is music that challenges, reflects, probes, dazzles and delights.

Along with John Adams and Philip Glass, Reich is one of the Americans credited with creating a movement in music called 'minimalism' – all repeating patterns, driving rhythms and shapeshifting melodies. He certainly created a language that sounded and felt – and still sounds and feels – thrillingly new.

And yet for all his ultra-modern impression, Reich is often playing with old tricks from the classical playbook. In this hypnotic piece for electric guitar virtuoso and tape, he constantly teases our expectations about tune and accompaniment in a way that would have been familiar to composers of, say, the eighteenth century. And when it comes to those mesmerizing patterns that develop and build in our ear, he's walking a direct line from J. S. Bach.

Consider this a supreme January mood-booster . . .

20 January

An die Musik – To Music
by Franz Schubert (1797–1828)

Du holde Kunst, in wieviel grauen
    Stunden,
Wo mich des Lebens wilder
    Kreis umstrickt,
Hast du mein Herz zu warmer
    Lieb entzunden,
Hast mich in eine beßre Welt
    entrückt.

You, noble art, in how many
    grey hours
Where life has ensnared and
    encircled me
Have you kindled my heart to
    warm love,
Have you transported me to a
    better world!

Yep. That is all.

21 January

Trauermusik
by Paul Hindemith (1895–1963)

What happens when you're an international viola soloist and composer, merrily making your way to give a concert in London with the BBC Symphony Orchestra, and the King of England suddenly drops dead?

Spare a thought for poor Paul Hindemith, a German composer and former soldier. The man who made a fascinating contribution to twentieth-century tonality (laid out in his 1930s book *The Craft of Musical Composition*) also played a unique role in the commemoration of a deceased British monarch. On 19 January 1936, he set off for London, intending to give the British premiere of his new viola concerto on the 22nd. And then, shortly before midnight on the 20th, King George V died. The concert was immediately cancelled, but it was decided that Hindemith should nevertheless be prevailed upon to write something to reflect what had happened. Gamely, he agreed – no pressure! – and at 11 a.m. the next morning he walked into an office that the BBC had provided for him, took a seat and got his head down.

It seems unbelievable given that it takes some composers years to write a single work, but by 5 p.m. on 21 January it was done: Hindemith had come up with a haunting and evocative piece called *Trauermusik* – 'mourning music' – in homage to the late king. British musicians are legendary the world over for their ability to 'sight-read' (i.e. perform something without any previous knowledge of the piece) and luckily this tradition didn't let them down: that very same evening the newly minted *Trauermusik* was performed in a live broadcast from a BBC radio studio, with the great English maestro Adrian Boult conducting and the composer as soloist. Pretty impressive stuff.

22 January

Adagio from *Lady Macbeth of the Mtsensk District*
arranged for strings
by Dmitri Shostakovich (1906–1975)

Media trolling is no millennial phenomenon. Shostakovich's opera *Lady Macbeth of the Mtsensk District*, premiered on this day in 1934, depicts a nineteenth-century Russian woman who falls for one of her husband's workmen and is driven to murder. It's a ferocious mix of sex, violence and passionate music. Describing it as a 'tragedy-satire', Shostakovich saw in his heroine the *'destiny of a talented, smart and outstanding woman, "dying in the nightmarish atmosphere of pre-revolutionary Russia" . . . I feel empathy for her'*.

The opera was initially a hit: for two years it was rarely off the stage. And then, in January 1936, Stalin went to see it. Two days later, an anonymous editorial (attributed to Stalin himself) appeared in the Communist Party rag *Pravda*; it condemned the work as 'Muddle Not Music'. The opera was described as *'fidgety, neurotic'* (which is a bit rich, coming from a totalitarian regime); it was *'coarse, primitive and vulgar'*; music that *'quacks, grunts and growls'*. Such a *'game'*, the writer warned, ominously, *'may end very badly'*.

It was indeed bad news for Shostakovich. The opera was banned and all his music denounced. He was declared an enemy of the people. He lived in fear for his life – and that of his wife and their unborn child. Still in his twenties, he withdrew his fourth symphony and took a pragmatic approach to his fifth, calling it 'A Soviet Artist's Response to Just Criticism'. The rest of his career was characterized by this struggle between artistic integrity and wariness of the Soviet regime. It was only after Stalin's death that Shostakovich could again unleash something true to himself (see 17 December). But he would never again write an opera.

23 January

Clarinet Concerto no. 1 in F minor, op. 73
3: Rondo – Allegretto
by Carl Maria von Weber (1786–1826)

A change of mood today thanks to this spirited little number from the heart of the woodwind repertoire. The German composer Carl Maria von Weber had been a bit of a rebel in his former life – getting arrested, joining a secret society, that sort of thing – but by the time he wrote this in 1811 he was busy earning a reputation as one of the leading founders of German Romanticism. Weber's favourite instrument was the clarinet and he dashed off this playful and virtuosic concerto in less than a month for the leading clarinettist of the day, who as it happened was also a great friend. This 'rondo' movement is a pyrotechnic romp that shows off the terrific range of the instrument and demonstrates how far the development of clarinet writing had come in the two decades since, say, Mozart's time (see 5 September).

24 January

Mass for Five Voices
5: Agnus Dei
by William Byrd (c. 1539/40–1623)

This beautifully distilled setting of the Agnus Dei, the invocation to the Lamb of God, was composed around 1594/5 but was lost and forgotten until its rediscovery in the early twentieth century.

Although it's probable that his parents were Protestant (and he certainly contributed richly to the Anglican musical repertoire), Byrd was shaped by his staunch adherence to the Catholic faith. He probably intended this to be sung in the domestic chapels that were maintained by families who remained loyal to the Pope and the Roman Catholic church. They would have been taking considerable risk in doing so, given the 1593 statute of penalties against 'Popish recusants'.

Byrd was one of the undisputed masters of European Renaissance music and taught many of the shining lights of the next generation. His music has also had a profound influence on some modern composers, as we will discover next month (see 10 February). I love how the writing here is supremely controlled yet somehow sensual in its clarity. Listen how, for example, with each successive invocation of the Agnus Dei, he seamlessly folds in a new vocal line, as though we are listening in on a private conversation which eventually unspools to a magnificent, moving climax involving all the voices.

25 January

~~~

My love is like a red, red rose
Traditional

It's Burns Night! For all the haggis and tatties, the bagpipes and the whisky, today is, above all, about the poetry of Robert 'Rabbie' Burns. Composers through the years have been drawn to his words, including such luminaries as Beethoven, Schumann, Mendelssohn, Ravel and Shostakovich. I have a particular soft spot for this traditional setting of 'A Red, Red Rose':

> *O my Luve's like a red, red rose,*
> *That's newly sprung in June:*
> *O my Luve's like the melodie,*
> *That's sweetly play'd in tune.*

Burns described this as a *'simple old Scots song which I had picked up in the country'*. Simple it may be, but it's also touching and evocative – and has played its own part in musical history: when Bob Dylan was asked for the source of his greatest creative inspiration, it was the lyrics of this song, he said, which had had the biggest effect on his life.

26 January

Unsent Love Letters
by Elena Kats-Chernin (b. 1957)

Today is Australia Day, so it seems an opportune moment to celebrate one of the most exciting classical composers to have emerged from down under in modern times. Elena Kats-Chernin writes operas, ballets, vocal music, orchestral works and film scores, but I'm particularly smitten with her meditations on the unsent love letters of avant-garde French composer Erik Satie.

Satie was one of music's true originals (see 1 June, 1 July, 3 September) and lived a life of seeming paradox and contradiction. A virtuosic showman on stage, in private he was introverted and shy. Dapper in public, favouring fine silks and velvets, at home he lived in slovenly chaos. Derided by his professors as being *the laziest student in the Conservatoire*, he yet wrote some of the most gorgeous, inventive and memorable music of the twentieth century.

It was some years after Satie's death in 1925 that a group of his friends were finally able to enter his cramped apartment at 22 rue Cauchy in Arcueil, just outside Paris, to which he had not allowed anybody access for twenty-seven years. There amongst the chaos they found, in no particular order: two grand pianos placed one on top of the other, seven velvet suits, multiple umbrellas, a chair, a table and stacks upon stacks of love letters to his muse, lover and neighbour Suzanne Valadon – which he had never sent. Inspired by these, Kats-Chernin has written a suite of twenty-six exquisite piano miniatures, each one reflecting some element of Satie's wholly unique art, love and life. If you can listen with a classic French cocktail in hand, so much the better . . .

27 January

Symphony no. 41 in C major, K. 551 ('Jupiter')
4: Molto allegro
by Wolfgang Amadeus Mozart (1756–1791)

Oh, happy day, this one, when into the world came Mozart. It's a clichéd word, genius, and so hard to quantify, but I think we can all agree that this guy was the real deal: a child prodigy, probably the most gifted writer of melody there has ever been or will ever be, a composer of music so profound, so wise, so witty and tender and empathetic and human that its being in the world simply makes things a little bit better.

We're going to be hearing a lot of Mozart this year, so I hope you're with me on this one. Not *enough* Mozart – I could probably have filled 366 days with his works alone – but sufficient amounts to give you a flavour, I hope, of just how skilled he was at writing anything he turned his attention to. He wrote his first symphony when he was eight, and his forty-first when he was thirty-two. It was to be his last; he would be dead within three years.

By the time he got to this one he was dashing them off monthly: no. 41 was written in August, hot on the heels of no. 39 in June and no. 40 in July. Always one for hustling up some sideline cash, the entrepreneurial but eternally penniless Mozart had been intending for it to be performed in a new casino in the Spiegelgasse in Vienna, but that never happened, for whatever reason. Nevertheless, the work has become one of the shining cornerstones of the symphonic repertoire. This fourth movement in particular is a glorious thing and I hope that wherever you are, whatever you're doing today, it works its cheering magic on you.

28 January

'L'Heure exquise' – 'The Exquisite Hour'
from *Chansons grises*, no. 5
by Reynaldo Hahn (1874–1947)

Time for another lush poetry setting: this one from the world of the French *Belle Époque* courtesy of the Caracas-born composer Reynaldo Hahn. Part Venezuelan, part German Jew, Hahn made his permanent home in Paris, where he was taken under the wing of fellow composers Charles Gounod and Jules Massenet, and became the lover and long-time muse of the great French writer Marcel Proust.

In this exquisite song, Hahn sets poetry by Paul Verlaine from the 1869 anthology *Fêtes galantes*. The title is a nod to the Rococo painter Antoine Watteau's early works: think gorgeously dressed young men and women frolicking in pastoral landscapes. Underlying all that languorous splendour, though, is a persuasive note of melancholy, reflected in the tender vocal line, which occasionally swoons heavenward. It is indeed the 'exquisite hour' . . .

Rêvons, c'est l'heure . . .	*Let us dream! It is the hour . . .*
Un vast et tendre	*A vast and tender*
Apaisement	*Calm*
Semble descendre	*Seems to descend*
Du firmament	*from a sky*
Que l'astre irise . . .	*made iridescent by the moon . . .*
C'est l'heure exquise.	*It is the exquisite hour!*

29 January

Trio from Act 3
Der Rosenkavalier
by Richard Strauss (1864–1949)

The history of classical music is littered with broken marriages and tempestuous love affairs, but Richard Strauss was a composer who bucked the trend, remaining happily married to his wife Pauline for fifty-six years. It may be coincidence, but Strauss also happened to write many operas that revolve around strong female protagonists. There's Salome, Elektra, Ariadne, Helena, Arabella, Daphne – and perhaps the most magnificent of all, the Marschallin in his opera *Der Rosenkavalier*, a romantic comedy set among the Viennese aristocracy which received its UK premiere on this day in 1913.

The unhappily married Marschallin has taken a seventeen-year-old count, Octavian, as her lover. In a (made-up) household engagement ritual, he is later selected to present a silver rose to the lovely Sophie on behalf of the Marschallin's lecherous old cousin Baron Ochs, who intends to marry her. Alas, Octavian and Sophie fall helplessly in love; the Marschallin must yield to the younger woman; and the Baron is revealed to be the buffoon he is.

Strauss, along with Gustav Mahler, represents the zenith of late, post-Wagnerian German Romanticism and, while the opera's music is unashamedly rich throughout, it hits an emotional peak in this highly charged and melodically splendid trio, in which the Marschallin, Octavian and Sophie all reflect on their ideas and ideals of love.

The opera was a storming success: to accommodate public demand a special Rosenkavalier Express ran from Berlin to Dresden; canny marketeers started producing Rosenkavalier merchandise, including branded champagne; and a certain *New Yorker* cartoon depicts a man on his deathbed begging to hear this trio one last time. I can't say I blame him.

30 January

Violin Sonata no. 1 in A major, op. 13
1: Allegro molto
by Gabriel Fauré (1845–1924)

I adore this sonata for the way it immediately and unapologetically thrusts us into the middle of a conversation between the violin and piano. Fauré was a student of Camille Saint-Saëns (see 25 February, 2 December), went on to teach Maurice Ravel (7 March, 14 July), and is generally considered one of the geniuses of late nineteenth-/early twentieth-century music, bridging as he does the fascinating period between the Romantic and Modernist eras. Here he unleashes a mood of passionate ardour that somehow manages, in characteristic fashion, to stay on just the right side of elegant restraint. A few minutes in, the vibe (and the key) modulates dramatically and Fauré takes us somewhere unexpected in what's known as the 'development' section – somewhere that, no matter how many times I hear it, I always want to follow.

At the premiere in January 1877, Fauré was at the piano and the solo violin part was taken by the pioneering young violinist Marie Tayou, leader of an all-female string quartet. *'The sonata had more of a success this evening than I could ever have hoped for'*, he admitted to a friend. *'Mademoiselle Tayou was impeccable.'* His teacher Saint-Saëns was in the audience that night and wrote a rave review, reserving particular praise for the composer's boldness: *'In this sonata you can find everything to tempt a gourmet'*, he enthused in one of France's leading music publications. *'New forms, excellent modulations, unusual tone colours, and the use of unexpected rhythms. And a magic floats above everything, encompassing the whole work, causing the crowd of usual listeners to accept the unimagined audacity as something quite normal.'*

31 January

Echorus
by Philip Glass (b. 1937)

This should give hope to anyone currently holding down an unrewarding job or two while secretly harbouring dreams of artistic greatness.

Philip Glass, who was born on this day, worked for many years as a taxi-driver and plumber in New York before finally being able to give up the day job(s) and concentrate wholly on his music. He's gone on to become one of the most influential and boundary-hopping creative artists of any genre, credited with the founding of minimalism in music – although he has always resisted the term, preferring the description *'music with repetitive structures'*. His many collaborators include the iconic pop star David Bowie, the visionary Indian classical musician Ravi Shankar, the Oscar-winning filmmaker Martin Scorsese and the writer Allen Ginsberg. Glass is ludicrously prolific: alongside epic symphonies, pioneering string quartets and groundbreaking instrumental works, he has written more than fifteen operas and fifty film scores, including *The Truman Show*, *The Hours* and *Notes on a Scandal*. His influence can be heard across any musical genre you might care to name, from classical to rock and pop, film to video game soundtracks.

This lovely piece, derived from the word 'echo', was composed in the winter of 1994 for violinists Edna Michell and Yehudi Menuhin. It's based on the old Baroque form of the chaconne (see 16 May, 27 July, 28 July). According to Glass himself, *Echorus* was *'inspired by thoughts of compassion and is meant to evoke feelings of serenity and peace'*.

I don't know about your life, but serenity and peace are in critically short supply in mine, so I'll take it where I can get it.

FEBRUARY

1 February

'Che gelida manina' – 'What a frozen little hand'
from *La Bohème*
by Giacomo Puccini (1858–1924)

A few weeks ago we were with poor old Cavaradossi awaiting his execution in *Tosca*; we open this month with another supremely romantic tenor aria from Puccini. It's from Act I of *La Bohème*, which premiered in Turin on this day in 1896 (and went on to inspire Baz Luhrmann's film *Moulin Rouge* as well as the musical *Rent*).

It's Christmas Eve in 1830s Paris. The young bohemian poet Rodolfo is hanging out with his friends in his freezing garret (they are having to burn pages of his latest manuscript for warmth). When his friends go off to the café, having successfully staved off the landlord for another rent cheque, Rodolfo hangs back – which is serendipitous, because it is at that point that a knock on the door reveals his neighbour Mimi, a seamstress. She is after a light for her candle, which has gone out.

Che gelida manina,	*What a frozen little hand.*
se la lasci riscaldar.	*Let me warm it for you.*

Their hands touch – his candle goes out too – she drops her key – they try and find it – and in one of opera's great *coups de foudre*, under the light of the moon, these two human beings fall fast and hard in love.

When opera gets it right, nothing comes close for emotional impact. Puccini invariably gets it right. The two arias that follow this one, in which Mimi tells him her name, and Rodolfo tries to convince her to come with him to the café, are also outstanding pieces of songwriting. We are with them every step of the way, as the world falls away around them and it's just Mimi for Rodolfo for ever, for always. (Or not – because it's opera, and that's how these things go . . .)

2 February

String Quartet in E flat major
1: Adagio ma non troppo
by Fanny Mendelssohn (1805–1847)

When Fanny Mendelssohn was fourteen, she memorized J. S. Bach's forty-eight Preludes and Fugues and played them to her father for his birthday. Mr Mendelssohn was apparently impressed, charmed even, by this astonishing feat of memory and technical prowess. But his response to his sensationally gifted daughter can essentially be summed up as 'very nice, dear – but leave music-making to the boys'.

With the exception of some fierce pioneers (see e.g. 3, 4 February), the history of women in classical music is pretty much this, right up until the late twentieth century: talented human is compelled to express herself through music but is repressed by a patriarchy that forbids her from composing except behind closed doors.

What's so infuriating is that Fanny was in a supposedly supportive environment. Felix was well aware of his sister's genius: they shared every piece they wrote, and he adored her. Yet even he prevented her from publishing her work. (Presumably he was trying to be helpful when he put out lots under *his* name or simply 'F. Mendelssohn' – meaning that music which for years was attributed to Felix is only now being revealed as Fanny's. Even Queen Victoria, when asked which of Felix's pieces she liked best, named a song by Fanny.)

When Felix set off on a grand tour of Europe, Fanny stayed at home and got married. Thankfully, her husband, painter William Hensel, encouraged her: he supplied her with manuscript paper every day before he went to his own studio. Fanny probably never believed her music would be heard beyond the confines of her own home. Many of the 450 pieces she produced are miniatures, but here she breaks out onto a more expansive musical canvas – and more than holds her own.

46

3 February

'Il cavalier di Spagna' – 'A Spanish Knight'
from *La liberazione di Ruggiero dall'isola d'Ancina*
by Francesca Caccini (c. 1587–1641)

A significant date in the history of classical music, today: it was on this day in Florence in 1625 that the work generally regarded as the first opera ever composed by a woman was given its premiere. (And there have not, as it happens, been that many since.)

La liberazione di Ruggiero was Francesca Caccini's take on the sixteenth-century Italian epic *Orlando Furioso* – a forty-six-part poem about an eighth-century military leader who served the Frankish warrior King Charlemagne and was seduced by a sorceress. Catnip to composers, many have turned their hand to this colourful tale – including, a century or so later, Handel in his famous opera *Alcina* (16 April).

Francesca Caccini was the daughter of the Renaissance composer Giulio Caccini (10 December) and a talented singer, lutenist, poet and teacher. In the opera, she adopts what were then ultra-modern techniques, inspired by the likes of Claudio Monteverdi (20 March, 29 November). She also employed a compositional scheme in which female characters are associated with 'flat' keys and male characters with 'sharp' keys, which has led modern critics to wonder whether Caccini was deliberately making a statement about gender through her music. As a member of the court of the Grand Duchess of Tuscany, Maria Maddalena, she would almost certainly have been considered one of the most influential female European composers of her time. Sadly, very little of her music survives.

4 February

Fantasie nègre
by Florence Price (1887–1953)

Seeing as we're talking female musical pioneers, just consider for a moment the intersectional odds that would have been stacked against the American composer Florence Price. Born in Little Rock, Arkansas, her childhood was marked by racial tension and a climate in which local lynchings were commonplace. Yet she went on to become the first African-American woman symphonist and the first whose music was considered worthy of being performed by a major orchestra.

Price was one smart cookie, graduating from high school at the age of fourteen. She won a place at the New England Conservatory, an esteemed music college on the East Coast of the US, where her training was very much shaped by the European tradition. Nevertheless Price found ways of incorporating her deep Southern roots into her music. She also avoided the worst of the racism that her fellow African-American students faced by passing herself off as Mexican.

The music of the African-American church was a strong influence, as were early blues and the spirituals whose rhythms and syncopations have captivated so many classical composers, both black and white – including Frederick Delius (30 March) and Michael Tippett (2 June). It was the spiritual 'Sinner, please don't let this harvest pass' which inspired this piece from 1929, an ambitious blending of American and European styles that Price dedicated to her student Margaret Bonds, another important African-American female composer.

In the 1930s, while balancing her career with the demands of being a single mother to two children, Price became friends with some of the leading artists of the day, including poet Langston Hughes, one of the architects of the Harlem Renaissance. Hers is a unique voice in twentieth-century music and deserves to be more widely heard.

5 February

Trumpet Concerto in D major
1: Adagio
by Georg Philip Telemann (1681–1767)

You have to feel a bit sorry for poor old Telemann. Over the course of his long life, this multi-talented law school dropout racked up at least 3,600 musical works that survive (and countless more that were destroyed); he was also a novelist, poet, flautist, singer, musical theorist and a highly regarded director of church music. And yet during his lifetime and beyond, he was somewhat sidelined by critics who dismissed his work as almost too effortless, too plentiful. It was only in the twentieth century, when a vast cache of his unheard works was discovered after the Second World War, that his reputation started to recover and his music to be taken seriously.

Telemann was a contemporary and friend of J. S. Bach – and godfather to his son Carl, whom we'll be hearing from later this month (15 February) – but in a way they represent opposing musical approaches. Whereas Bach was the king of complex 'contrapuntal' textures, in which separate musical lines work in counterpoint with each other, Telemann was much influenced by his work as a singer and was all about the straightforwardly lyrical melodic line – of which this stately trumpet concerto is a terrific example. In this way, he can be seen as looking ahead to what would become the refined melodic elegance of the Classical period which was right around the corner.

6 February

Composer, conductor, theatre director, musical visionary – Wagner's artistic achievements are unparalleled. But if his genius altered the course of music for ever, his reputation is often overshadowed by the uglier aspects of his personality (his overweening megalomania; his rabid anti-Semitism; his being Adolf Hitler's favourite composer; his being appropriated by the Nazi party as their unofficial bandleader . . .).

How is any principled listener to reconcile the repellent philosophy with the astonishing music? I've taken my cue from Daniel Barenboim, a leading (Jewish) interpreter of Wagner, who urges that the music be treated on its own terms. (This is in no way to excuse Wagner, but it's worth pointing out he died before Hitler was born and had been dead for half a century before Hitler came to power.)

The Mastersingers is unusual for Wagner in that it's set in a defined time and place – Nuremberg in the mid-sixteenth century. Unlike his famous *Ring Cycle*, and in fact most of his operas, it features no supernatural powers, no fairytale legends or magical forces. Depicting the world of the Mastersingers and their guild, it's a comedy celebrating the solace of songwriting in a world of delusion and folly.

The opera was a hit from its first performance – at which Franz Strauss played the French horn. The composer (12 July) and father of Richard, whom we met last month, led the orchestra on strike after one rehearsal at which Wagner apparently made so many interruptions, it was still going on after five hours. There's a pervasive stereotype among the orchestral community that it's the brass players who are always keenest to wrap up and get to the pub; 'twas seemingly ever thus.

7 February

Miserere
by Gregorio Allegri (c. 1582–1652)

The story goes that a fourteen-year-old Mozart heard Allegri's haunting and mysterious setting of Psalm 51 – which it had been forbidden to transcribe outside the Vatican for almost 150 years – whilst visiting the Sistine Chapel. He was apparently so struck by the beauty of the music that he afterwards scribbled the whole piece down – from memory. He then returned to the chapel two days later to make a few minor corrections, and it was subsequently published in a version that, unlike the single previous authorized transcription, captured the work's innate power. Shortly after, Mozart was summoned back to Rome by Pope Clement XIV, who awarded him the Chivalric Order of the Golden Spur.

To be fair, the now iconic *Miserere* was already well known in musical circles, so Mozart would have heard it on other occasions, but there is no doubting his love for it, given the way it influenced his own sacred choral writing. And what's not to love? In a polyphonic masterstroke, Allegri has one group of voices singing a simple *Miserere* chant and the other group interweaving theirs around them.

Miserere mei, Deus: secundum magnam misericordiam tuam.
Have mercy upon me, O God, after Thy great goodness.

Allegri, who died on this day, composed it for the Tenebrae service in Holy Week which began at dusk (*tenebrae* is Latin for 'shadows' or 'darkness'). During the service, all the candles in the chapel would have been slowly extinguished, one by one, until finally there was a lone candle burning – which was then hidden. It must have been incredibly atmospheric.

As an alto in the papal choir, by the way, Allegri used to job-share with a man named Stefano Landi. We'll be meeting him tomorrow.

8 February

Homo fugit velut umbra (Passacaglia della vita) by Stefano Landi (1587–1639)

As well as sharing a singing position in the papal choir with yesterday's composer, Gregorio Allegri, Stefano Landi was a rhetorician, philosopher, multi-instrumentalist and songwriter who made an impact in the early Baroque Roman school by writing the first major opera based on a historical subject (in this case, the fifth-century St Alexis).

Largely forgotten now, in his day Landi had some seriously powerful patrons, including the wealthy and influential Borghese and Barberini families, who, in the manner of the super-rich at the time, liked to surround themselves with the most talented musicians at court. (So much more fun than a yacht!) The environment, filled as it was with brilliant young artists all competing for the attention of their patrons, would presumably have been as inspiring as it was ruthless.

This work, *Homo fugit velut umbra* – 'Man flees like a shadow' – shows Landi absorbing the ideas of that musical melting pot. Throwing together the lute, theorbo, guitar and harp, plus a number of violins, a viola da gamba, a cornet and some percussion, he writes a stylish and rhythmically captivating 'passacaglia' – variations over a repeated bass-line – that, while reminding us that our time here is brief and we all must die, does at least make a highly persuasive case for the fullest possible living of life:

si more cantando, si more	*We die singing, we die*
sonando . . . morire bisogna.	*playing . . . yet die we must.*
si muore danzando, bevando,	*We die dancing, drinking,*
mangiando . . . morire bisogna.	*eating . . . yet die we must.*

9 February

Piano Sonata, op. 1
by Alban Berg (1885–1935)

The Austrian composer Alban Berg, who was born on this day, had a taste for the lyrical late-Romantic idiom but was far from immune to the onslaught on tonality that was being wrought by his teacher Arnold Schoenberg (13 September). Along with Schoenberg and Anton Webern (15 September), Berg is a leading figure in the group of composers known as the 'Second Viennese School' (the 'First' being Mozart, Haydn and Beethoven). These composers adopted what is known as 'twelve-tone technique'. Music written in this style – also know as 'serialism' or 'dodecaphony' – questions and destabilizes the whole structure of Western harmonic tradition by avoiding being in a particular 'key'. Schoenberg himself described the system as a *'method of composing with twelve tones which are related only with one another'*.

Used, as we are, to the chromatic palette in Western music which has prevailed for the best part of a millennium, such compositions can sound very unfamiliar and strange indeed to our ears. That said, there are moments of great beauty to be found, and I find the philosophy behind the music fascinating. If serialism is viewed as a way of ensuring that all twelve notes of our chromatic scale are used as often as one another, without emphasizing any one note, it becomes almost idealistic.

In this piece Berg is emulating Schoenberg's theory of 'developing variation': he begins with a single musical idea to which, after a considerable amount of drama, a lot of shifting musical sands and restless tonality, we eventually return. It is Berg's first major work, which makes its confidence and bravura all the more impressive.

10 February

Agnus Dei
by Charlotte Bray (b. 1982)

First performed on this day in 2016, Charlotte Bray's setting of the Agnus Dei is a compelling example of how classical music exists in dialogue across the centuries. Bray was directly inspired, she says, by the striking *'beauty and tranquillity'* of William Byrd's five-part Mass, and in particular the Agnus Dei movement, which we heard last month.

Bray starts with a fragment of Byrd's theme and builds her own piece with 'tone clusters' that are constructed, as she puts it, *'from a germ of the harmonic language of the Byrd'*. She was also influenced by his architectural structure: like him, she at first uses just three voices of the ensemble, layering them until finally, in the third section, all five parts of the ensemble are heard together in a powerful, uplifting climax.

11 February

Nocturne for violin and piano
by Lili Boulanger (1893–1918)

The prejudice against female composers until comparatively recently makes the achievements of the Boulanger sisters, Nadia (22 October) and Lili, even more remarkable. Growing up in a musical family, they entered the Paris Conservatoire at a young age, where their teachers included Gabriel Fauré (30 January, 15 May). Nadia went on to have an extraordinary career as a teacher, shaping some of the twentieth century's greatest musical minds, from conductor/pianist Daniel Barenboim and tango pioneer Astor Piazzolla (11 March) to Philip Glass (31 January, 4 October) and legendary pop producer Quincy Jones.

Lili was a prodigious composing talent. Aged nineteen, she became the first woman to win the coveted Prix de Rome for composition. That led immediately to a deal with one of the leading music publishing houses of the day, Ricordi. A glittering future beckoned, but within five years she would be dead, her life cut short by intestinal tuberculosis (known these days as Crohn's Disease).

Lili published around thirty pieces before her death. Written in the impressionist style, this nocturne contains a hauntingly beautiful violin melody as well as quotations from the *Prélude à l'après-midi d'un faune* by Claude Debussy and *Tristan and Isolde* by Richard Wagner. And yet, while she openly acknowledged her influences, this piece remains intensely personal.

It was on this day in 1929, by the way, that a Russian-French astronomer named Benjamin Jekhowsky discovered a minor planet, a dark asteroid from the middle of the asteroid belt. He named it 1181 Lilith in her honour. As memorials go, it's not the worst.

12 February

6 Consolations
No. 3 in D flat major
by Franz Liszt (1811–1886)

It is mid-February. Be consoled by this – just this.

13 February

Symphonic Dances from *West Side Story*
4: Mambo
by Leonard Bernstein (1918–1990)

'*Suddenly it all springs to life. I heard rhythms and pulses and – most of all – I can sort of feel the form*', Leonard Bernstein wrote in his diary. Not long after, in 1957, *West Side Story* emerged – and in what is arguably the greatest musical ever written, those 'rhythms and pulses' would incorporate everything from classical music to cool jazz to hot latin dance (swing, mambo, cha-cha) to the infectious sounds of the street and of New York's Tin Pan Alley. Taking Shakespeare's *Romeo and Juliet* as its inspiration, Bernstein and his collaborators – including lyricist Stephen Sondheim and choreographer Jerome Robbins – transport us to the world of rival street gangs and to the timeless love story between Tony, a former member of the Jets and best friend of the gang leader Riff, and the Puerto Rican Maria, sister of Bernardo, the leader of the Sharks.

By 1960, *West Side Story* had been a huge hit on Broadway and beyond, transforming musical theatre for ever. With a Hollywood film in the works, Bernstein extracted key moments from his score and, with the help of colleagues, turned them into this vibrantly orchestrated concert suite. It premiered in Carnegie Hall on this day in 1961.

This Mambo section depicts competitive dances between the Jets and the Sharks; if you can manage to stay still in your seat while listening, I'll be amazed.

14 February

Concerto for two violins in D minor, BWV 1043
2: Largo ma non tanto
by Johann Sebastian Bach (1685–1750)

Ah, St Valentine's Day. And if music be the food of love – etc., etc. – we had better play on. I weighed up love songs; I considered break-up songs – of which Franz Schubert wrote some corkers. In the end, though, I decided that this day deserved a piece that, to me, represents the very essence of love.

The 'Bach Double', as it is fondly known, is quite simply the ultimate musical dialogue. Think of the two soloists passing back and forth melodic ideas as in an extended, intimate conversation. There are moments of the sort of sublime soul-matey harmony you feel when you first fall in love – *How can I be so understood!* – and there are moments of tension and dissonance – *How can I be so misunderstood!* There are moments when the two violins get lost in each other's thoughts or finish each other's sentences without even being conscious of it; then there are those passages that turn unexpectedly into heated debates. There are the ecstatic highs – and the undeniably cooler periods where the two interlocutors seem as though they would really rather talk to the orchestra than each other. In short, it feels to me like a pitch-perfect evocation of what it's like to be in a relationship. (And Bach knew, by the way; he knew.)

For my money, this second movement might just be the most beautiful piece of music we have. Bach renders – and rends – the human heart in a way that very few other composers have ever come close to. And seeing as we're talking about love: let me just say that mine for this piece knows no bounds. For what it's worth, it's the desert island disc I'd be rushing to save from the waves.

15 February

Flute Concerto in A minor
1: Allegro assai
by Carl Philipp Emmanuel Bach (1714–1788)

If J. S. Bach is now considered the godfather of all classical music, there was a time in which his reputation was far eclipsed by that of his son, Carl Philipp Emmanuel (C. P. E.), who in his day was known as the 'Great Bach'. Where his father's supposedly mathematical fugues were disdained as *'music for the eyes'* by some late eighteenth-century critics, audiences, cultural influencers and fellow composers were going mad for the fluid self-expression of C. P. E. His music represents a fascinating bridge between the Baroque and Classical eras: you can practically hear him wriggling free of the constraints of the Baroque era and seeking out a mode that would come to be known as the *'Empfindsamer Stil'* or 'sensitive style' of the early Classical period. *'He is the father and we are all the children,'* said none other than Mozart. *'Whoever among us can do something right has learned it from him.'*

C. P. E. worked as an accompanist at the court of Frederick the Great, who, as King of Prussia from 1740 to 1786, was celebrated across Europe as a uniquely enlightened, multifaceted, polymathic, polyglot monarch (he was dubbed the 'Philosopher King'). He spoke and wrote in French; he was close to writers such as Voltaire; he refounded the Berlin Academy, inviting thinkers and intellectuals from all over the continent to stay in the city; and he planned magnificent new opera houses and theatres for the city.

Above all, Frederick was a talented flautist and passionate about music. His beloved flute, nicknamed *'principessa'*, accompanied him everywhere, even on military campaigns. As a result, he commissioned from C. P. E. Bach and others some of the finest music ever written for the flute, including this demanding but deliciously mischievous concerto.

16 February

~~~~~

Piano Quartet in E flat major, op. 47
3: Andante cantabile
by Robert Schumann (1810–1856)

Here's a thing. At the start of June 1842, Robert Schumann (Clara's husband) had never written a piece of chamber music, other than a very early stab at a quartet when he was still in his late teens. By the end of 1842, his so-called 'year of chamber music' – although it had actually been only six months – he had produced no fewer than three complete string quartets and a piano quintet (13 May) as well as this splendid piano quartet. How did this happen? Was it something he was drinking? Whatever inspired and enabled this veritable frenzy of chamber-writing genius, I am very grateful for it because these pieces are some of my closest musical companions.

Schumann – who suffered from devastating bouts of depression, who tried to take his own life, who ended his days in an asylum and was dead by forty-six – is an intensely autobiographical composer: into his music he pours his heart and soul, taking us into his confidence and revealing aspects of his personality in a way that is all the more remarkable given how reserved and shy he was in public. The early months of 1842 had been tough on him and Clara: they were on tour, they were under pressure, and Robert writes in his diary of feeling *'very ill . . . always sick and melancholy'*. It strikes me that to write music like this is, then, an act of the very greatest creative generosity – and of trust. Here is Schumann, getting his private anguish down on paper, writing his way out of his own head, saving himself, yes, but in the process of the music being received by us, received and processed and felt and loved, saving *us* too.

Take, if you can, the next seven and a half minutes just to listen – just to listen to this.

17 February

Mélancolie
by Francis Poulenc (1899–1963)

And here is Poulenc in 1940, once again, writing music during the Nazi occupation of France that reminds us what a fierce and formidable musical intellect he is. On the surface, this is a brief lyrical, improvisatory, neo-romantic pastorale – but the clue is in the title. As befits a man who was depressed by the occupation and at constant risk of persecution for being openly gay, the shadows gradually lengthen over its surface; a tender but potentially crushing beauty hovers in its wings.

18 February

Theme from *Schindler's List*
by John Williams (b. 1932)

We're taking two trips to the movies this month, no questions asked. Some of the finest composers of the past hundred years have been those who write for film; the history of the cinema has always been closely bound to classical music. It was Camille Saint-Saëns (25 February, 2 December) who wrote the first ever film score, for a silent movie called *L'Assassinat du duc de Guise*, in 1908; in the decades that followed, many classical giants were drawn to write for Hollywood, including Prokofiev, Satie, Korngold, Walton, Shostakovich, Britten and Glass.

Film soundtracks are a terrific gateway to the wider wonders of the classical world: for many people, it'll be their first experience of hearing music from a non-pop genre. To write a decent film score you have to be a musical storyteller extraordinaire; your music has to touch vast numbers of people in a very particular way. I can't think of a better exemplar than John Williams, the man behind such iconic film scores as *Star Wars*, *E.T. The Extra-Terrestrial*, *Indiana Jones*, *Jaws*, *Jurassic Park*, *Harry Potter* and *Superman*.

Williams's music for Stephen Spielberg's film *Schindler's List*, which was released in the UK on this day in 1993, is a case in point. Incorporating traditional aspects of Jewish music that, irrespective of culture, seem to vibrate atavistically in our collective consciousness, in less than five minutes he manages to transmit the unspeakable tragedy of the Holocaust. The result is an infinitely more powerful film. I would go so far as to say the music is a critical part of what made audiences of all generations everywhere connect to *Schindler's List*, and why it endures in our minds long after the final credits roll.

That the leading classical violinist Itzhak Perlman wanted to play it on the original recording says it all. We'll be back with more movie music in a few days' time, too, so stay tuned.

19 February

'The Spheres' from *Sunrise Mass*
by Ola Gjeilo (b. 1978)

Right. I thought some atmospheric choral music inspired by the February borealis might provide a bit of inspiration at a point in the year which can be a bit bleak – in the northern hemisphere, at least.

Ola Gjeilo is a New York-based Norwegian composer (his surname is pronounced Yay-lo) who was inspired to write the album *Northern Lights*, from which this track comes, one wintry night back home. He was looking out from a high window over a lake under the stars, he says, when he started thinking about the *'terrible beauty'* of the northern lights and the *'powerful, electric quality'* of the aurora borealis. *'It must have been both mesmerizing and terrifying to people in the past, when no one knew what it was.'*

With his layered vocal textures and gleaming dissonances that seem almost to dissolve as they resolve, Gjeilo manages to paint in music one of the world's most elusive natural phenomena. From where I'm listening – near the somewhat less picturesque Harrow Road in London – I find this music utterly transporting: I'm conveyed to another world.

20 February

Handel in the Strand
by Percy Grainger (1882–1961)

There's a lot to be said for the occasional piece of music that simply puts a smile on your face. And here you go, here's one: a musical snapshot of George Frideric Handel careening down the Strand, in London, accompanied by the pop music of the day, courtesy of the Australian-born composer Percy Grainger, who died on this day.

What Grainger does in this vignette is more skilled than it may sound on the surface. It's not going to change the world, but I do find it cheering when it accompanies me on any number of domestic tasks – emptying the dishwasher, putting on a load of laundry, sorting the bins, etc.

21 February

Ein deutsches Requiem – A German Requiem
1: 'Selig sind, die da Leid tragen' –
'Blessed are they that mourn'
by Johannes Brahms (1833–1897)

A change of mood today. Felled with grief after the death of his mother, the great Romantic composer Johannes Brahms began to compose this in February 1865 and it's fair to say he takes a somewhat distinctive approach to the writing of a Requiem. Sacred but non-liturgical, shunning Christian dogma and ignoring the standardized Latin of the traditional Roman Catholic Requiem Mass, he instead chooses texts derived from the German Lutheran bible. Its unusual title – which he first mentioned in a letter to Clara Schumann (the great muse and perhaps love of his life; we'll come to that later) – was, he explained, a reflection of the language in which it was written, rather than a comment on its intended audience. Brahms later said he might just have happily called the work *Ein menschliches Requiem* ('A Human Requiem').

And it *is* a human requiem; a profoundly consoling and empathetic work of art for all humanity that reveals Brahms's capacious heart. Where the Requiem Mass in the Roman Catholic liturgy begins with prayers for the dead (*'Grant them eternal rest, O Lord'*), for example, Brahms decides to place the living front and centre; the words of this movement come from the Beatitudes: *'Blessed are they that mourn, for they shall be comforted.'*

What a thing, Brahms seems to say, in his own luminous way. What if such a thing were possible? That those who mourn might truly be comforted. This motif, of turning anxiety to comfort, recurs throughout the work. A human requiem, eh? It may never have been more urgently needed.

22 February

Sonata for two pianos in D major, K. 448
2: Andante
by Wolfgang Amadeus Mozart (1756–1791)

It can't be easy being a concert pianist: aside from the formidable technical demands and endless hours of practice, it can be a lonely life – you don't generally play in orchestras; if you're a soloist you're on your own much of the time; you can't even take your own instrument with you. Mozart would have known this all too well, touring as he did around Europe, playing one court's random keyboard after another.

What a gift, then, that as well as writing for every other conceivable musical form he turned his attention to the relatively narrow genre of music for multiple pianists. (He also wrote a concerto for two pianos, one for three pianos, and plenty of duets for four hands.)

I once heard a critic dismiss this as 'pure entertainment', which pretty much sums up why classical music has got an image problem. (Heaven forfend we should be entertained!) Mozart wrote it in 1781 for a pupil, Josepha von Auernhammer, who apparently had a crush on him. He was still a bachelor, but I hear no courtship ritual in its notes, no flirtation between the instruments: what I hear is a most beguiling musical depiction of the joys of friendship.

This sonata, by the way, is the piece used by the scientists who investigated the phenomenon known, for shorthand, as the 'Mozart effect'. They found that listening to this music for just ten minutes each day could sufficiently rewire our brains to make us smarter. It could also help treat those suffering from epilepsy and other neurological conditions. The research is freely available online if you feel like diving in. Frankly, I'll take any excuse to listen again.

23 February

Love theme from *Cinema Paradiso*
by Ennio Morricone (b. 1928)

A trumpeter by background, the Italian composer Ennio Morricone entered Rome's storied classical music conservatoire, the Santa Cecilia Academy, in 1940. Having enrolled for a four-year harmony degree, he completed it within six months. He was twelve years old. That should give us some indication of his singular musical brain.

Morricone has gone on to compose over a hundred classical works, but it is the five hundred-odd (classically influenced) film scores he has produced over the course of his career that have made him legendary. His scores invariably make a film, as the directors he works with know all too well. Sergio Leone, for example (the director with whose 'spaghetti western' films Morricone's music is synonymous), only began shooting *Once Upon a Time in the West* after Morricone had written his magnificent score. The music came first. That never happens.

It was on this day in 1990 that Giuseppe Tornatore's postmodern Italian classic *Cinema Paradiso* was released in the USA – where it went on to win the Best Foreign Language Film Oscar. Telling the tale of a little boy who forges a friendship with the projectionist at his local village cinema and goes on to become a great director, it is blessed with a score by Morricone and his son Andrea. Touching and unapologetically sentimental, the theme perfectly reflects the central premise of Tornatore's film: namely that art matters; that filmmaking matters; that cinema, as a communal experience that builds bonds between people across generations, across time and space, matters. The same might be said for music itself.

24 February

Spiegel im Spiegel
by Arvo Pärt (b. 1935)

It's Estonian Independence Day: a good moment to hear from one of that country's most musical sons, Arvo Pärt. As reclusive now as he was pioneering in his day, Pärt started his career by embracing the avant-garde. Growing up in communist Estonia, he experimented with atonality, with dissonance, with serialism. And then, in the late 1970s, he went in a more minimalist and meditative direction – even coining his own word, 'tintinnabular', to describe a new style which was less intellectually complex, more spiritual; less challenging, more immediately sensory.

This piece for solo violin and piano, meaning 'mirror in the mirror', was one of the first compositions he wrote after changing tack and it remains one of his most enduringly popular. Needless to say, there's a lot more to Arvo Pärt's sound world than this glistening reverie, but it's a good place to start. I hope it delivers a moment of stillness and serenity to your day.

25 February

Le carnaval des animaux – The Carnival of the Animals
13: 'The Swan'
by Camille Saint-Saëns (1835–1921)

As procrastination techniques go, this is a classic. In February 1886, the French composer Saint-Saëns was holed up in a small Austrian village trying to concentrate on finishing his Third Symphony. Instead, he distracted himself from the task at hand by composing a fourteen-movement suite called *The Carnival of the Animals*, complete with tortoises, kangaroos and donkeys. Writing to his publishers, Durand, in Paris, he apologized for dilly-dallying . . . *'mais c'est si amusant!'* – 'but this is so much fun!'

Saint-Saëns never intended for his *Carnival* to go public. For years, it was heard only behind behind closed doors, at private gatherings, and he specified that it should never be published in his lifetime. (Presumably he was concerned that it would detract from his reputation as one of France's musical heavyweights; classical music snobbery being what it is.) He did relent, however, for this penultimate movement, 'The Swan', which he arranged for publication in 1887 with cello and piano (it was originally written for two pianos). Moving and elegiac, it became world-famous as a ballet called *The Dying Swan*, choreographed by Mikhail Fokine and danced by the great ballerina Anna Pavlova some four thousand times.

Saint-Saëns died in December 1921. The first ever public performance took place, on this day, the following year. (He did eventually get round to writing the Third Symphony, by the way, and it's terrific – see 27 May.)

26 February

Vladimir's Blues
by Max Richter (b. 1966)

The German-born, UK-based composer Max Richter is a fascinating figure in contemporary classical music. A graduate of the famous Royal Academy of Music in London, he is signed to Deutsche Grammophon, one of the most august classical music labels ('since 1898'). His first album, *Memoryhouse*, was published by Boosey & Hawkes, who also publish Edward Elgar, Richard Strauss and Igor Stravinsky. He composes, old-school, with manuscript paper at a piano, part of an analogue lineage that goes all the way back to J. S. Bach.

Yet his is a hybrid musical language that draws in crowds of listeners who wouldn't normally go near a concert hall, often much younger than the average classical punter. Whether intentionally or not, Richter has come to be seen as the architect of a post-minimalist electronic revolution at the borderlands of classical music that has also seen composers such as Ólafur Arnalds reimagine the music of Chopin (9 August), and Nils Frahm play at the ultimate classical musical festival, the BBC Proms (29 March).

Richter works across a variety of genres, including film music, and constantly pushes at the boundaries of what music with classical roots might be capable of in a digital age (see also 22 March).

Like many composers before him, Richter also uses his music to explore political ideas and ideals. In the run-up to the 2003 allied invasion of Iraq, for example, he produced *The Blue Notebooks*, which he describes as *'a protest album about Iraq, a meditation on violence . . . [and] at the utter futility of so much armed conflict'*. The album, which features this arresting piano piece, was recorded about a week after mass protests against the war; it came out on this day in 2004.

27 February

String Quartet no. 2 in D major
3: Nocturne: Andante
by Alexander Borodin (1833–1887)

It seems unlikely to me, because I can barely add two plus two without a calculator, but the compelling links between science, mathematics and music are well documented and backed up by hard science. For Albert Einstein, for example, music wasn't just a relaxing sideline after a long day of figuring out, say, general relativity: it was central to his mode of thought. '[It] helps him when he is thinking about his theories,' revealed his second wife, Elsa. 'He goes to his study, comes back, strikes a few chords on the piano, jots something down, returns to his study.' The physicist himself believed that if he hadn't been a scientist he would have been a violinist. 'Life without playing music is inconceivable for me,' he declared. 'I live my daydreams in music. I see my life in terms of music. I get most joy in life out of music.'

And yet as complementary as music and science are, few manage to combine them as professional careers. Alexander Borodin, who was born on this day, is a shining exception. He wrote symphonies and operas and painted vast orchestral tableaux such as *In the Steppes of Central Asia*. He also composed chamber music of great beauty, such as this nocturne, which his biographer Serge Dianin suggests was intended as a twentieth-anniversary gift to his wife, Yekaterina.

Meanwhile, he was equally celebrated in the chemistry community. In 1862, he described the first nucleophilic displacement of chlorine by fluorine in benzoyl chloride in a process later promoted by the Soviet Union as the 'Borodin reaction'.

My own Borodin reaction was further improved when I discovered he was an ardent advocate of women's rights, promoting equality of education in Russia and founding the School of Medicine for Women in St Petersburg. What a guy.

28 February

Symphony no. 2 in E flat major, op. 63
2: Larghetto
by Edward Elgar (1857–1934)

In some circles, Edward Elgar has a reputation for being something of a buttoned-up Edwardian, conservative and quintessentially English.

If anything should dispel that, it's his Second Symphony, completed on this day in 1911 and described as *a passionate pilgrimage of the soul*.

The piece is dedicated to the memory of King Edward VII, who had died the previous year. This movement takes the form of a funeral march, befitting the monarch's death – but also likely reflecting Elgar's personal grief at having recently lost two close friends. The movement surges with feeling that is all the more powerful for having been unleashed from the genteel confines of an Edwardian English symphony.

Conducting a rehearsal, Elgar urged his players:

> *Strings, you must play those semiquaver figures of yours like the sigh of an immense crowd . . . Oboe, I want you to play your lament entirely free, with all the expression you can get into it.*

Inscribed on the original score of the symphony are lines from 'Song' by Percy Bysshe Shelley (published shortly before his death in 1822).

> *Rarely, rarely, comest thou,*
> *Spirit of Delight!*
> *Wherefore hast thou left me now*
> *Many a day and night?*
> *Many a weary night and day*
> *'Tis since thou art fled away.*

Elgar was not to know it, but this symphony would be the last one he'd complete. In a letter to a friend he admitted: *'I have written out my soul.'*

29 February

Petite messe solennelle
1: Kyrie
by Gioachino Rossini (1792–1868)

Born on the Leap Year, Gioachino Rossini published his first opera at eighteen, and by the age of twenty-one was acknowledged as a genius of the form. He would go on to write thirty-nine operas, as well as hold illustrious posts in theatres around Italy.

Unlike most classical musicians, Rossini was a shrewd businessman: as music director of an opera house in Naples he negotiated a monthly salary of 200 ducats plus a share of the theatre's gambling tables, amounting to a whopping 1000 ducats per annum. Adjusted for today's rates, it's a financial set-up most composers could hardly dream of.

He was worth it, though. Speedy and prolific, Rossini was once quoted as saying *give me the laundress' bill and I will even set that to music* – and it's true, the melodies seemed to fly out of him; hence his nickname, 'The Italian Mozart'. Beethoven wrote to him, saying, '*Ah, Rossini. So you're the composer of* The Barber of Seville. *I congratulate you. It will be played as long as Italian opera exists.*' (So far, so good.)

Like many of the best composers, Rossini took existing musical trends and made them his own (he also stole mercilessly from his own back catalogue: deadlines will do that to you). This was written towards the end of his life. He labelled it '*Petite*' with a dash of irony, writing on the final page of the manuscript:

> *Dear Lord, here it is finished, this poor little mass . . . I was born for opera buffa, as you well know. Not much technique, a little bit of heart, that's all. Blessings to you and grant me Paradise.*

MARCH

1 *March*

〜

Ar hyd y Nos – *All through the Night*
Traditional Welsh

For as long as there have been humans needing to communicate with each other, music has been among the most powerful ways of doing it, and perhaps nowhere more so than in Wales. In 1187, for example, the medieval chronicler Giraldus Cambrensis records that across the country, music can be found wherever there are people; he also notes that even very small children can harmonize with aplomb. No wonder Wales is often called the 'land of song'.

Despite the best efforts of the Nonconformists, the English and mass-market entertainment, extremely rich choral, vocal and instrumental traditions continue to flourish in Wales. The days in which every single town or village could boast its own choir and music society may be gone, but for such a tiny country it still punches far above its weight when it comes to producing world-class musicians.

For St David's Day, then, here's a much loved traditional song, first recorded in the 1784 collection *Musical and Poetical Relicks of the Welsh Bards*, as assembled by the legendary Welsh bard, harpist, poet, composer and arranger Edward Jones (a.k.a. 'Bardd y Brenin').

Dydd Gŵyl Dewi Hapus!

2 March

Missa prolationum
1: Kyrie Eleison I
by Johannes Ockeghem (c. 1410–1497)

The name Johannes Ockeghem may be largely unknown outside niche Renaissance-enthusiast circles, but in his day this singer, choirmaster and teacher was a pillar of the Franco-Flemish circle, that tight-knit community of fifteenth-century composers (none of whom we know much about) who traded musical ideas, built on polyphonic trends coming out of places like England, and developed a rich, complex, sensual approach to what a small group of human beings singing together could do.

As a composer, Ockeghem produced some of the earliest examples of Renaissance polyphony that are still in the general choral repertoire today, although older examples do exist. (The earliest surviving polyphonic compositions, found in an anonymous ninth-century treatise called the *Musica enchiriadis*, date from AD 900 – a fact that gives me actual goosebumps.)

Ockeghem was so admired by his contemporaries that his death unleashed an outpouring of feeling from the next generation, including a moving tribute from another Franco-Flemish giant, Josquin des Prez, which we'll be hearing later in the year (26 July).

3 March

Carmen Suite no. 1
3: Intermezzo
by Georges Bizet (1838–1875)

I find it heartbreaking that Georges Bizet died believing his opera *Carmen* to be a failure. The premiere took place on this day in 1875 and was badly received by the critics, who had no taste for its supposedly 'low-life' subject matter. Exactly three months later, the composer dropped dead from a heart attack. He was only thirty-six; it was also his sixth wedding anniversary.

It was not long, however, before *Carmen* began to be recognized for the exceptional piece of lyric theatre that it is. Saint-Saëns and Tchaikovsky were ardent admirers; even Wagner, not exactly one to lovebomb his fellow composers, gave it grudging praise. Brahms, meanwhile, attended over twenty performances and apparently considered it the best thing that had been seen on a stage perhaps ever.

I'm with them. Bizet blends nuanced and attractive music with an unerring instinct for drama. By operatic standards, the characters are subtly drawn; here's the gypsy Carmen in all her reckless vulnerability, there's Don José (we'll meet him later in the year) in his journey from young, love-struck soldier to misogynistic abuser; neither of them the empty operatic caricatures they might easily have been.

Carmen went on to become one of the most successful operas of all time. After Bizet died, two concert suites of music from its score were assembled; they too have remained favourites in the orchestral repertoire. This gorgeous intermezzo, reflecting Don José's state of love-struck bliss, is taken in a rare moment of calm before Act 3. (Although don't be fooled – it's opera: it's all going to go horribly wrong . . .)

4 March

Concerto for two trumpets in C major, RV 537
1: Allegro
by Antonio Vivaldi (1678–1741)

The mighty Antonio Vivaldi, one of the all-time musical greats, was born on this day: we shall celebrate with some sparkling double trumpets. I love the bright, fanfare-like opening of this concerto and the call-and-response exchange he creates between both the solo lines and the ensemble. With the exception of Bach, it's hard to think of another Baroque composer – or indeed any composer – who writes better for multiple solo instruments. (Vivaldi also wrote concertos for double mandolins, double violins, double cellos and all sorts of other combinations.)

This crisp yet freewheeling concerto is also significant for being one of the earliest concertos to feature brass instruments in a solo capacity. In Vivaldi's day, unlike the modern era, trumpets were valveless, or 'natural'. This meant their expressive range was very limited and they were fiendishly difficult to control – and thus terrifying to play as a soloist. Those early performers must have had some formidable lip technique!

5 March

Symphony no. 1 in D major, op. 25 ('Classical')
1: Allegro
by Sergei Prokofiev (1891–1953)

Always a bit of a renegade spirit, Prokofiev, who died on this day, is doing something really interesting here – writing an almost satirical pastiche of a 'Classical' symphony from the vantage point of 1917, the year of the Russian Revolution, when all around him established aesthetic forms (not to mention whole nations, empires) were fragmenting and falling apart. He wrote this cheering, cheeky symphony at the age of twenty-six, whilst on holiday in the country, and was very deliberately seeking to emulate Joseph Haydn (6 April, 13 July, 28 December), whose music he had studied at the conservatoire in St Petersburg.

This nod to Viennese formality was a deliberate provocation, marking as it did a shift from Prokofiev's youthful adventures in much more avant-garde and dissonant twentieth-century sound worlds. But it also happened to correspond with a shift towards similar preoccupations among other composers such as Igor Stravinsky (29 May) who were intrigued by what would happen if they meshed radical twentieth-century harmonies and ideas with Classical norms such as four-movement symphonies.

Prokofiev, though, had no interest in being part of this burgeoning 'neoclassical' movement; he saw his clever, witty symphony as a one-off experiment and slammed Stravinsky for merely doing 'Bach on the wrong notes'. Ouch.

6 March

Piano Trio no. 5 in D major, op. 70 no. 1 ('Ghost')
1: Allegro vivace e con brio
by Ludwig van Beethoven (1770–1827)

No matter how many times I hear this – and it's a lot – I am never not electrified by how Beethoven just catapults us, no warning, into a magnificent three-way conversation. Right from the outset we're on a tumultuous musical trip and he keeps us on our toes (if ears can be said to be on toes) with fantastically varied textures, dynamic surprises and even notes that sound somehow 'wrong' – yet are somehow right.

It's no exaggeration to say that Beethoven absolutely towers over this period; a tortured, complex, beleaguered musical giant bridging the structural elegance of the Classical era and the wilder emotion of the Romantic era – overcoming immense personal struggles (such as his deafness from the age of twenty-eight) to radically transform music. His innovations are endless. Previously, for example, it would have been a given that the two string parts in a trio would play an inferior role to the keyboard; now all three instruments communicate as equals and it makes for a thrilling listen, raising the piano trio genre to heights that some leading lights of the next generation would take it upon themselves to try and scale (see e.g. 21 March).

If you're thinking, by the way, that this trio does not sound particularly 'ghostly', its nickname reflects the fact that Beethoven was working on some ideas for incidental music to a production of Shakespeare's *Macbeth* at the same time. (There are notes to this effect scrawled at the end of the admittedly much more eerie-sounding second movement.) Some historians believe that passage was possibly meant for a scene in the play depicting the three witches; regardless, classical music loves a nickname and the appellation has stuck.

7 March

Piano Concerto in G major
2: Adagio assai
by Maurice Ravel (1875–1937)

There are before-and-after pieces of music in life, aren't there? Things that, once heard, change everything. These are the pieces I find myself temporarily unable to live without; ones I find myself compelled to play over, and over, and over, again.

This is one such piece. I was sixteen, and playing in my school orchestra. There was a really good pianist in the year above, and at the end-of-year recital, she was performing it. I'll never forget the first rehearsal – it blew my mind. I remember feeling a giddy combination of relief that it was now in my life and a sort of mute outrage that I'd existed all these years without knowing it existed. I bought the CD and played it on constant repeat for about the next six months. It's never left my side since.

Ravel, who was born on this day, had in mind Saint-Saëns and Mozart when in 1929 he turned his attention to writing a new piano concerto. His dream was to be able to play it himself, but he knew his own technique wasn't good enough. So he set out to write something less challenging, then changed his mind and decided not to hold back, to write the piece he wanted, and instead practise so hard that by the time it was ready, he'd be up to the job.

As goals go it was impressive, but alas he was still defeated by his own ambition. Despite practising the studies of Chopin for months, by the time the concerto was ready Ravel was not. He asked its dedicatee, the sensational Marguerite Long, to play the piano part at the premiere in 1932 instead, and settled for merely conducting.

I'm thankful Ravel didn't temper his vision for the piece, as it's one of the jewels of the twentieth-century piano repertoire. I hope you fall as hard for it as I did.

8 March

~~~~~

'O dolce mio tesoro' – 'O my sweet treasure'
from *Sesto libro di madrigali*
by Carlo Gesualdo (1566–1613)

'*Irrefutably badass*' is not an obvious phrase to reach for when discussing a late-Renaissance lute player and composer whose output was chiefly a cappella madrigals and settings of sacred texts. But that's how Alex Ross, esteemed music critic of *The New Yorker*, views Don Carlo Gesualdo, and I've never yet found a better description.

For better or worse, classical music has a reputation for being a rather staid affair; its practitioners well-behaved servants at court who busy themselves with, say, counterpoint and harmony. Gesualdo, who was born on this day, rather obliterates this stereotype. He suffered from manic depression, he murdered his wife, he was embroiled in the Spanish Inquisition and a witchcraft trial, and was eventually beaten to death by his servants in a kind of masochistic rampage.

But then he goes and writes this insanely beautiful music. Gesualdo was astonishingly – perhaps diabolically – inventive. His unhinged harmonies were revelatory. No wonder Stravinksy (29 May) and Schoenberg (13 September) cited him as a model for their own radical innovations. Describing Gesualdo as '*one of the most personal creators ever born to my art*', in 1960 Stravinsky reworked at least a dozen of his madrigals by hand and compiled them in his *Monumentum pro Gesualdo di Venosa*, which was later turned into a ballet by the choreographer George Balanchine.

His is music with its nerve-endings sometimes disturbingly close to the surface. I'm breaking you in gently here, but if you have the stomach for it, there's a whole new world to discover.

9 March

Violin Concerto, op. 14
2: Andante
by Samuel Barber (1910–1981)

Not all the game-changers in music actually change much. Here's someone who, by resisting the intellectual glitter of Modernism, became himself something of a radical. In the mid-twentieth century, many American composers were drawn to the breakaway atonal and arhythmic trends that were sweeping Europe. Samuel Barber, who was born on this day, preferred to hold fast to things that probably felt somewhat 'old-fashioned' by then – lyrical melodies, consoling harmonies, sumptuous orchestration, traditional forms. (Things, in other words, that people really like to listen to.) Many of his contemporaries have faded into obscurity; Barber's reputation only grows.

It was on the cusp of calamity, in 1939, that he undertook to write a violin concerto for one of the talented young artists on the scene at that time. From a cornucopia of influences, including Korngold (2 September) and Puccini (14 January, 1 February, 14 October), Barber directly draws on the inspiration of the Bruch (6 January) and Sibelius (20 September) violin concertos. Yet he infuses the piece with his own emotional sensibility. The language is wholly Barber's own – and wholly wonderful.

10 March

Zigeunerweisen, op. 20
by Pablo de Sarasate (1844–1908)

More violin today, but in a very different mode to yesterday. As a fiddle player myself, I sometimes fantasize about what it must have been like to see some of the great violinists of history in action: Fritz Kreisler, Joseph Joachim, Niccolò Paganini, Marie Hall, Jascha Heifetz and Pablo de Sarasate, who was born on this day. Celebrated for his virtuosic technique as a performer, he composed pieces of great stylistic panache that are as exhilarating to listen to as they are hair-raising to play.

Like many composers of the time, Sarasate was aware of the growing trend for incorporating traditional folk idioms into modern pieces. The title of this piece means 'gypsy airs', and was probably inspired by a trip he took to Budapest in 1877, where he visited the great Hungarian musician Franz Liszt, gave a few concerts, and generally soaked up the music of popular local bands. And classical music being the free-for-all melodic treasury that it is, Sarasate apparently felt no compunction about lifting wholesale one of the folk tunes that had caught his attention, the song *Csak egy szép lány van a világon* ('There's only one lovely maid in the world').

When a rather disgruntled Hungarian composer known as Elemér Szentirmay got in touch with Sarasate's German publisher after the publication of *Zigeunerweisen* to point this out, Sarasate feigned ignorance, got his assistant to write an apologetic letter on his behalf in German, and from there on acknowledged on the manuscript the originator of the main melody: *'used with the composer's kind permission'*. Cheeky.

11 March

Libertango
by Astor Piazzolla (1921–1992)

To a different musical world altogether now and the grand tango master Astor Piazzolla. Born in Argentina on this day, he spent his childhood in New York City, studied in Paris under the legendary Nadia Boulanger (22 October) and later returned to his homeland, where he revolutionized its seductive national dance by infusing it with elements of jazz and classical music.

As a kid, Piazzolla had availed himself of his father's extensive record collection, which included lots of Bach, and by the time he was in his late teens was trying his hand at writing classical music. Back in Buenos Aires, he found himself increasingly fascinated by the process of orchestration – essentially the arrangement of how a piece is divvied up for orchestra; which instruments play what, where, when. In his early twenties, he would often spend his mornings watching the rehearsals of the orchestra of the Teatro Colón, before playing the tango clubs at night. It proved a heady mix.

Piazzolla also took lessons with the eminent classical composer Alberto Ginastera (11 April) and was much influenced by the briefly Buenos Aires-based classical pianist Arthur Rubinstein, who urged Piazzolla to absorb himself in the music of Stravinsky (29 May), Bartók (25 March) and Ravel (7 March, 14 July). They would all have their influences on his compositional style, but as ever with the true greats, there's some alchemical element in his music that makes it all his own.

This classic tango in the 'new style' was first published in 1974 and has since been recorded at least five hundred times.

12 March

Miserere in C minor
by Jan Dismas Zelenka (1679–1745)

My penchant for epic choral music may be obvious by now, and I just can't get enough of the high drama and emotional charge of this rarely performed, much neglected Bohemian composer – especially in this piece, which the original manuscript tells us was completed on this day in 1738.

Colourful and urgent, expressive and angular, I love how Zelenka's maverick chord progressions turn this into something unexpectedly modern. It is a brilliant example of a sacred choral work that feels as though it originated from an actual human being who cared what he was writing about; rather than someone at court simply joining the musical dots. (Although Zelenka was a court composer, as it happens, in Dresden; and therefore one in the curious position of being a passionate Catholic stuck in a zealously Lutheran city.)

He may be largely forgotten now, but in his day Zelenka was greatly admired. Telemann, for example, was so in awe of his abilities that he was drawn into a complex plot to try and steal copies of his work (which is ironic, as Telemann himself campaigned for exclusive publication rights for his works and was an early advocate of intellectual property rights for composers). J. S. Bach, meanwhile, tirelessly lobbied Zelenka's employers to get an appointment at the same court, just to be closer to his hero. Zelenka is hardly ever heard today, which just goes to show what a fickle old thing history can be.

13 March

~~~~~~~~

'Kashmiri Love Song'
from *Four Indian Love Lyrics*
by Amy Woodforde-Finden (1860–1919)

From the world of Baroque Bohemia we shuttle now to the sultry climes of nineteenth-century India and Amy Woodforde-Finden, who died on this day, allegedly while composing at her beloved piano. Born in Chilé to American parents, she later moved to London and became a British citizen before marrying the rather excellently named Lieutenant-Colonel Woodford Woodforde-Finden, a brigadier and surgeon in the Indian Army.

Celebrated for her 'Eastern ditties', Woodforde-Finden wrote songs blending colonial British base notes with Asian flavours, a generous dash of sentimentality and an Orientalist twist. Although very much 'of their time', they make for a lovely listen and have always been popular with audiences: although she'd originally had to self-publish this one – based on a poem by Laurence Hope, nom de plume of Adela Florence Nicolson – such was the demand that it was eventually bought by the high-profile music publisher Boosey & Hawkes. Good on her.

I recommend listening with a cold gin and tonic or equivalent in hand. Shalimar, here we come.

14 March

Tarantella: 'La Carpinese'
Traditional

Doing the tarantella has been a custom in Southern Europe for centuries, allegedly since the villagers in the Italian seaside port of Taranto discovered that a certain kind of whirling, high-octane dance could act as an antidote to the deadly bite of the local 'tarantula' spider. It's possible this was actually a front for people who just wanted to get out of their heads dancing in a kind of post-Dionysian/pre-rave frenzy, which would otherwise have been frowned upon, but whatever the case, the legend of the tarantella's power spread far and wide. Even the famous English diarist Samuel Pepys refers to it in his 1662 volume: come harvest time in Southern Europe, he is told, and duly reports, *'fiddlers go up and down the fields everywhere, in expectation of being hired by those that are stung'.*

Magical antidotal properties aside, the tarantella invariably makes for an adrenaline-pumping listen and it crops up again and again in classical music (as well as in more mainstream pursuits, such as Francis Ford Coppola's *The Godfather*, released on this day in 1972, with its famous wedding tarantella). Romantic composers were particularly drawn to its alluring rhythms: those who had a crack at tarantellas in the nineteenth century include Chopin, Rachmaninov, Mendelssohn, Tchaikovsky, Verdi, Rossini and Debussy.

15 March

'Va tacito e nascosto' – 'Go silently and stealthily'
from *Giulio Cesare*
by George Frideric Handel (1685–1759)

Beware the Ides of March! On this day, associated for ever with the assassination of Julius Caesar in 44BC, I thought we should hear from the man whilst he's still alive – in Act I of Handel's smash-hit late opera, whose action takes place a few years before that fateful day.

Handel seems to have an apparently effortless skill as a dramatist. Without ever labouring the point, his music perfectly illustrates the situation that a wary, distrustful Caesar finds himself in. Convinced he is about to be betrayed, Caesar describes himself as a hunter tracking his prey – and lo and behold, this is exactly what we hear in the music.

Va tacito e nascosto,	*The wise hunter*
Quand'avido è di preda,	*seeking prey*
L'astuto cacciator.	*goes silently and stealthily.*
E chi è a mal far disposto,	*And he who intends evil*
Non brama che si veda	*will not wish to show*
L'inganno del suo cor.	*the deceit in his heart . . .*

It's also got a fantastic part for the solo French horn; worth the price of admission alone.

16 March

String Quintet in C major, D. 956
2: Adagio
by Franz Schubert (1797–1828)

The ever-inventive Schubert confounds tradition here by calling for an extra cello to complement the standard string quartet forces of two violins, viola and cello. It's his only string quintet, and I'm touched by how insecure he was about it – sending it to his publisher with a pitch that will feel all too familiar to anyone in the creative world who has ever peddled their wares: '*Should it by chance commend itself to you,*' he beseeches, '*please let me know . . .*'

The publisher wrote back ignoring the quintet and essentially asking for more pop songs. (Schubert was the originator of the three-minute ballad, as we'll see.) For all his lavish compositional talents, and despite the fact he had already published no fewer than fifteen string quartets, he simply wasn't taken seriously as a writer of chamber music in his day. Now he's regarded as one of the great geniuses of the form, but he never lived to see this sublime masterpiece published; just two months later, at the age of thirty-one, he would be dead.

17 March

Nocturne no. 5 in B flat major
by John Field (1782–1837)

It's St Patrick's Day: time to hear from the first Irishman to make a significant impact on the European classical scene. Born in Dublin, John Field was a pianist and composer whose combination of formal creativity and deeply felt lyricism earned him the admiration of many fellow composers, including Brahms, Schumann, Mendelssohn – and above all Chopin, who was apparently ecstatic when the pianist and composer Freidrich Kalkbrenner observed that Chopin's touch *'reminded him of Field's'*. Chopin was particularly inspired by Field's set of 'nocturnes', a musical form that many credit the Irishman with inventing, although other composers, including Haydn, had previously employed the term. (Field certainly took the form and ran with it; we'll hear how Chopin developed it still further on 28 November.)

Trends in piano playing in Field's day tended to prioritize virtuosity of technique, but he was unafraid to go in a different direction, cultivating an ideal of poetic expression and heartfelt emotion that prefigures the prevailing winds of Romanticism. Nowadays, Field's music sounds very familiar to us in mood at least, inspiring as it has vast amounts of lush piano music, but it's worth bearing in mind that this sort of thing had never been heard before. As the great Franz Liszt, another Field superfan, wrote in the preface to an edition of the *Nocturnes*:

> *None have quite attained to these vague . . . harmonies, these half-formed sighs floating through the air, softly lamenting and dissolved in delicious melancholy. Nobody has even attempted this peculiar style, and especially none of those who heard Field play himself, or rather who heard him dream his music in moments when he entirely abandoned himself to his inspiration.*

18 March

Polonaise de Concert in D major, op. 4
by Henryk Wieniawski (1835–1880)

In 1843, the administrators of the famous Paris Conservatoire, the French music college par excellence, found themselves facing a dilemma when they encountered the young Polish violinist Henryk Wieniawski. Despite not being French, and only nine, such was his talent that they felt they had no choice but to accept him as a student. Their decision was roundly vindicated: he went on to graduate at eleven, and two years later started publishing his compositions.

Wieniawski writes music to delight; to persuade. He fell in love with a girl called Isabel and proposed to her, but her parents forbade the union. Then he wrote his *Légénde*, played it to them, and they promptly changed their minds (see 16 October).

In 1852, at the peak of his career and fame, Wieniawski composed this effervescent Polonaise (and its accompanying Adagio) as a gift for King William III of the Netherlands. He himself gave the first performance on this day that year; it must have been a dazzler.

19 March

Cello Suite no. 1 in G major
1: Prelude
by J. S. Bach (1685–1750)

It's hard to imagine now, but back in Bach's day, the cello was considered an extremely lowly instrument; certainly not one worth writing solos for. ('Mwah-hah-hah!' I hear him chortle. 'Just you wait, people. Just you wait.') Seriously, though, an air of mystery surrounds his six cello suites because the original manuscript has long disappeared. For centuries they were barely known, and generally assumed to be études or studies rather than solo works.

That we have them firmly back in the repertoire now is down to one of history's great instances of serendipity, a 'What if . . . ?' moment whose counterfactual does not bear imagining. In 1890, the thirteen-year-old Catalan cellist Pablo Casals was out strolling with his father near the port in Barcelona. They stopped to browse in a local junk shop, and the young cellist happened upon an edition of the cello suites that had been made in the nineteenth century by someone called Grützmacher. Intrigued, he bought it, took it home, started practising, and the rest, as they say, is history.

Each of the six suites has its own distinct personality, its own story, its own blend of heart-stopping beauty and high-jinks joy. I could have chosen any movement, but I have started at the very beginning, with the opening movement of the opening suite, in the ardent hope that at some point, maybe now, maybe later, you'll find the time to go on and listen to them all – to take them into your life and let them enrich your every day.

20 March

Zefiro torna e di soavi accenti – Return, O Zephyr
by Claudio Monteverdi (1567–1643)

Straddling the Renaissance and Baroque eras, Monteverdi was the most important composer of his time and in many ways the first modernist. The architect of a number of musical revolutions, he practically invented opera as we know it, creating, in works such as *Orfeo* and *The Return of Ulysses*, the mass popular entertainment of the day; always rooted, critically, in authentic human experience. On a smaller scale, his settings of madrigals – secular songs for multiple voices, invariably written in elaborate counterpoint – are equally filled with surprises, with dynamic ups and downs and moments of such spontaneity and naturalness that we take for granted now what would have sounded impossibly new in his day.

This one is a classic. Monteverdi sets a rhapsodic ode to spring by the poet Ottavio Rinuccini, in a work celebrating the bountiful promise of the season. As ever with Monteverdi, the music serves its text with infectious exuberance:

Zefiro torna e di soavi accenti	*O Zephyr, return softly,*
l'aer fa grato e'il pié discioglie a	*Sweeten the air and sprinkle grass*
l'onde . . .	*across the waves . . .*
fa danzar al bel suon su'l prato i	*Make fields of flowers dance to your*
fiori.	*gentle sound.*

Today, meteorologically speaking at least, is the day that the west wind ushers in spring. Here's hoping . . .

21 March

Piano Trio no. 1 in D minor, op. 49
2: Andante con molto tranquillo
by Felix Mendelssohn (1809–1847)

As we saw earlier this month, Beethoven paved the way for the development of the piano trio, extending its possibilities as an exciting creative canvas that, while intimate, could tell a rich and varied story through music.

Mendelssohn was one of the composers of the following generation to pick up Beethoven's baton and run with it. He took the genre still further, especially in the way he treats the three distinct voices as equal partners, rather than following the old model in which strings are always subservient to the keyboard.

His revolutions did not go unnoticed at the time: Robert Schumann, who dubbed Mendelssohn 'the Mozart of the nineteenth century', wrote of this piece:

> *This is the master trio of our age . . . It is an exceedingly fine composition which will gladden our grandchildren and great-grandchildren for many years to come.*

Yup.

22 March

Recomposed: Vivaldi Four Seasons
'Spring 2'
by Max Richter (b. 1966)

Even if you have only the most fleeting previous acquaintance with classical music, the chances are you'll have heard Vivaldi's *Four Seasons*. A lot. Beloved of on-hold telephony operators, generic Italian restaurants, TV adverts and classical compilations everywhere, it's one of the most famous pieces of music, of any genre, ever written. And such is the work's ubiquity it's easy to forget how radical, how thrillingly inventive it actually is. Because we hear it all the time, it's easy to forget to *listen* to it.

That's why I so love what Max Richter, who was born on this day, does with his ingenious reworking of the *Seasons* from 2012. We've already seen how the finest composers throughout history raid the riches of the canon to remake something wholly new; how they are all in dialogue with each other across time and space, chucking around ideas and inspiration and insights into what the twelve little notes they have at their disposal can do. This is a particularly inspiring example. With a mixture of irreverence and respect for the original – Richter talks of *'throwing molecules of the original Vivaldi into a test tube with a bunch of other things, and waiting for an explosion'* – he finds his own distinctive way through a sonic landscape with which we are all overfamiliar. In the process, he both creates a modern masterpiece and enables us to hear Vivaldi's anew. That's no small thing.

23 March

Heal You
by Anna Meredith (b. 1978)

Born in London, raised in Scotland and a former resident composer with the BBC Scottish Symphony Orchestra, Anna Meredith writes music of so many different genres that any attempt to label her is soon revealed for the folly it is.

As well as opera, vocal, orchestral and instrumental music, Meredith has turned her fierce intelligence and playful imagination to beatboxer symphonies, pop music and film scores. Her music has been performed everywhere from the hallowed Royal Albert Hall during the Last Night of the Proms to a service station off the M6 (in a particularly memorable body-percussion flash-mob performance).

This short, evocative choral piece sets words by the storyteller Philip Ridley and is a real mind-cleanser, in the best possible way.

24 March

Viola Concerto in G major
1: Largo
by Georg Philip Telemann (1681–1767)

Telemann in a mellow mood today, his birthday, writing for the instrument that some say is closest to the human voice (and others are just mean about; the viola having long been the butt of orchestral jokes). Of the seventy-eight instrumental concertos that this hugely prolific composer wrote, this is the one for which he's best known.

I mentioned in our encounter with Telemann last month that he was a law school dropout; what I'm always touched by is how in private, despite having been forced onto a professional path that his heart was not in, he never gave up hope: he taught himself multiple musical instruments and kept writing music, in secret, on the side. I think you can hear that compulsion to express himself in pretty much everything he writes – this is music with its heart on its sleeve.

25 March

Romanian Folk Dances
2: 'Sash Dance'
by Béla Bartók (1881–1945)

Born on this day, Béla Bartók's contribution to musical history goes far beyond the compositions he left us. Influenced by figures from the past such as Bach, Beethoven, Brahms, Strauss and Debussy, he was also fascinated by the breakdown in traditional Western tonality as instigated by Schoenberg & co. in the Second Viennese School, the ramifications of which could be heard all around him.

Most importantly, as an assiduous collector, curator, arranger and analyser of the folk music of his native Hungary and beyond (Turkey, Algeria, the Carpathian basin), Bartók was an early pioneer in 'comparative musicology'. Now known as ethnomusicology, this discipline studies music from the perspective of those who actually make it (rather than just what it sounds like in an isolated context). In this way, his gift to the diverse soundscapes of the twentieth century is immeasurable.

It was a moment of pure chance that sparked Bartók's lifelong passion for folk music. In the summer of 1904, while on holiday, he overheard a young nanny called Lidi Dósa singing some traditional Transylvanian songs to the children she was looking after. He was captivated. As we saw with Sarasate (10 March), by the late nineteenth century there was a growing trend among classical composers to draw on national musical traditions. Spearheaded by the likes of Glinka (4 June), Dvořák (21 July, 29 August, 8 September) and Liszt, Bartók took this preoccupation to a new level, absorbing, as he himself puts it, the very *'idiom of peasant music'* to the point where it *'has become his musical mother tongue'*.

This vibrant, fleeting movement is based on a dance from Igris in the Banat region of Romania, in which the dancers traditionally wear a distinctive sash or waistband; Bartók brings the picture vividly to life.

26 March

12 Notations pour piano, arranged for orchestra
1: Fantasque – Modéré
by Pierre Boulez (1925–2016)

Speaking of ethnomusicologists, here's a composer who might nearly have become one, had the pull of his other gigantic talents not taken him in the direction of the manuscript paper, the conductor's podium and the cutting-edge institution, sometimes all at once. It was in the winter of 1945 that Frenchman Pierre Boulez was introduced to Balinese and Japanese music and African drumming at the Musée Guimet in Paris. *'I almost chose the career of an ethnomusicologist because I was so fascinated by that music,'* he later admitted. *'It gives a different feeling of time.'*

Boulez, who was born on this day, was all about creating 'different feelings' in musical textures, sounds and time. A pupil of Olivier Messiaen (15 January), even as a young man Boulez exhibited absolute certainty about what he wanted the future of music to sound like – and suffice to say, it was like nothing that had been before.

Over the course of his long and varied career, he balanced stints as chief conductor at many leading international orchestras with founding an institute in Paris, IRCAM, that specializes in the science behind avant-garde electro-acoustical art music, as well as with writing the most revolutionary music of the day. More than anyone else, Boulez can be said to have transformed the landscape and soundscape of twentieth-century classical music.

Like that of any great innovator, his work may sound strange and unfamiliar at first. Messiaen once remarked that Boulez *'totally transformed the sonority of the piano'* – and it can take some getting used to. The suite of twelve *Notations* dates from the time he was being bewitched by those Balinese sounds and shows him well on his way; it's a good place to start.

27 March

Overture
from *La clemenza di Tito*, K. 621
by Wolfgang Amadeus Mozart (1756–1791)

Based on a libretto that had already been set to music by various other composers, *La clemenza di Tito* was an opera with a nakedly political agenda – and one that resonates just as loudly in our own day. (Put simply, Titus is a populist leader who learns the price of power to great personal cost.) Written in the last year of Mozart's outrageously short life, it may just hold the record for the fastest significant opera ever composed. According to his first biographer, he dashed off the entire work in just eighteen days.

La clemenza, opening with this vital and dramatic overture, was the first of all Mozart's twenty-two operas to reach London. It was premiered on this day in 1806 at His Majesty's Theatre on the Haymarket. It has sometimes been dismissed as inferior to some of Mozart's earlier works – perhaps because of the breakneck pace in which it was produced – but in recent years the critical tide has turned; it is now generally considered a late masterpiece.

Mozart, for what it's worth, called *La clemenza* his *'true opera'*.

28 March

In the month of March
by Toru Takemitsu (1930–1996)

Following thirteen-year-old Pablo Casals' chance discovery of the Bach cello suites in a junk shop earlier this month, here's another story about a teenage boy and a serendipitous musical encounter.

It's 1944. In the mountains west of Tokyo, a fourteen-year-old child soldier named Toru Takemitsu is stationed in one of the dugout fortresses that have been constructed along the Japanese home front in case of invasion. One day, in an unexpected breach of the soul-destroying labour routine they have been subjected to until now, an officer invites Toru and his fellow soldiers into a room at the back of the fortress. There, he reveals a windup record player with a makeshift bamboo needle. And he plays them some music. It is a simple gift – the very simplest, in some way, to exchange music like this; humans have been doing it for as long as we have been here. But what a gift.

Toru listens in what he later describes as a state of *'enormous shock'*. For the rest of his life, this moment will represent the beginning of his musical consciousness. Later, when he begins teaching himself instruments and the basics of composition; when he wins the admiration of giants like Stravinsky; when he goes on to write hundreds of celebrated pieces, and score ninety films, and publish twenty books; when he is recognised as one of Japan's most celebrated composers and cultural figures, it is always to this point that he will return in his mind – this musical offering, this gesture of common humanity, this gift.

29 March

❧

Ambre
by Nils Frahm (b. 1982)

Along with Max Richter (26 February, 21 June) and Ólafur Arnalds (9 August), pianist and composer Nils Frahm is one of the musicians I get most excited about when I think about how classical music is a living, breathing, evolving thing and not some ossified art form of centuries past.

The Berlin-based millennial – who previously held down jobs as a postman, in a coffee shop, and cleaning houses, even toilets – takes an unconventional approach to what he does. He makes meticulously produced music across a number of genres, and incorporates electronic and vintage recording equipment into his sound. A mixer, producer, DJ and engineer, Frahm appears to be curious about everything, including psychology: he's fascinated, for example, by how the emotional experience of music can actually alter people. '*We can change people's attitudes with tones*', he has said. '*After I've played a good concert, people leave the room happy. This is something we can give back to the world. That's my religion.*'

A few years ago Frahm instituted 'Piano Day', a global celebration of all things keyboard that takes place on either 28 or 29 March, the eighty-eighth day of each year (standard concert pianos have eighty-eight keys). The idea is that everyone can get involved, irrespective of their experience.

This sense of music as a shared, communal property reflects Frahm's attitude that making music is a much more collaborative process than some classical composers would have you believe. For Frahm, his audience is absolutely key. '*Without the listener*', he points out, '*it would all be nothing.*'

30 March

'La Calinda' from *Koanga*
by Frederick Delius (1862–1934)

We've heard from many of the great European Romantics already this year: time now to meet one of their English number. That said, Frederick Delius, though he was born in Bradford and studied in Isleworth, had German parents and actually lived and travelled all over the place, including France, Germany, Norway and America. Cosmopolitan and curious, he was friends with many of the leading artistic lights of the day: playwright August Strindberg, painters Paul Gauguin and Edvard Munch, and fellow composers Edward Grieg (17 May, 4 November) and Percy Grainger (20 February).

As a young man, Delius had a formative experience that set his life on a particular course. In 1884, he left Bradford and headed to America to work as a fruit-picker in a Florida orange grove (perhaps as a way of escaping the family wool business, where he was otherwise destined to spend his days). In Florida, dreaming of becoming a professional composer, he got his first piece published. It was also in Florida that he was exposed to the African-American sounds that would have such an impact on his own compositional style.

Captivated by the spirituals being sung by out-of-hours waiters and by deckhands as they worked on nearby ships, he incorporated these and other non-European musical sounds into his opera *Koanga*, which had its first public performance on this day in 1904. Based on a story of Creole life, it centres on an African prince and voodoo priest who has been enslaved on a Mississippi plantation. It's generally understood to be the first time a composer working in the European tradition ever based melodic material on African-American music.

31 March

O Jesu Christ, meins Lebens Licht –
Oh Jesus Christ, light of my life, BWV 118
by J. S. Bach (1685–1750)

J. S. Bach was born on this day. Repeat: J. S. Bach was born on this day.

Before I expire in rhapsodic gratitude at this light of my own life, let's just stick the record on and raise a toast to the man who, when it comes to music, has given us everything.

APRIL

1 April

Piano Concerto no. 1 in B flat minor, op. 23
1: Allegro non troppo e molto maestoso
by Pyotr Ilyich Tchaikovsky (1840–1893)

The history of classical music, like that of pop, is riddled with instances where people failed to recognize brilliance staring them in the face. On Christmas Eve, 1874, Tchaikovsky went to pianist Nikolai Rubinstein's house to play him a new concerto, in the hope that the famous Russian virtuoso would premiere it. It didn't go so well. In a letter to his benefactress, Nadezhda von Meck, the composer recalled:

> I played the first movement. Never a word, never a single remark. Do you know the awkward and ridiculous sensation of putting before a friend a meal which you have cooked yourself, which he eats and then holds his tongue? Oh, for a single word, for friendly abuse, for anything to break the silence! For God's sake say something! But Rubinstein never opened his lips.

Tchaikovsky gamely carried on. But afterwards, the abuse flowed – and it wasn't so 'friendly':

> A torrent broke from Rubinstein's lips . . . My concerto was worthless, absolutely unplayable; the passages so broken, so disconnected, so unskilfully written, that they could not even be improved; the work itself was bad, trivial, common; here and there I had stolen from other people; only one or two pages were worth anything; all the rest had better be destroyed. I left the room without a word.

This puts me in mind of A&R man Dick Rowe, allegedly saying, 'Guitar groups are on their way out, Mr Epstein', as he declined to sign The Beatles. Tchaikovsky, like Brian Epstein, had the presence of mind to hang tight – and guess who had the last laugh.

2 April

Violin Sonata no. 5 in F major, op. 24 ('Spring')
1: Allegro
by Ludwig van Beethoven (1770–1827)

By the time he turned thirty-two, Beethoven had written – alongside dozens of other works – no fewer than ten violin sonatas. In the early ones, you can almost hear him becoming increasingly impatient with the constraints of Classical form. By the time he gets to this one, in 1801, he seems fully poised to jump off the genteel bridge of true Classicism into the wild, roiling abandon of the Romantic period. Amid the grace and formality are passages of great vigour and zest, and while its nickname had nothing to do with the composer, it delivers joyfully on its promise.

Wherever you are, may your day be full of the delights of spring.

3 April

Intermezzo in B flat minor, op. 117 no. 2
by Johannes Brahms (1833–1897)

Towards the end of his life, with symphonies, concertos, large-scale instrumental works and plenty of chamber music behind him, Brahms seems to have wanted to focus his energies on something more intimate. In his final years he produced dozens of piano miniatures, including sixteen extremely beautiful intermezzi. Perhaps this is what he meant when he talked of wanting to write *'for himself alone'*, as he told Clara Schumann in a letter shortly after his fifty-ninth birthday.

(Ah yes – Clara. The great love of Brahms's life. Brahms had met and become a protégé of Robert Schumann in 1853; before long he was writing to Schumann's wife, saying, *'I can do nothing but think of you . . . What have you done to me? Can't you remove the spell you have cast over me?'* In 1856, after years of mental illness, Robert died and Brahms immediately went to Clara, to whom he was already extremely close. An affair was fervently denied, but letters were written that were then destroyed by both sides, so who knows? What is beyond speculation is the profound impact their relationship had on each other's music – for which we can all be grateful.)

The many late intermezzi, including the triptych of opus 117, exude a lullaby-like tenderness (Brahms once referred to 'cradle songs of my sorrows') and take us on wistful flights of the imagination. For all their gentleness, though, Brahms had a certain inner steel and they also remind us of this man's astonishing ability to process raging torrents of messy human emotion into disciplined musical forms.

Some music critics are a bit snide about Brahms, who died on this day. I don't know why. I find his music profoundly expressive and moving, enlightening, generous, joyful: the whole kit and caboodle. To me, he's as true a musical communicator as we've ever had.

4 April

Symphony no. 3 ('Symphony of Sorrowful Songs')
2: Lento e largo – Tranquillissimo
by Henryk Górecki (1933–2010)

Classical music in Poland underwent something of a renaissance after the Second World War. Leading the charge was Henryk Górecki, who once issued this timeless piece of advice for would-be composers:

If you can live without music for two or three days then don't write – it might be better to spend the time with a girl or with a beer.

Górecki, whose surname is pronounced 'Goretsky', initally emulated modernist trends of Western Europe, but his early dabblings in dissonance were later replaced by a style described as 'sacred minimalism'. This is exemplified in his Third Symphony, which received its premiere on this day in 1977 and which has gone on to sell over a million copies – a rare accolade for a classical work. A highly unusual work, it asks us to look tragedy directly in the eye. In each movement, a solo soprano sings a Polish text: the first a fifteenth-century lament by Mary; the third a Silesian folk song in which a mother searches for her son, who has been killed by Germans. This middle movement sets the words of a prayer inscribed by an eighteen-year-old girl on the wall of a Gestapo prison in 1944.

The work is all the more moving for the fact that Górecki had lost members of his own family in concentration camps. His grandfather had been in Dachau; his aunt in Auschwitz. *'You know how it is between Poles and Germans,'* he once noted. *'But Bach was a German too – and Schubert, and Strauss. Everyone has his place on this little earth.'*

5 April

Fanfare for the Common Man
by Aaron Copland (1900–1990)

Now to the man dubbed the 'the Dean of American composers', Aaron Copland – yet another leading light to emerge from the miraculous conservatoire that was no. 36, rue Ballu in the ninth *arrondissement* of Paris, otherwise known as the home of Nadia Boulanger (22 October). He spent three years studying with Boulanger and her eclectic tastes helped shape his own musical curiosity. '*It was wonderful*', he later wrote, '*for me to find a teacher with such openness of mind, while at the same time she held firm ideas of right and wrong in musical matters. The confidence she had in my talents . . . were crucial to my development at this time of my career.*'

Copland described his musical style as 'vernacular', capturing as it does something of the pioneering spirit and epic landscapes of his country. This work dates from 1942, when conductor Eugene Goossens commissioned a series of fanfares to boost patriotic morale and reflect the American war effort. The title was inspired by a speech given by Vice President Henry Wallace. '*Some have spoken of the American Century*', declaimed Wallace. '*I say that the century which we are entering, the century which will come out of this war, can be, and must be, the century of the common man.*'

Upon hearing Copland's plan for the title, Goossens wrote: '*It deserves a special occasion for its performance*', and suggested that they premiere it at income tax time.

Today is the last financial day of the year in the UK, so a good time to hear it.

6 April

Symphony no. 101 in D major ('Clock')
2: Andante
by Joseph Haydn (1732–1809)

As classic a Classical symphony as they come, this one, displaying exactly the sorts of formal finery that Prokofiev was satirizing last month (5 March). This was part of the set of twelve late works by Haydn known as his 'London' symphonies. Having already produced a hundred symphonies – a hundred! – by this stage, you might expect him to be mining familiar ground, but somehow Haydn manages to convince us that he's having a whole new adventure, as if he'd never tried one of these symphony things before.

It was premiered in Mayfair in 1794, and prompted raptures from critics. This one, for example, writing in the London *Morning Chronicle*, declared:

> As usual the most delicious part of the entertainment was a new grand [symphony] by HAYDN; the inexhaustible, the wonderful, the sublime HAYDN! The first two movements were encored; and the character that pervaded the whole composition was heartfelt joy. Every new [one] he writes, we fear, till it is heard, he can only repeat himself; and we are every time mistaken.

(Capitals journalist's own.)

At least the reason for this piece's nickname should be obvious from the outset. *Tick-tock . . .*

7 April

'Walking the dog'
from *Shall We Dance?*
by George Gershwin (1898–1937)

In his all-too-brief life George Gershwin produced some of the best-loved works of the past one hundred years across multiple genres, from operas such as *Porgy and Bess* to orchestral works such as *Rhapsody in Blue* and *An American in Paris.* He himself spent time in the city of light in the 1920s, but, interestingly, Nadia Boulanger (22 October) turned him down as a student and Maurice Ravel (7 March, 14 July) was so wowed by the American's gifts that he also refused his request for lessons, saying *'it is better to write good Gershwin than bad Ravel, which is what would happen if you worked with me'.*

A preternaturally talented writer of melody, Gershwin was catnip for Hollywood directors. In *Shall We Dance?*, the seventh collaboration between Ginger Rogers and Fred Astaire, this delightful musical interlude takes place on an ocean liner bound for New York, during passenger dog-walking hour, when Fred Astaire's character Peter, an American ballet dancer posing as 'Petrov', contrives to meet Ginger Rogers' Linda Keene, a celebrated tap dancer. (They will later fall in love, obviously, but many hoops will have to be danced through before a happy ending is eked out.)

Gershwin died from a brain tumour aged thirty-eight, just a year after *Shall We Dance?* was released. As with Schubert, as with Mendelssohn, as with Mozart, it's too painful to contemplate what he might have done had he lived on.

8 April

Le Printemps – Spring, op. 18
by Darius Milhaud (1892–1974)

The artistic stereotype of the tortured creative genius is a pervasive one, but if anyone can challenge it, it's Darius Milhaud, one of the group of Paris-based composers known as 'Les Six'. Milhaud was actually famous among the classical community for being a nice guy, with some commentators expressing their suspicions that anyone of such a sunny disposition could produce art of any real complexity. (Milhaud proves time and again that depth need not derive from darkness.)

He was a highly prolific composer, but had wide interests beyond the realm of classical, including jazz (he taught Dave Brubeck, of *Take Five* fame) and Brazilian music (see 22 June). Milhaud was a legendary teacher: some other notable students include Steve Reich (19 January, 8 August, 26 November), William Bolcom (26 May), Philip Glass (31 January, 4 October) and the pop legend Burt Bacharach – to whom he apparently said: *'Don't be afraid of writing something people can remember and whistle. Don't ever feel discomfited by a melody.'*

My kinda guy.

9 April

En la Macarenita
Traditional, arranged by Bob Chilcott (b. 1955)

For something completely different today, we say happy birthday to one of British choral music's contemporary heroes, Bob Chilcott – a composer, arranger and choirmaster who works all over Britain with vocal ensembles and has an eclectic and unfussy approach to the notion of what 'classical' choral music can be.

Later this year we'll hear his gorgeous arrangement of music by William Walton; meanwhile, here's Chilcott's take on a traditional Spanish folk song – in which a girl heads down to the Macarena and catches the wooing eyes of a dancing stranger . . .

(This song has nothing, by the way, to do with the 1990s pop smash by Los del Rio, in case you were considering dusting off your Macarena moves.)

10 April

Concerto no. 7 in F major for three pianos, K. 242 ('Lodron')
1: Allegro
by Wolfgang Amadeus Mozart (1756–1791)

Another shining example, after February's double-piano delight, of Mozart writing for multiple keyboards and showing off his uncanny ability to create something that feels like animated musical conversation in real time.

This concerto came about because one of his patrons, a certain Countess Antonia Lodron, fancied having a piece that she could play with her two daughters, Aloysia and Josepha. Mozart, who was just twenty at the time, duly obliged, and helpfully tailored each part to the technical proficiencies of the soloist in question. He later turned it into a version for two pianos which he performed with his own sister, Nannerl.

Mozart's music does many things, but rare are the times, I find, when listening to him does not improve one's day at least a little bit. This piece is an excellent case in point.

11 April

Tres piezas, op. 6
1: 'Cuyana'
by Alberto Ginastera (1916–1983)

More piano today, but of a markedly different flavour. I'm fascinated by the continuum of twentieth-century musical thought: how ideas get exchanged down the line from students to teachers and back again. Alberto Ginastera, who was born on this day, taught Astor Piazzolla (11 March) and was himself taught by Aaron Copland, whom we met earlier this month (5 April). He is considered one of the most important classical composers from the Americas, and integrated traditional musical elements from Argentina in his work in a variety of ways, some more explicit than others.

This atmospheric solo piano piece dates from 1940, during Ginastera's earliest compositional phase, which he dubbed his 'objective nationalism' period (1934–1947). No matter how many times I hear it, I never quite know what's coming next – in the best possible way. I love how the composer takes us on a meandering melodic journey and just at the moment when you feel you know exactly where you are, he picks you up and deposits you somewhere else, somewhere completely unexpected.

12 April

Metamorphosen
by Richard Strauss (1864–1949)

It took Richard Strauss just one month to pull off one of the most haunting pieces of the twentieth century. It was on this day in 1945 that he completed his emotionally searing work for twenty-three strings, *Metamorphosen*, towards the end of the Second World War and just a few years before his death.

To call it elegiac would be an understatement. *Metamorphosen* is largely understood to be a meditation on the destruction of Germany during the war, and in particular a comment on the bombing of towns such as Munich and Dresden. Some critics make the point that Strauss would have been better off writing something that reflected on the Nazi party's systematic destruction of human life, rather than dwelling on the decimation of an inanimate city. I understand why, but I think this misses the point. In the dejection it enacts, the intensity of the feelings it evokes, this piece for me distils some quintessence of universal human loss and never leaves me anything other than utterly shaken.

It is a singularly moving musical response to the senselessness of war – any war.

13 April

Overture
from *Tannhäuser*
by Richard Wagner (1813–1883)

To the man, now, who paved the way for Strauss's intense, chromatic post-romantic musical language. Almost exactly one hundred years before Strauss finished *Metamorphosen*, the piece we heard yesterday, Wagner was completing, on this day, the full score of what he described to his wife Cosima as his *'consummate drama'*.

Set in the thirteenth century, *Tannhäuser and the Singers' Contest on the Wartburg*, to give it its full name, traverses the sorts of fantastical plots and supernatural characters that would preoccupy Wagner throughout his career, as well as positing a classic Wagnerian conflict between the spiritual and the sensual. It also contains some of the most stirring music he ever wrote – which is a big call, given that he wrote so much.

The overture, which Wagner worked on last, is the perfect introduction to all the knights and nymphs, pilgrims and troubadours, goddesses and sirens that are to come; it also stands alone as a concert piece of exceptional drama. If you're in need of musical motivation today, I hope this will be just the ticket.

14 April

Frühlingsglaube – Faith in Spring
by Franz Schubert (1797–1828)

Yet another gift to our lives from Franz Schubert; this time a glowing, quiet beauty of a song that sets words by Ludwig Uhland encapsulating the bittersweet promise of spring.

The second verse is particularly wistful:

Die Welt wird schöner mit jedem Tag, Man weiß nicht, was noch werden mag . . .
Nun muss sich Alles, Alles wenden.

With each day the world grows fairer,
One cannot know what is still to come . . .
Now all, all must change.

Schubert was such a melodic genius that his 'lieder' or songs have invited reams and reams of academic music criticism over the years. While much of it is illuminating, I often find the songs are the most powerful explanations of themselves and simply listening opens up the world.

15 April

Piano Concerto no. 2 in F minor, op. 21
2: Larghetto
by Frédéric Chopin (1810–1849)

In 1829, when he was working on this first ambitious attempt at a piano concerto (although it was published later, hence being cata-logued as no. 2), the nineteen-year-old Chopin had recently lost his heart to a young singer named Constantia Gladkowska – to whom he was yet to actually speak. *'I have . . . found my ideal',* he wrote to a friend, *'whom I worship faithfully and sincerely . . . But in the six months since I first saw her I have not exchanged a syllable with her of whom I dream every night.'*

Mate, we've all been there. Unlike most lovestruck youngsters, though, Chopin at least had the ultimate outlet for his unrequited feelings: he poured his ardour into this radiant larghetto, confirming to his friend, she *'was in my mind when I composed [it]'.*

It's hard to imagine a more persuasive love note. Shame, then, that the romance with Constantia went no further. At least this heavenly music endures.

16 April

'Tornami a vagheggiar' – 'Return and desire me'
from *Alcina*
by George Frideric Handel (1685–1759)

Back in February, we met Francesca Caccini, whose opera *La liberazione di Ruggiero*, based on Ariosto's epic poem *Orlando Furioso*, was the first to be composed by a woman (at least, the first that survives). A century or so later, Handel was drawn to the same story, producing, in quick succession, a hat-trick of operas based on the poem. Hot on the heels of *Orlando* and *Ariodante*, his *Alcina* was premiered at the Covent Garden Theatre in London on this day in 1735.

It takes place on the enchantress Alcina's island, where she has created, through her magic powers, a magnificent palace amid a beautiful landscape to lure in her unsuspecting prey – of which one such 'victim' is the warrior Ruggiero.

Handel packed *Alcina* with lavish sets and great tunes, including this sparkling showstopper from Act 1. The public went mad for it. After attending a rehearsal at Handel's house in Brook Street, Mayfair, his neighbour Mary Pendarves wrote in her diary: *'I think it is the best he ever made . . . 'tis so fine I have not words to describe it.'*

17 April

Ellis Island
by Meredith Monk (b. 1942)

When the multi-talented American composer, choreographer, director and filmmaker Meredith Monk was invited to make a film about Ellis Island, which had been the iconic point of entry for millions of immigrants to the USA, she applied her characteristically imaginative and original vision to the process, weaving documentary material around contemporary images and writing an evocative and atmospheric soundtrack to accompany what is otherwise pretty much a silent film. The film, which intercuts the historic and modern, is like a distillation of Monk's work in microcosm.

Like so many millions of Americans, Monk's own grandparents had made the journey through Ellis Island many decades previously. Making the film, she says, '*was a very painful process. Human beings were commoditized at Ellis Island. [The film] is all about dealing with the "other" . . . and the fact that you can make another person into an object.*'

The all-time record for immigrants received at Ellis Island was on this day in 1906, when a total of 11,747 immigrants were processed. In that year alone, 1,004,756 immigrants were received into the US.

18 April

Stabat mater

7: 'Eia mater, fons amoris' – 'Oh mother, fount of love'
by Antonio Vivaldi (1678–1741)

One of the fascinations of immersing oneself in a thousand years of music is the opportunity it affords for comparing distinct approaches to identical sources. Dozens of composers, for example, have set music to the thirteenth-century text *Stabat mater doloroso*. Nobody knows who wrote the poem, although it's often attributed to an elusive Franciscan friar called Jacopone da Todi; wherever it came from, it's a deeply moving meditation on the crucifixion of a beloved child.

Over the course of the year we'll be hearing three versions, each of which takes the original material in diverse directions. Vivaldi's timeless setting was written in 1712 on a commission from the Santa Maria della Pace church in Brescia.

He sets the work in nine parts, of which this wrenching movement is the seventh.

Eia Mater, fons amoris,	*Oh, mother, fount of love,*
me sentire vim doloris fac	*make me feel the force of your sorrow*
ut tecum lugea	*that I may grieve with you*

I found this piece deeply moving *before* I had a child; these days, it's liable to reduce me to a sobbing wreck. Yet, in the way of the greatest music, its beauty is somehow, simultaneously, its own redemption.

19 April

Valse lente – slow waltz
by Germaine Tailleferre (1892–1983)

There is a terrific picture of the French composer Germaine Tailleferre standing amid a cluster of male composers, and everything in her expression, her demeanour, says, 'Yeah? And what?' Born on this day, Tailleferre was the only woman to be included in the group of acclaimed early twentieth-century French composers known as 'Les Six', which also included Francis Poulenc (7 January, 17 February) and Darius Milhaud, whom we heard earlier this month (8 April; also 22 June).

By all accounts, Tailleferre was not someone to let her gender stand in the way of anything. Through the twentieth century's many shifts in musical style, she held her nerve and navigated her own distinct path. Over a long and varied career, she produced instrumental concertos, operas, chamber works, and some magnificent ballet music for the likes of Serge Diaghilev's *Ballets Russes*. I love the fact that she was still composing and playing the piano until the day she died, aged ninety-one.

20 April

'Music for a while'
from *Oedipus*
by Henry Purcell (1659–1695)

Music for a while
Shall all your cares beguile . . .

John Dryden, *Oedipus*

Why yes, it shall. This supreme statement on the power of music comes from two of Restoration London's artistic heroes: playwright John Dryden and composer Henry Purcell. They worked on a number of projects together, including *King Arthur* (1691), an opera (of sorts) that is considered the first ever professional partnership between a librettist and a composer.

Captivated by music, Dryden subscribed to the Pythagorean notion of a 'music of the spheres', which held that music, as an expression of mathematical relationships in sound, could encode its own explanation of the universe. Deliberately shaping his texts so that they could be set to music, he found in Purcell the ideal collaborator; someone *'in whose person we have at length found an Englishman equal with the best abroad'* and a man capable of writing music *'with so great a genius that he has nothing to fear but an ignorant, ill-judging audience'*. (Interesting to note that new music was just as likely to draw the bafflement/criticism of audiences then as now.)

Dryden was right. Purcell is one of the most important musicians England has ever produced, and his reach over modern music remains profound. You can also hear his harmonies, his bold suspensions and resolutions, and his formal structures – such as the ascending 'ground bass' that underpins this piece – reimagined and reanimated not just in later classical compositions but in modern pop songs and film soundtracks galore.

21 April

Khovanshchina
Prelude: Dawn over the Moscow River
by Modest Mussorgsky (1839–1881)

Mussorgsky was six when he started taking piano lessons from his mother; by the age of ten he was giving concerts of music by the likes of John Field (17 March) and Franz Liszt (12 February, 31 July).

Aged seventeen, he met the twenty-two-year-old Alexander Borodin (27 February) while both were serving at a military hospital in St Petersburg. They became friends, and later Mussorgsky fell in with Borodin's St Petersburg-based crowd of composers. Known as the 'Mighty Handful', the group also included Nikolai Rimsky-Korsakov (14 September). All these young men were committed to shaping a musical identity that could be considered uniquely Russian, drawing on themes from Russian history and folklore in their bid to loosen the grip of Western music over their culture.

Mussorgsky's 'national music drama' *Khovanshchina* took as its background the Moscow Uprising of 1682 and the Khovansky affair a few months later. He died before he could finish the work. Rimsky-Korsakov completed, revised, and orchestrated it in 1881; in 1913 Igor Stravinsky and Maurice Ravel made a further arrangement of this version on commission from the great ballet impresario Sergei Diaghilev; Dmitri Shostakovich then revised it again in 1959 based on Mussorgsky's original score. The whole thing is laced with noble melodies but I particularly love this opening movement, which paints, in gently atmospheric music, a picture of dawn breaking over the Moscow River.

22 April

Danza gaya
by Madeleine Dring (1923–1977)

Madeleine Dring was an early proponent of the sort of 'slash' career now popular among millennials. A talented composer, actress and cartoonist, she studied at the Royal College of Music and managed to balance a successful career on stage in the West End with writing music for theatre, radio and television.

Her influences include Francis Poulenc (7 January, 17 February) and her style is refreshingly unpretentious – impressive for a woman trying to make her voice heard in a landscape still overwhelmingly dominated by men. I imagine she must have been under considerable pressure to do something 'different', but instead she sticks to her guns and writes pieces of rhythmic vibrancy and great charm.

Her husband Roger Lord was an oboist, so it's not surprising that Dring wrote so many pieces for his instrument – including this rumba-inflected dance. This is not music that's going to change the world, but if it doesn't set your toes tapping I'll eat my hat.

23 April

'How Sweet the Moonlight' from *The Merchant of Venice* by Jocelyn Pook (b. 1960)

Composers throughout the centuries have been drawn to the words of Shakespeare, who was born – and died – on this day, which also happens to be St George's Day. For Hector Berlioz, for example, the discovery of Shakespeare *'struck like a thunderbolt'*, revealing *'the whole heaven of art, illustrating it to the remotest corners'*. Other composers who have worked with Shakespearean material include – to name but a few – Mendelssohn, Tchaikovsky, Verdi, Prokofiev, Sibelius, Vaughan Williams, Finzi, Adès and Bernstein.

There are in fact more than twenty thousand Shakespeare-related pieces listed in the *Shakespeare Music Catalogue* published by Oxford University Press. These include operas, ballets and song-settings, as well as incidental music to dozens of his plays. Shakespeare on celluloid has also drawn leading lights of the classical world (see e.g. 10 October), including Jocelyn Pook, one of the most in-demand women working in film music either side of the Atlantic.

Her score for *The Merchant of Venice* (2004), which starred Al Pacino and Jeremy Irons, manages to capture the atmosphere of early Renaissance music yet gives it a modern twist. Her setting of the luscious poetry of Act 5, scene 1 creates a particularly atmospheric mood:

> *How sweet the moonlight sleeps upon this bank!*
> *Here will we sit and let the sounds of music*
> *Creep in our ears. Soft stillness and the night*
> *Become the touches of sweet harmony . . .*

24 April

Symphony no. 5 in C minor, op. 67
4: Allegro – Presto
by Ludwig van Beethoven (1770–1827)

It's hard to imagine a time when this epic symphony had never been heard: it opens with what are now the most famous four bars in musical history – 'da-da-da-daah' – and has entered mainstream consciousness in a way that most classical works will never do. But spare a thought for the poor orchestra who had to give the premiere of this piece, in freezing conditions, in Vienna in December 1808. Boy, it must have been something to sight-read. They had only one rehearsal and the concert, which also included a number of other major works, was a disaster.

Despite that, it didn't take long for Beethoven's Fifth to be recognized as the monumental thing it is and cement its place in the canon for all eternity. Owing an obvious debt to the symphonies of Mozart, it marks the end of the Classical symphony, and its influence on the Romantic symphonists waiting in the wings – Brahms, Mahler, Tchaikovsky, Bruckner, Berlioz – is unparalleled. In this rollicking, exuberant final movement, where he switches to the triumphant major key, I think you can also hear its impact on other genres such as pop and film music (here's looking at you, John Williams).

It's worth recalling that Beethoven by now was entirely deaf. If ever there were a reminder that we underestimate any human being at our peril, it's surely epitomized in him.

25 April

6 pieces from *Kuolema*, Op. 44
1: 'Valse triste'
by Jean Sibelius (1865–1957)

Handy, if you're a playwright, to have one of the sharpest musical minds of the twentieth century as your brother-in-law, able and willing to furnish your theatrical productions with fabulous incidental music.

The Finnish composer Jean Sibelius wrote six pieces for his wife's brother Arvid Järnefelt's 1903 play *Kuolema* ('Death'), including a waltz which, according to a friend of Sibelius, was dreamed up by the composer upstairs at the Kämp restaurant in Helsinki – which is still there – aided by plenty of oysters, quinine and soda. (Sibelius was a famously heavy drinker, but on that day he was apparently suffering from a nasty cold, hence sticking to the unadulterated quinine.)

It is, perhaps unsurprisingly, the music rather than the drama that has endured. The following year, Sibelius revised his moody waltz from the play and it was first performed in its own right on this day in 1904 as 'Valse triste'. The Finnish public lapped it up; it was soon heard in European concert halls and has never left the orchestral repertoire since.

26 April

Caprice in A minor, op. 1 no. 24
by Niccolò Paganini (1782–1840)

Composers often dedicate their works to specific people – patrons, benefactors, lovers, friends, family, even pets. (Chopin's famous 'Minute' Waltz, for example, was originally known as 'The Little Dog Waltz' in honour of Marquis, the beloved pet of his lover George Sand.) When the virtuoso Italian violinist Paganini published his 24 Caprices, however, he dedicated them to *'agli Artisti'* – to 'all the artists' rather than to anyone in particular.

This would all be very charming and democratic, were it not for the fact that you have to be an artist of an extremely rare talent to actually play them. Paganini, who was one of the earliest classical superstars, wrote music for himself to play in concert so it's no surprise they were so difficult. Fiendishly demanding from a technical point of view, but also full of wit and mischief, the caprices are some of the most exhilarating works for the solo violin. They transformed our understanding of what the instrument – and its players – might be capable of, and raised the bar for generations of violinists to come.

With its pure tonality of A minor and clean-line structure, this caprice in particular has been used as a jumping-off point by a number of composers – including Liszt, Brahms and Rachmaninov – from which they could develop their own ideas and spin new, ingenious variations. We'll be meeting one of the most famous examples later this year (see 3 July).

27 April

Prélude in G flat major, op. 11 no. 13
by Alexander Scriabin (1872–1915)

The Russian pianist and composer Alexander Scriabin, who died on this day in 1915, is one of music's great eccentrics. It seems he had a bit of a God complex: he once tried to walk on water at Lake Geneva to preach to some fishermen, and he fervently believed that his work would bring about apocalypse.

These fixations may well be discernible in later pieces such as his *Mysterium* – which he specified had to be performed for seven days at the foothills of the Himalayas – and the 'Black Mass' Sonata, which has some pretty bonkers moments. But you'd never know it from his early preludes, which are un-apocalyptically pleasant to listen to. I've chosen a lovely one in G flat major, a particularly rich and expressive key, but truly they're all a delight.

28 April

Lay a garland
by Robert Lucas de Pearsall (1795–1856)

We hear today from one of Bristol's most musical sons. That said, Pearsall was never recognized as a professional composer and most of his work remained unpublished at the time of his death.

As well as music, Pearsall wrote poetry and translated works by Goethe and Schiller. He had a wide range of interests, most of them rather antiquated, including heraldry and Renaissance polyphony. While the rest of music-minded Europe was being intoxicated with the notion of Romantic freedoms, Pearsall penned earnest articles promoting the early music of the Roman Catholic and Anglican churches and its trademark conventions such as plainsong and polyphony.

He was a compelling advocate for what he believed in and composed some ravishing music based on his preoccupations. This exquisite 1840 madrigal, for example, was based on a poem from *The Maid's Tragedy* by Beaumont and Fletcher, which was entered into the Stationers' Register on this day in 1619.

It's sung, heart on sleeve, in Act 2 by the character Aspasia, at the moment she realizes that her betrothed has been forced into a marriage of convenience with the King's mistress.

> *Lay a garland on her hearse*
> *of dismal yew.*
> *Maidens, willow branches wear,*
> *say she died true.*
> *Her love was false, but she was firm*
> *Upon her buried body lie*
> *lightly, thou gentle earth.*

29 April

String Quartet with Didjeridu, no. 14 ('Quamby')
1: Prelude
by Peter Sculthorpe (1929–2014)

The didgeridoo is not an instrument you regularly find in classical compositions, but then again, Peter Sculthorpe is not your average classical composer. Born in Tasmania on this day, over the course of a seven-decade career he played a significant part in bridging disparate musical worlds, and arguably did more than anybody of his generation to explore what a classical music identity might mean in an Australian context.

Sculthorpe, who was one of the first Western-trained musicians to learn the didgeridoo, incorporated many Indigenous Australian elements into his compositions. In the manner of Sibelius with Finland (20 September) or Grieg with Norway (17 May), he somehow managed to articulate some essence of his land through sound, and was capable of evoking the dry, epic magnificence of the Australian landscape with unusual instrumental textures. Yet Sculthorpe was equally intrigued by Asian music and by the trends that emerged from Europe in the Romantic and modernist eras. Gustav Mahler's song cycle *Das Lied von der Erde*, for example, was a major inspiration (18 May).

30 April

Violin Concerto in E minor, op. 64
3: Allegretto non troppo – Allegro molto vivace
by Felix Mendelssohn (1809–1847)

Throughout the course of the history of music, there are pieces studding the landscape that can be seen as landmarks. Pieces that change everything, that throw into relief all that has gone before in getting us to this point, and to which all future examples will somehow have to refer back, whether consciously or not.

Brimful as it is with new ideas and formal features, Felix Mendelssohn's Violin Concerto in E minor is one such piece. He began writing it in 1838, in close consultation with his great friend, the violinist Ferdinand David, whom he had known since his teens. '*A violin concerto in E minor keeps running through my head*', he wrote to David, '*and the opening gives me no peace.*'

Mendelssohn worked hard on this concerto: it would take another six years before it was finished, with David having meanwhile suggested all manner of revisions and alterations.

It was worth the wait.

MAY

1 May

Children's Corner, L119
1: 'Doctor Gradus ad Parnassum'
by Claude Debussy (1862–1918)

Children's Corner may sound like something that belongs in the musical playground, but don't be deceived: the six pieces in this collection were never intended to be played by kids (unless those kids happened to be prodigies, which to be fair is always a possibility in the world of classical music). Debussy wrote this for his beloved three-year-old daughter Claude-Emma, known as 'Chouchou', and the suite as a whole is meant to be evocative of scenes from childhood. With the exception of this thrilling little opener – whose title, curiously, refers to *The Steps to Mount Parnassus*, an arcane study of counterpoint dating from 1725 – the movements are named after Chouchou's toys. (There's also a serenade for a doll, a lullaby for a stuffed elephant called Jimbo, a little shepherd, and so on.)

Debussy wrote *Children's Corner* in 1908, four years after he had divorced his first wife and taken up with his longtime muse and lover Emma Bardac. His abandoned wife Lilly had tried to kill herself, very publicly, in the Place de la Concorde, so to escape the scandal and the worst of Paris's gossipmongers the lovers had temporarily relocated to the unlikely haven of Eastbourne, on the south coast of England. Chouchou was born the following year. Debussy and Emma were finally married the same year this suite was published.

It's so easy to forget that these legendary composers were actual human beings, with domestic pressures, messy love lives, adorable kids. I enjoy these occasional reminders of their regular humanity: at its heart, here is a devoted dad writing some music for his daughter. It is made all the more powerful for me by the knowledge that within a decade, Debussy would be dead. Poor Chouchou would succumb to diphtheria less than a year later.

2 May

'Mother of God, here I stand'
from *The Veil of the Temple*
by John Tavener (1944–2013)

It must be quite a thing, as a composer, to be asked to write something *'absolutely extraordinary'* – no pressure! – but that's what Director of Music and Organist Stephen Layton wanted as a musical 'calling card' for London's historic Temple Church in the year 2000, and that's what he got.

Tavener responded to the commission with an 850-page, eight-hour-long masterpiece about the *'Cosmic Ascent of Christ'* called *The Veil of the Temple*. A man of profound faith, the composer envisaged his score as a *'journey towards God'* and, in a nod to a tradition that would have been standard in AD 1000, composed it as a 'Vespers' or all-night vigil, intended to reconcile people as they come together in an act of communal devotion from dusk to dawn. At the premiere in 2003, the performance began at 10 p.m. and at 6 a.m. the following day the audience emerged as one into the streaming sunlight of a July morning. It must have been extraordinary.

Tavener regarded the *The Veil of the Temple* as *'the supreme achievement'* of his life and the *'most important'* work he ever composed. About halfway through, he sets words by the nineteenth-century Russian poet Mikhael Lermontov, a contemporary of Pushkin who was highly influenced by Lord Byron. Whatever your faith, or if you have none, this sublime interlude provides a pause; a reset; a moment of intense stillness and beauty.

> *Mother of God, here I stand now praying,*
> *Before this icon of your radiant brightness . . .*

3 May

Piano Trio in E flat major, K. 498 ('Kegelstatt')
3: Rondo – Allegretto
by Wolfgang Amadeus Mozart (1756–1791)

Kegelstatt means, in German, 'a place where skittles are played'; in other words a sort of bowling alley. Legend has it – thanks to some scribbling on the score – that Mozart composed this playful trio after a game of skittles in Vienna in 1786. Whether or not that's true, you can certainly hear him having fun with it, especially in the clarinet part. The clarinet was a relatively new instrument in Mozart's day, but its uniquely mellow and expressive sound charmed him sufficiently that he also explored its considerable solo potential in major works such as the Clarinet Concerto and Clarinet Quintet (5 September).

In Mozart's hands, the piano, viola and clarinet may sound like the most natural combination of instruments in the world, but before he wrote this piece, nobody had ever thought of putting them together like this. It was an inspired idea. Many later composers, including Robert Schumann and Max Bruch, duly followed suit with their own pieces of chamber music for the same combination.

4 May

'Ellens Gesang III', D. 839 ('Ave Maria') by Franz Schubert (1797–1828)

Over the course of just eleven years, Schubert wrote a staggering six hundred-plus songs and set the words of dozens of poets – some of whom were very well known, such as Johann Wolfgang von Goethe and Heinrich Heine; some of whom were close friends from his tight-knit social circle, such as Franz von Schober, his housemate on the Speigelgasse who wrote the text to *An die Musik*, which we heard back in January.

Sir Walter Scott was a wordsmith much admired by Romantic composers (he was also set by Bizet, Donizetti, Rossini and Mendelssohn, to name but a few). In 1825, Schubert composed a cycle of seven songs based on Scott's epic poem *The Lady of the Lake*. In this one – Ellen's third song – the title character Ellen Douglas has gone with her exiled father to a goblin's cave, as he has declined to join the rebellion against King James. Things are not exactly going to plan, and with the rebels approaching, Ellen sings an impassioned prayer to the Virgin Mary, begging her for help.

The song begins with the words *'Ave Maria'* and Schubert's ravishing music proved so popular that it was later turned into a setting for the whole Roman Catholic prayer, taking its place amid a host of other gorgeous settings (see e.g. 3 June, 19 September, 10 December).

5 May

The Yellow Cake Revue
3. 'Farewell to Stromness'
by Peter Maxwell Davies (1934–2016)

Never, surely, in the course of history has a protest against a uranium mine been turned into a thing of such loveliness.

It was in 1971 that the Salford-born composer Peter Maxwell Davies (later Master of the Queen's Music) moved to Orkney. Towards the end of that decade, he became aware that the South of Scotland Electricity Board was intending to mine Yellowcake uranium deposits near Stromness, a town on the largest island. The objective was to fuel a nuclear power plant, and for sound environmental and ecological reasons, local residents stood in unilateral opposition to its going ahead.

Maxwell Davies, by now very much an honorary Orcadian, poured his own objections into a unique work of art. *The Yellow Cake Revue* comprises politically charged cabaret-style songs and recitations as well as a pair of piano interludes. First performed on Orkney in 1980, it had its world premiere on this day in 1990 and has been beloved of audiences ever since.

Maxwell Davies was nothing if not a pioneer – and his music is not always, it must be said, to everyone's taste. In 1969, for example, the premiere of his work *Eight Songs for a Mad King* had been heckled with cries of 'rubbish', and the first performance at the BBC Proms of *Worldes Blis* that same year prompted a mass desertion from the Royal Albert Hall.

Yet Max, as he was affectionately known in the music world, was ultimately a warm and generous musical communicator. He was cheered that this affecting *'little piano piece'* (as he described it) touched so many. It has almost *'become a folk tune'*, he observed before he died. *'People just say, "I like that piece," and they don't know who wrote it . . . And that's very unusual, for a so-called serious composer, to write a piece that people like so much.'*

6 May

Maiblumen blühten überall –
May-flowers are Blooming Everywhere
by Alexander von Zemlinsky (1871–1942)

To fin-de-siècle Vienna today and a highly unusual bouquet of May blooms, scored for the rare combination of string sextet and soprano.

Alexander von Zemlinsky doesn't get much airtime these days, which I think is a shame because he sits within a nexus of one of the most fascinating periods of modernist culture. As well as enjoying the patronage of Johannes Brahms (21 February, 3 April, 7 May, 3 August), he was a student of Anton Bruckner (11 August, 11 October) and taught a number of prominent composers, including Erich Korngold (2 September). As a young man, he fell passionately in love with Alma Schindler (13 August), who would in turn go on to marry Gustav Mahler (18 May; see also 7 July, 9 October).

Like his friend and brother-in-law Arnold Schoenberg (13 September), as well as numerous other Jewish musicians, Zemlinsky was forced to flee Nazi Austria for the USA. Unlike many of his counterparts, though, he never received the recognition for which he longed – and which Mahler and Schoenberg publicly stated he deserved.

For me Zemlinsky's hyper-expressive music is most interesting in the way it reflects the tumultuous shifts in Western music between 1890 and 1940. He pushes and pushes his harmonies to breaking point, but never takes the plunge into full-blown atonality, à la Schoenberg. This piece, which sets words by the leading German poet Richard Dehmel, starts off all languid and atmospheric, but with the entrance of the soprano, Zemlinsky ramps up the intensity. It's a one-of-a-kind listen, and invariably has the effect of transporting me, as only music can, to another time and another place.

7 May

Violin Sonata no. 1 in G major, op. 78
1: Vivace ma no troppo
by Johannes Brahms (1833–1897)

Yesterday we heard from Zemlinsky, one of the many late Romantic composers to be both inspired and actively encouraged by Johannes Brahms. Today, to the man himself, who was born on this day – and a piece that always feels to me like the sun coming out in musical form.

In 1853, Brahms was taken under the wing of Robert Schumann, who later recalled hearing from his young protégé, *'sonatas, veiled symphonies rather, songs, the poetry of which would be understood even without words . . . Sonatas for violin and piano, string quartets, every work so different that it seemed to flow from its own individual source.'* That innocuous line *'the poetry of which would be understood even without words'* gets directly to the heart of what is most magical about all music for me.

Though prolific, Brahms was ruthlessly self-critical and unforgiving: he tore up at least four violin sonatas that did not survive in the process of creating the three that do. While part of me regrets this, greedily wishing he'd written more, you just can't argue with the ones he left behind.

8 May

Spitfire Prelude & Fugue
1: Prelude
by William Walton (1902–1983)

It was on this date in 1945 that the Allies of World War Two formally accepted Nazi Germany's unconditional surrender of its armed forces, so I thought we could indulge, on VE Day, in a wartime classic by William Walton. This rousing Prelude was extracted from his score to the 1942 film *The First of the Few*, about the aviation engineer R. J. Mitchell, who designed the Spitfire fighter plane that was to form the backbone of RAF Fighter Command and play such a pivotal role in the eventual Allied victory. The film's title refers to a speech Winston Churchill made about the heroic Spitfire pilots in the Battle of Britain: *'Never in the field of human conflict was so much owed by so many to so few.'*

Walton was a leading composer of the day who also wrote acclaimed concertos, large-scale vocal pieces such as cantatas and oratorios, symphonies, an opera and film music. He was dubbed *'English music's head prefect'* by his contemporary Benjamin Britten, so it's little wonder that the British government exempted him from military service on the condition he compose music for their morale-boosting propaganda films. Right from the opening brass fanfare in this iconic piece, Walton delivers the goods.

9 May

Act 1 'letter scene'
from *Eugene Onegin*
by Pyotr Ilyich Tchaikovsky (1840–1893)

I was fifteen and had just been dumped by the first great love of my life. A few nights later I got dragged to see *Eugene Onegin* by my mum.

There was nowhere on earth I would *less* rather have been than at the stupid opera. All I wanted to do was lock myself in my bedroom, listen to pop songs that reminded me of our relationship, wrap myself in the one T-shirt I still had of his (it smelled of him!), cry my heart out and write him a letter – no mobiles yet – begging him to take me back.

So there I am, slumped in my seat, wretched with heartbreak and barely paying attention. But then – wait – I'm watching a girl pull out a piece of paper and start to sing. And now she's writing a letter, to this man who has heartlessly crushed her love, and she's singing each bit of the letter as it comes to her, seemingly spontaneously, and it's so beautiful, such transparently expressive music, and I'm sitting forward, and reading the subtitles, and listening, really listening now, and I can't help but be transfixed. It's like this girl is singing my life. Suddenly it's all laid bare on stage before my very eyes and ears, and the consolation I feel is real. And now I get it, why opera – for all its ridiculousness – can sometimes be the very truest and most powerful art form there is.

Eugene Onegin is based on Pushkin's masterpiece in verse, the very first chapter of which he started on this day. Tchaikovsky's portrait of Tatyana, spurned by Onegin only for him to realize too late his mistake, is heroically sympathetic and nuanced. '*I loved Tatyana*', the composer wrote to a friend, '*and was furious with Onegin who seemed to me a cold, heartless fop.*'

10 May

Piano Concerto no. 2 in F major, op. 102
2: Andante
by Dmitri Shostakovich (1906–1975)

After Debussy's musical gift to Chouchou earlier this month, here's another example of a parent seriously raising the birthday-present game. It was for his son Maxim's nineteenth birthday, on this day in 1957, that Shostakovich produced this tremendous concerto.

Shostakovich had a grisly time of it, living and composing as he did under the repressive Soviet regime (see e.g. 22 January). But by the time he wrote this, Stalin had been dead for four years and there's a lightness of touch, a shift in sensibility that invests the piece with an inner warmth we don't usually hear in his otherwise wracked and complex music. And yet, perhaps as a result of the censure to which he was still regularly subjected and to pre-empt criticism, the composer himself dismissed it as having *'no redeeming artistic merits'*.

That's patently not true, as generations of leading pianists will testify. And Shostakovich clearly felt a great deal of affection for the work. While Maxim, quite rightly, gave the premiere at his graduation from the Moscow Conservatoire, Shostakovich chose to perform the work a number of times himself and recorded it alongside his first concerto.

11 May

Harlem Symphony
3: 'Night Club'
by James P. Johnson (1894–1955)

James P. Johnson will always have his place in musical history as a jazz pioneer, the father of a technique called 'stride piano' and the teacher of such luminaries as Thomas 'Fats' Waller. But this ragtime-era legend also studied classical music, and even as he transformed New York's jazz scene, strove to be considered as a serious composer of symphonic music.

A distinctive feature of his music was the way he incorporated the African-American musical themes that surrounded him in his home neighbourhood, Harlem. While the likes of George Gershwin (and, when visiting New York, Maurice Ravel) would head to Harlem of an evening to hear pianists like Johnson do their thing before retreating back downtown and riffing on what they'd heard in their own scores, Johnson's use of jazz and African-American idioms in his classical music comes from a place of considerably greater authenticity. Nevertheless, despite writing sixteen musicals, more than two hundred songs, a symphony, a piano concerto, two tone poems and an opera, he received little recognition from the classical world and has only recently begun to be taken seriously by classical practitioners.

Before his death, Johnson invited the music critic Rudi Blesh to come and take a look at his many unpublished scores. *'These are long works with a feeling of breadth and sweep and with a racial pungency . . .'* notes Blesh. *'. . . Their African rhythms move with a forthright nobility. One feels none of these qualities as borrowed – they all reside in the . . . composer himself.'*

12 May

'Una furtiva lagrima' – 'A furtive tear'
from *L'elisir d'amore*
by Gaetano Donizetti (1797–1848)

Along with Gioachino Rossini (29 February) and Vincenzo Bellini (23 September), Donizetti was a leading proponent of a fashionable early nineteenth-century operatic style known as 'bel canto', which literally means 'beautiful singing'. He wrote his first opera at nineteen and produced some seventy-five during the course of his career, in addition to 16 symphonies, 19 string quartets, 193 songs, 45 duets, 3 oratorios, 28 cantatas and a slew of instrumental concertos, sonatas and chamber music.

To be this prolific, Donizetti had to be fast. *L'elisir d'amore*, his comic masterpiece which premiered in Milan on this day in 1832, was dashed off in just six weeks. Between 1838 and 1848 it became the most frequently produced opera in all of Italy.

This aria from Act 2 is sung by the character Nemorino, a village peasant, upon seeing his beloved Adina, a rich landowner, weeping. He believes that the magical love potion he has bought to win her heart (actually a bottle of crappy red wine sold by the charlatan Doctor Dulcamara) has 'worked'. (Spoiler alert: it hasn't.)

Despite his glittering career, Donizetti's life was marred by grief and debilitating mental health problems. He and his wife lost all three of their children. And then in 1836, just a year after both his parents died, he lost his wife. No wonder he suffered an emotional collapse. In February 1846, his doctors described him as *'the victim of a mental disease that brings disorder into his actions and his decisions'*. Against his wishes, he was institutionalized; he died two years later.

13 May

Piano Quintet in E flat major, op. 44
1: Allegro
by Robert Schumann (1810–1856)

Today's musical offering was also written in a matter of weeks – between September and October 1842 – in that near-miraculous 'Chamber Music Year' of Schumann's that we discussed earlier in the year (see 16 February).

As may be obvious by now, I love chamber music that feels conversational rather than contrived; that creates a mood of exchange and dialogue between autonomous musical voices. This is another cracking example. Although piano quintets did exist prior to this one, they tended to be written for keyboard plus violin, viola, cello and double bass. Schumann decides to combine a piano with a standard string quartet (i.e. two violins, viola and cello), an ensemble that was gaining in cultural prestige all the time and even starting to be heard in concert halls rather than small private salons (or 'chambers').

It says a lot, I think, about Schumann's intuitive communicative gifts that he foresaw what these two mighty forces could do in combination. In his hands, the piano quintet becomes its own unique genre, walking a line between the public and the private, and balancing both bold symphonic statements and intimate chamber-like textures.

Schumann dedicated the work to his wife, Clara. One of the most talented pianists of the age, it was she who played the fiendishly difficult piano part in its first public performance the following year.

14 May

6 Mélodies, op. 5
No. 3 in E flat major: Andante soave
by Fanny Mendelssohn (1805–1847)

More now from Fanny Mendelssohn, who died on this day and whose death, it has been argued, triggered her traumatized brother Felix's equally untimely demise a few months later. (Just imagine what they might have produced, these two sublimely gifted siblings, had they lived beyond their early forties and late thirties, respectively.)

Of the almost five hundred pieces Fanny was compelled to write, more than one hundred were for her own instrument, the piano. (Felix, by the way, was the first to admit his sister was a better pianist than he was.) Fanny had a particular genius for melody and mood. This lovely piece contains fewer punchy harmonies and suspensions than the string quartet we heard back in February, but it's still got it going on.

When I listen to it unspool, when I follow its fluid emotional lines, I can't help but picture Fanny – perhaps sitting at home at her keyboard, dreaming about her brother off on his grand tour around Europe getting to meet royalty, getting to mix with fellow composers, getting to hear everything he possibly could and soak it all up to put back into his music while she was forced to stay at home and wait to get married. I hear a young, brilliant woman pouring her curiosity and her intelligence and her empathy into outstandingly good music that would remain neglected and underrated for the best part of another one hundred and fifty years, and still has to fight to be heard.

15 May

Cantique de Jean Racine, op. 11
by Gabriel Fauré (1845–1924)

Fauré was just nineteen when he submitted this short choral work for a composition competition at the École Niedermeyer de Paris – and won. I was a teenager too when I first encountered it (being sung by the school choir in an assembly one morning) and like Ravel's piano concerto, which we heard back in March, it was another one of those 'before-and-after' pieces for me. I was arrested by its other-worldly beauty: these impeccably layered, lush vocal lines, tinged as they are with subtle flecks of modernist colour.

Fauré dedicated the piece to César Franck, who first conducted it on this day in 1875. The text, *'Verbe égal au Très-Haut'* ('Word, one with the Highest'), is a paraphrase of a Latin hymn by the French playwright Jean Racine. When I first heard this piece, sitting in my school hall, I had no idea what the words being sung meant but this did not stop me being profoundly moved by the music's 'meaning'. That's one of the great mysteries of music, and a principle I'll hold fast to: if a piece speaks to you, for whatever reason, whoever you are, that response is valid – what it means to you is what it means.

16 May

~~~~

Chaconne in G major
by Andrea Falconieri (c. 1585–1656)

An irresistibly cheering little dance today from an unfairly neglected early seventeenth-century composer and virtuoso lutenist. Like most of the jobbing freelance musicians of the day – and now – Falconieri had to be prepared to go where the work was: he travelled around Italy, Spain and France, picking up different musical trends and influences and absorbing them into his music as he went. From 1647, he managed to swing a permanent gig back in his native town of Naples, which in those days was under Spanish rule – hence, perhaps, the infectious Spanish-inflected rhythms of this chaconne.

I imagine Naples would have been a hugely exciting place to live at that time: cosmopolitan, stuffed full of art and music and literature and commerce; no wonder it was dubbed a 'golden age'. It was to be a fleeting moment, however: in the 1650s an outbreak of bubonic plague tore through the city, wiping out half of its population – including, in 1656, poor Signor Falconieri himself.

17 May

~~~~~~

Lyric Pieces Book 5, op. 54
No. 4: Notturno
by Edvard Grieg (1843–1907)

Today is Norway Day, and it is to the ultimate poster-boy for Norwegian classical music that we turn. Edvard Grieg (whose family, originally 'Greig', actually had their roots in Scotland) incorporated traditional Norwegian folk melodies into many of his compositions, and in doing so put his country firmly on the classical music map. Yet, like many of the composers who were committed to reflecting their national character in music (see e.g. 25 March, 4 June), he was gratifyingly cosmopolitan in outlook and travelled all over Europe, winning the admiration of Tchaikovsky and Brahms, Delius and Grainger.

(The feeling was definitely mutual. Of Grainger, for example, Grieg joked in 1907: *'I have written Norwegian Peasant Dances that no one in my country can play, and here comes this Australian who plays them as they ought to be played! He is a genius that we Scandinavians cannot do other than love.'*)

Grieg's *Lyric Pieces* do rather brilliantly what it says on the tin. Between 1867 and 1901 he published some sixty-six of these vignettes across ten collections. Poetic, folksy, nostalgic without ever being cloying, they are among the most charming miniatures of the nineteenth-century piano literature: the perfect quick classical fix.

18 May

'Der Trunkene im Frühling' – 'The Drunkard in Spring' from *Das Lied von der Erde* – *The Song of the Earth* by Gustav Mahler (1860–1911)

The summer of 1907 was a litany of horrors for Gustav Mahler. Amid a toxic culture riven with anti-Semitism, he was forced to resign as Director of the Vienna Court Opera. Then his four-year-old daughter died from scarlet fever and diphtheria, and he himself was diagnosed with the heart defect that would kill him a few years later. '*With one stroke*', he confessed in a letter to his friend, disciple and former assistant Bruno Walter, '*I have lost everything I have gained in terms of who I thought I was, and have to learn my first steps again like a newborn.*'

It was work that wrenched Mahler out of the gloom and helped him not just to walk, but soar. Earlier that year, a friend had given him a collection of ancient Chinese poetry translated into German. Chancing upon it again, he set about writing music to some of its verses in a creative frenzy. The epic song cycle that ensued is often described as his greatest 'symphony'; alas the composer, who died on this day in 1911, did not live to hear it performed.

Und wenn ich nicht mehr singen kann,	*And when I can sing no more,*
So schlaf' ich wieder ein.	*I fall asleep again,*
Was geht mich denn der Frühling an!?	*for what is springtime to me?*
Laßt mich betrunken sein!	*Let me be drunk!*

Legend has it that the poet, Li T'ai Po, died after rowing on a lake one night when he leant over to try and kiss the moon. That's probably a fable, but I've never been able to shake the image. Ever since, for me, Mahler's has been music that kisses the moon.

19 May

Symphony no. 1 in C minor
4: Allegro maestoso
by Alice Mary Smith (1839–1884)

Women in the nineteenth century who were brave enough to try and make their way in the world as writers of music invariably stuck to forms considered just about respectable for 'lady-composers', such as art songs, chamber works or piano miniatures.

Not so the heroic Alice Mary Smith, who was born on this day. Before she even hit thirty, Smith had had the temerity to produce two substantial orchestral symphonies. Much influenced by the Classical period, despite the prevailing winds of Romanticism of the time, Smith's music is full of energy and grace. This vibrant piece, composed when she was just twenty-four, carries the estimable title of being the first symphony ever written by a British woman. Strong work, sister.

20 May

Scherzo no. 2 in C minor, op. 14
by Clara Schumann (1819–1896)

Another day, another nineteenth-century female coolly busting through prejudices against her gender. Clara Schumann, who died on this day, was initially obliged to publish her music under a male pseudonym – and funnily enough, nobody questioned it, nobody went 'hang on, this sounds like "women's music", it can't have been written by a man.' because it sounds just like music, sigh. Anyway. As we have already seen, Clara was a force of nature. There was seemingly nothing she couldn't do: she was as accomplished a pianist as Liszt; as gifted a composer as her husband Robert; as impressive a wife, mother, grandmother and general show-on-the-road-keeper as I've come across, past or present.

For anyone to operate under the circumstances Clara did, even today, would be remarkable. That she achieved what she did in the face of such adversity – from her over-protective father, from society, from Robert's devastating mental illness – is all the more astonishing. Not every piece she wrote is a masterpiece, of course, but much of it is distinctive and beautiful and more than holds its own against what her male counterparts were producing. I love it when Clara's musical personality appears to shine through, as in this fierce yet elegant scherzo.

21 May

'Vesti la giubba' – 'Put on your costume'
from *Pagliacci*
by Ruggiero Leoncavallo (1857–1919)

Well, I sure hope you're in the mood for high drama.

Pagliacci, which was first performed on this day in 1892, is a shining example of the nineteenth-century operatic style known as 'verismo' – literally, 'true'. Like the literary movement of the same name, whose adherents wrote about subjects that had not previously been regarded as 'suitable' for high literature, verismo composers sought to put on stage operas with a greater fidelity to ordinary life as it was actually lived.

This was supposedly based on a story from Leoncavallo's own background: the murder in 1865 of one of his family servants who'd been involved in a fiery love triangle. The brief, gripping work is a heady distillation of small-town jealousy, romance, obsession and violence. This aria takes place at the end of Act 1, just after Canio, a clown, has discovered his wife's infidelity. Decimated, he must nevertheless get dressed and get on with it. Rarely has the sentiment 'the show must go on' been communicated with such emotion; at one point you can actually hear the poor guy sobbing . . .

Vesti la giubba e la faccia infarina.	*Put on your costume, powder your*
La gente paga, e rider vuole qua.	*face. People are paying, and*
	come to laugh.
Ridi, Pagliaccio,	*Laugh, clown, at your fractured love!*
sul tuo amore infranto!	*Laugh at the grief that poisons*
Ridi del duol, che t'avvelena il cor!	*your heart!*

22 May

Au Gré des ondes – Along the waves
5: 'Hommage à Bach'
by Henri Dutilleux (1916–2013)

Classical music has its fair share of perfectionists, and the French composer Henri Dutilleux is a prime example. He was ninety-seven when he died, on this day in 2013, but despite a long and illustrious career, left relatively few pieces behind. What he did contribute to the twentieth- and twenty-first-century musical canon, though, reminds us that for all the dominance of Pierre Boulez throughout this period (26 March) there was another way: a way that did not adhere to the 'necessity' of serialism and the inevitability of atonality, but one which extended a musical line from Bach and Mendelssohn, Debussy and Ravel, Stravinsky and Bartók, to produce work of vivid immediacy and great structural clarity.

This relatively early piece comes from a suite of six pieces that Dutilleux was commissioned to write in 1946 to be used as continuity music on French radio (some seriously classy jingles, basically; he may also have been punning on both radio and sea 'waves' in his title). If he acknowledges his debt to great keyboard masters of the past – especially Bach – he also prefigures much of the music that was to come. To my ears, this sounds as though it could have been written yesterday, and I find that pretty exciting indeed.

23 May

~~~

Romance for violin and piano, op. 23
by Amy Beach (1867–1944)

Amy Beach is often described as 'the first female American composer'. It is patently not the case that no American women before her had been compelled to write music, but, as we've seen, conditions for women who wanted to become professional composers were fairly dire until relatively recently. That makes the considerable impact that Beach had on America's musical scene all the more significant. As well as miniatures such as this one, she also wrote large-canvas works, including symphonies, masses and instrumental concertos.

It would have been outrageous had Beach not been able to find an outlet for her preternatural music gifts. Apparently, she was able to sing forty songs by the age of one – and I don't mean 'The Wheels on the Bus', either; by her second birthday she was able to improvise a counter-melody to anything her mother sang to her; a year later she could read music; by five she'd composed her first waltz, and so on.

Beach grew up to be a phenomenal pianist, despite the fact that, in childhood, her mother had forbidden her from playing the family piano, supposedly because indulging her would 'damage' her parental authority. (This is *so* not the reason I stop my toddler son from playing ours; I just value my eardrums.) When in 1885 Beach married an eminent Boston doctor almost twenty-five years her senior, he too discouraged her from playing. She was allowed to give two public recitals per year, with the proceeds going to charity. And although Mr Beach deigned to let his wife continue composing behind closed doors, she was not allowed to take lessons. The result is a self-taught genius with her own unique voice; her music deserves to be far better known.

24 May

Piano Concerto no. 5 in E flat major, op. 73 ('Emperor')
1: Allegro
by Ludwig van Beethoven (1770–1827)

Beethoven's final piano concerto is a colossus, no other word for it. He catapults the soloist into the action, with just a single chord of support from the orchestra, and basically cries, 'Let's go!' I can think of few more thrilling musical rides.

There are myriad technical reasons why this concerto, bestriding as it does the Classical and Romantic eras, is such a monumental achievement; reams of academic musical theses exist to unpick every one of Beethoven's radical ideas – from the bonkers fun he has with octave passages to the heart-wrenching harmonies he undoes us with in the sublime second movement.

As valuable as these analyses are, I honestly think they are an added bonus and largely superfluous for the general listener. This is a tremendous, joy-emitting example of a major piece of classical music that contains multitudes and can connect to anyone. This first movement lasts for twenty electrifying minutes, so perhaps not today, but some day, if you give yourself permission to dive in, to listen, know that you have as much right to this music as anybody. Have a listen and see what it does to you, what it says to you. It's yours – to embrace, to fall in love with, to discard, to reject, to do whatever you want with. But yours.

25 May

Milonga
by Jorge Cardoso (b. 1949)

Today is Argentina Day, so I've chosen music by one of that country's leading contemporary classical composers. A multi-talented musician, Cardoso is a guitarist, composer, teacher and prolific author – as well as a qualified medical doctor. (Seriously.)

A *'milonga'* is a place or a gathering where people go to dance the tango; it may also mean a particular type of dance or a particular tune to which *tangueros* dance. You'll be aware by now that one of my very favourite things about music is its ability to be, as well as so many other things, a magic carpet.

And here we go: I close my eyes, listen to this, and I'm not in Kansas anymore, or even in Kensal Rise; I'm not standing in my kitchen filling the dishwasher, oh no; I'm not scooping up endless peas off the floor under my son's highchair, no thanks; I'm not passed out on the sofa in my pyjamas at 9 p.m., knackered, with an unanswered email mountain to climb; oh no, not me, see I'm actually somewhere in sultry downtown Buenos Aires, it's after midnight, and I'm wearing a red dress. See you on the dance floor, *milongueras*.

26 May

~~~

'Waitin'
from *Cabaret Songs*
by William Bolcom (b. 1938)

Last month, we met the composer, teacher and member of 'Les Six' Darius Milhaud; today we hear from one of his most talented students, the contemporary American composer William Bolcom, who also studied with Olivier Messiaen (15 January) and, among many other accolades, has Pulitzer Prizes and Grammy Awards to his name.

Like Milhaud, Bolcom is seemingly curious about every type of musical genre. Along with nine symphonies, twelve string quartets, four operas, and a number of instrumental concertos, he has composed four volumes of attractive and unpretentious cabaret-style songs, written for his wife, the singer Joan Morris, all of which set texts by his friend Arnold Weinstein:

> *Waitin waitin*
> *I've been waitin*
> *Waitin waitin all my life.*
>
> *That light keeps on hiding from me,*
> *But it someday just might bless my sight.*
> *Waitin waitin waitin*

In this particularly sensuous and intimate example, you can hear Bolcom's giddy and loving embrace of the Germanic song tradition over the years, from Kurt Weill (6 July) to Hugo Wolf (3 October), Richard Strauss (11 June, 4 August) and – of course – Franz Schubert (20 January, 14 April, 4 May).

27 May

Symphony no. 3 in C minor, op. 78 ('Organ')
Poco adagio
by Camille Saint-Saëns (1835–1921)

Remember earlier in the year (25 February) when we encountered Saint-Saëns avoiding writing a new symphony by allowing himself to be distracted by a certain carnival of musical animals? Well. *This* piece was the one he was 'supposed' to be writing at that time – and, thankfully, he did eventually get around to finishing it.

Epic in scope, varied in texture, it's a work of magnificence. He threw the kitchen sink at it, taking us on a journey far beyond standard symphonic fare by including dazzling passages for the piano and, as the title suggests, a four-pipe organ big enough for a cathedral. In this intensely romantic movement in particular, the organ feels to me like a sort of heartbeat, a grounding, the essential baseline of life. Saint-Saëns admitted that he *'gave everything to it I was able to give. What I have here accomplished, I will never achieve again.'* He was right.

28 May

French Suite no. 5 in G major, BWV 816
7: Gigue
by Johann Sebastian Bach (1685–1750)

Dance music, Bach-style, today. The name is a bit of a misnomer, because Bach actually composed the six suites of this group very much in the modish Italianate style. He wrote them in his late thirties, his most prolific period.

As with many of his other works, they are directly inspired by the hot dance forms of the day, the gigue being a highly fashionable thing to do with one's feet in the Baroque era. Derived from the traditional British jig, it had been imported into France in the mid-seventeenth century and Bach's suites across the instrumental board – cello, violin, keyboard – are littered with them. I defy you to stay still.

29 May

Le Sacre du Printemps – The Rite of Spring
Part 1: 'The adoration of the earth' – Introduction
by Igor Stravinsky (1882–1971)

It's a balmy night on this day in 1913. In the spectacular art-nouveau auditorium of the Théâtre des Champs-Élysées, le Tout-Paris gathers to witness the world premiere of a work from Diaghilev's Ballets Russes. Depicting the pre-historic spring rites of ancient Russia and the great sacrifice of a Slavonic tribe, the ballet features a score by Igor Stravinsky, a composer virtually unknown until Diaghilev, three years earlier, had asked him to write music for The Firebird and then Petrushka. The atmosphere is electric.

The music begins. A strange, strangled, alarmingly exposed wood-wind solo. And after a few bars:

'It's terrifying!' whispers Claude Debussy. 'I don't understand!'
'If that's a bassoon,' utters Camille Saint-Saëns in a neighbouring box, 'I'm a baboon!'

Others will not be so restrained. Before another bar has been played, the crowd launch into a frenzied riot that has gone down in history.

Some were possibly spoiling for a fight; some had possibly been planted deliberately to start trouble. This was, after all, an age in which a succès de scandale was a certain badge of honour: to be truly avant garde was to push audiences to the very limits of what they could comprehend or accept – and then go somewhat further.

Stravinsky later claimed that he'd had to enter into a sort of creative trance to write The Rite of Spring. 'I am the vessel through which The Rite passed.'

Listening to this mad music over a century on, I find it's lost none of its raw power.

30 May

Overture
from *Candide*
by Leonard Bernstein (1918–1990)

Bernstein's sparkling operetta was based on the hugely influential 1759 novella *Candide, or The Optimist* by Voltaire, the great Enlightenment writer and philosopher who died on this day in 1778.

The gently mocking lyricism of Bernstein's score ingeniously mirrors the satire of Voltaire's original, which, as in most of his work, targeted the Catholic Church and advocated freedom of speech and religion. (*Candide*'s original lyricist, playwright Lillian Hellman, had seen parallels worth drawing with 1950s America under the shadow of McCarthyism.) Just as in *West Side Story* (13 February), when Bernstein displayed an uncanny knack for being able to evoke the vibrant sounds of the New York City street in orchestral form, here he confects a delicate pastiche of eighteenth-century forms and styles that give the music a period feel whilst maintaining a stunning modernity.

Nonetheless, *Candide* was a disaster at the box office when it opened on Broadway in 1956 and had to close after just eight weeks. The show then underwent multiple substantial revisions. The version it's generally performed in now has become one of the sure-fire hits of the lyric theatre: intelligent, witty, thought-provoking, and with some of the most fabulous music you'll ever hear.

As a child, I was lucky enough to see it in London in a concert version in 1989, conducted by Bernstein himself. I was sitting in the front row and was completely transfixed. As he was taking his bow, he turned around and, I'm sure, gave me a wink. Now whenever I hear this, my day is duly winked at; I hope it has the same effect for you.

31 May

Piano Quintet no. 1 in A minor, op. 30
1: Allegro
by Louise Farrenc (1804–1875)

It probably won't surprise you to learn that women in classical music, as in practically any other industry you could care to name, are generally paid less than their male counterparts. The situation might have been even more iniquitous, though, had it not been for Louise Farrenc, who was born on this day in 1804.

As a young pianist she showed such talent that some of the leading artists of the day wanted to teach her, including famed composers Ignaz Moscheles and Johann Nepomuk Hummel. Aged fifteen, her parents allowed her to study composition with the celebrated Antoine Reicha, although not in his much coveted class at the Paris Conservatoire, obviously, as that was only open to men. (He taught, among others, the likes of Hector Berlioz, César Franck and Franz Liszt.)

In later life, Farrenc, who also had a particular talent for writing chamber music, was taken on as a professor at the conservatoire. Despite her success, with many of her pupils scooping the top prizes, she was paid considerably less than the male professors doing the same job. For a decade, she fought to close the gender pay gap and was finally awarded equal pay.

She'd still have her work cut out for herself today, but nevertheless, we should recognize this for the significant milestone for women that it is!

JUNE

1 June

Je te veux – I want you
by Erik Satie (1866–1925)

Whether we've been aware of it or not, we've already taken in the influence of Erik Satie over the past five months. He's there in the music of Debussy (1 May, 23 August), of Poulenc (7 January, 17 February), of Elena Kats-Chernin (26 January) and so many others – and finally here he is, one of classical music's great eccentrics and always wholly himself, in what is for me the ultimate cabaret song.

Satie earned his way in Paris in the early 1900s playing the piano in the bars and music halls on the rue Montmartre. He'd dropped out of music college after one professor described him as the *'laziest student in the [Paris] Conservatoire'* and another had denounced him as *'untalented'*. Yet Satie's nocturnal existence as a cabaret pianist was to furnish him with a comprehensive musical education of a different sort; his lack of formal training did not exactly hold him back.

This sensual, sentimental waltz sets words by Henry Pacory and was composed for Satie's great friend and frequent collaborator, the legendary Montmartre chanteuse and 'Queen of the Slow Waltz', Paulette Darty.

2 June

Divertimento on Sellinger's Round
2. 'A Lament': Andante espressivo
by Michael Tippett (1905–1998)

The idea that a group of ego-driven, highly individualistic classical composers might collaborate meaningfully on a single piece of music may seem unlikely, but it's happened on a few occasions. In 1872, for example, some of the Russian composers associated with the 'Mighty Handful' group – including Borodin, Mussorgsky and Rimsky-Korsakov – joined forces on *Mlada*; in 1909 Diaghilev commissioned five composers, including Igor Stravinsky and Alexander Glazunov, to provide music based on Chopin for the ballet *Les Sylphides*; and in 1952, Benjamin Britten saw the premiere of a composite work called *La guirlande de Campra*, assembled by seven French composers, including Francis Poulenc and Germaine Tailleferre.

That duly inspired him to rally a group of his own musical compatriots – himself, Lennox Berkeley, Arthur Oldham, Humphrey Searle, Michael Tippett and William Walton – to create a joint work called *Variations on an Elizabethan Theme*, celebrating the forthcoming coronation of Queen Elizabeth II, which was to take place on this day in 1953.

They'd each be working with an Irish dance tune called 'Sellinger's Round' or 'The Beginning of the World', which had been a hit at the time of Elizabeth I. Tippett contributed the second movement, a lament, which then became the basis for his own stand-alone *Divertimento on Sellinger's Round*, a haunting and unusual work with an undulating solo violin melody that insinuates itself into your consciousness.

This was music that stopped me in my tracks when I first heard it; despite its explicit rooting in the traditions of the past it remains quite unlike anything else I've ever heard.

3 June

Ave Maria
by Charles Gounod (1818–1893)
after J. S. Bach (1685–1750)

J. S. Bach was an inveterate transcriber and recycler of his own works, so I can't imagine he'd be anything other than delighted that so many later composers – Mozart, Beethoven, Busoni, Schoenberg, Webern, Elgar, Rachmaninov, Stravinsky, Walton, Tárrega, Birtwistle, I could go on – felt compelled to take it upon themselves to refashion his compositions anew.

From the mid-nineteenth century, here is Frenchman Charles Gounod in full-on Bach fanboy mode, superimposing his own soaringly lyrical melody over a brief but perfect keyboard prelude that Bach had written almost 140 years previously.

The first alternative version that Gounod created, for solo cello or violin and piano, was in 1853; he described this as a 'meditation' on the original. It turned out to be the gift that kept on giving. Two years later, that work was turned into a version for chorus and orchestra, setting words by the French poet Alphonse de Lamartine. And then, in 1859, the tune once again got repurposed, this time into a setting for the 'Ave Maria' prayer.

It's this version which has become such a blockbuster, heard at weddings and funerals all over the world and gracing classical compilations left, right and centre – but is no less affecting for its ubiquity.

4 June

Overture
from *Ruslan and Lyudmila*
by Mikhail Glinka (1804–1857)

Throughout this year we've been hearing from many of the composers who were influenced by Glinka's groundbreaking musical approach, including Bartók, Grieg, Mussorgsky and Tchaikovsky. High time we now met the man himself.

Glinka is often dubbed the 'Father of Russian Music' because of his unwavering determination to carve out for his own musical culture a distinct identity, rather than slavishly emulating the classical trends coming out of Europe. It's not that Glinka outright rejects these styles and forms, but he treats them as a foundation upon which he can create a whole new sort of music, made with an intoxicating combination of ingredients from his homeland and beyond.

Closer to home, as the conductor of a serf orchestra on his wealthy uncle's estate, Glinka was able to directly mine the thriving Russian folk music scene, whilst being simultaneously well versed in the world of Italian opera, which he could see performed by touring companies in St Petersburg. This exuberant overture to his opera version of Pushkin's fairytale story *Ruslan and Lyudmila*, first seen in the UK on this day in 1931, takes its cue from Rossini but almost immediately heads off in a direction that feels at once more rooted.

It was bold of Glinka to stick to his nationalist guns. The opera, which tells the story of the abduction by an evil wizard of a Kiev princess and the gallant knight who tries to rescue her, became the gold standard for the emerging generation of Russian opera composers.

(Pushkin, by the way, had been intending to write the libretto, but unhelpfully got himself killed in a duel with his brother-in-law after the latter attempted to seduce his wife.)

5 June

Ribers no. 8
Traditional Danish, arr. Danish String Quartet

On Danish National Day, a story both of music and of the inventive and dynamic musicians that keep breathing thrilling new life into very old traditions. I first encountered this fantastic piece when the superbly talented (though not-so-imaginatively-named) Danish String Quartet were members of the BBC New Generation Artists scheme. As well as the standard classical repertoire for string quartet, these three young Danish dudes plus Norwegian cellist had an infectious passion for Nordic folk music, so they decided to sod convention and include some of it in their concert programmes.

The reaction was good, so in September 2013, they spent a week in the Danish countryside, arranging and recording a handful of their favourite folk tunes. *'The setup was simple: we had no recording label, no long term plan, and we just barely managed to cover the costs via a crowd-funding campaign'*, they later admitted. But the gamble paid off: they sent the rough-and-ready album, which they called *Wood Works*, to a record label – who loved it, and promptly agreed to release it.

Now the Danish String Quartet performs music such as this along-side classic quartet fare such as Haydn, Schubert and Mozart in venues all over the world, from folk music festivals and alternative clubs to eminent classical venues and concert halls. For a while, Star-bucks was rotating the album in coffee shops across the world, and it even caught the ear of a Nordic-themed computer game developer.

I love this. As artists, the Danish String Quartet could not take so-called 'classical music' more seriously, yet they see absolutely no contradiction in building music such as this into their core repertoire. This piece speaks as honestly to who they are as musicians and the rich tradition from which they come as anything else they might care to play.

6 June

Adagio of Spartacus and Phrygia
from *Spartacus*
by Aram Khachaturian (1903–1978)

The lushest of musical love-letters today from Aram Khachaturian, a Russian composer of ethnic Armenian descent who was born in Tbilisi, Georgia, on this day in 1903. Khachaturian wrote such vivid, colourful, almost painterly music he was once nicknamed the '*Rubens of Russian Music*'. But like so many other composers and artists working under the Soviet regime, he fell in and out of favour with the authorities: flavour of the month one moment, he would find himself with no warning being denounced – alongside Shostakovich, Prokofiev et al. – the next.

Upon Stalin's death in 1953, Khachaturian found himself back in favour. The drastically altered political circumstances seemed to give him a new lease of creative life; the following year, he composed music for his third ballet, *Spartacus*, and it contains some of his finest work. Based on the story of a famous Roman slave revolt (and thereby offering endless possibilities for meaty subtext), it was a storming success, winning the composer the coveted Lenin Prize.

This unashamedly romantic episode comes from Act 2, as Spartacus manages to free his lover Phrygia and they are finally reunited. Amid the passionate celebrations, though, listen out for harmonic twists that warn us of the grief to come . . .

7 June

Raga Piloo
Traditional Indian
Version by Ravi Shankar (1920–2012) and
Yehudi Menuhin (1916–1999)

It was in June 1966 that one of the seminal cultural collisions of the twentieth century occurred. The American-Jewish violin virtuoso Yehudi Menuhin, then artistic director of the Bath Festival, invited his friend, the Hindustani classical sitar virtuoso Ravi Shankar, to join him at the festival. Menuhin became the first Western musician to perform a classical raga onstage with Indian musicians, and the collaboration went on to alter the musical soundscape for ever.

Menuhin had been the ultimate child prodigy, the most famous classical musician on the planet. As talented as he was, he was nervous about improvising these 'ragas', an Indian mode of structuring melody with particular motifs, which has no equivalent in the Western tradition. Yet as one of music's great empathizers and humanitarians, he ardently believed in the importance of introducing Western audiences to Indian classical sounds. The mutual respect between the two musicians is palpable and the project was a resounding success.

The following year, EMI's Angel Records released Menuhin and Shankar's landmark album, *West Meets East*, which went on to win a Grammy for Best Chamber Performance (making Shankar the first Asian ever to win a Grammy). It was the fastest selling LP in the history of the label. By December, Menuhin and Shankar were performing this piece at the United Nations Headquarters in New York for Human Rights Day.

It's hard to overstate the influence of the collaboration, and not just on classical music. In some way, every piece of East-West musical fusion over the past half-century owes a debt to these two great pioneers.

8 June

Abendlied – Evening Song
by Robert Schumann (1810–1856)

Robert Schumann was born on this day. I was originally going to suggest we hear something from the cheerier side of his vast output to celebrate his birth. Yet Schumann's was a life marked by intense sorrow and mad grief as well as ecstatic joy, love and beauty. He was a man riven by contradiction and complexity. A man possessed of infinite creative gifts and great musical and personal generosity. A man whose piano career was cut short by an accident to his hand in his early twenties and whose life was cut short by the mental illness we would now likely diagnose as bipolar disorder. He was a man of tremendous intellectual energy and curiosity, who wrote not just some of the most beautiful music ever produced, but founded a successful music magazine and wrote reams of insightful music and literary criticism. He was also a romantic dreamer, a lyric poet whose expressions of love can break your heart. He was a man who encouraged and supported so many artists of the younger generation – who helped make Brahms the composer he is, who helped make Clara the composer she is. He was a man who could finally endure it no more, the demonic melodies in his head, too, too much. A man who threw himself into the Rhine aged just forty-four, and died in an asylum two years later.

Far too much life – and death – to sum up within a few minutes of music, I know. And yet – and yet this unbelievably moving song without words for piano, this incandescent 'song of the evening', does somehow distill something of Schumann's spirit.

It's three and a half minutes long. I rest my case.

9 June

Sinfonia concertante for violin and viola in E flat major, K. 364
1: Allegro maestoso
by Wolfgang Amadeus Mozart (1756–1791)

I don't think I was aware, until I started writing this book, how deep my obsession with Mozart's music for multiple soloists goes, but time and again when trying to whittle down the hundreds of his pieces that I could have included, I'm drawn to these. I think it's because one of the luckiest and most life-affirming things we can do as musicians is play with other people. I love the ways in which these pieces seem to tease out the colours and textures of human relationships and friendships in all their playfulness, their messy contradictions, their turbulence, their peacefulness, their frailty, their grandeur, their sheer ordinariness.

And so, following the magnificent double and triple piano works we have already heard, comes this masterpiece for solo violin and viola plus orchestra. The sinfonia concertante was a highly fashionable form that emerged in the Classical period as a sort of crossover hybrid between (yup) a symphony and a concerto; a logical next step to the concerto grosso that had proved so popular in the Baroque era (see e.g. 8 January, 13 December). The form was particularly in vogue in France, so it's quite possible that Mozart, the ultimate musical magpie, got the inspiration to write it during a stay in Paris in 1778.

Wherever it came from, it was typically inspired. Mozart could so easily have let the viola play – um – second fiddle to the violin, but rather than let its dusky, husky timbre be overshadowed by the higher instrument's brilliance, he configures the whole thing to let the sonorous viola shine just as brightly. (The viola was apparently his favourite instrument.) In his heart, his big, capacious, wholly unpretentious heart, Mozart is the ultimate musical democrat. There's proof in every glorious bar.

10 June

Isolde's Liebestod – Love-Death
from *Tristan und Isolde*
by Richard Wagner (1813–1883)

Tristan and Isolde, premiered on this day in 1865, is sometimes described as 'the ultimate opera'. The first time I went to see it, I was secretly dreading it. Five hours! Firstly, I was convinced there was no way I'd be able to stay awake. I had never seen a Wagner opera before, and I imagined interminable spectacles, all shouty warrior women, un-followable plots about Vikings and dwarves and Valkyries, and far too long between the famous bits.

I was also, I have to admit, terrified of the audience. Hardcore Wagner fans are their own breed. Whether they mean to or not, many give off a vibe that you can't be part of the 'club' unless you've, say, seen every production at Bayreuth (Wagner's own opera house). That you have no right to enjoy this stuff at your own pace, but must be able to identify every single 'leitmotif' (a signature theme that recurs through-out) before it appears, then casually cross-reference them by bar number. I have no truck with these elitist attitudes towards *any* music, so I had always given these people – and the work itself – a wide berth.

What actually happened that night was that I sat at the edge of my seat, captivated by this extraordinary music and the drama in which it sits. On paper, *Tristan and Isolde* is just another love affair (between a Cornish knight and an Irish princess). In Wagner's hands it becomes this giant metaphysical and philosophical treatise on – well, every-thing. *'Life and death'*, he wrote, *'the whole import and existence of the outer world, here hang on nothing but the inner movements of the soul.'*

It also, by the way, includes the so-called 'Tristan chord', a har-monic ambiguity with which Wagner is said to have changed the entire course of Western music in just four notes. (As you do.)

11 June

Morgen! – Tomorrow!, op. 27 no. 4
by Richard Strauss (1864–1949)

Richard Strauss, who was born on this day, set this poem by his contemporary John Henry Mackay in 1894. He had just turned thirty, and it was part of a group of four songs that he gave to his wife, the soprano Pauline de Ahna, as a wedding present.

Und morgen wird die Sonne
  wieder scheinen,
und auf dem Wege, den ich
  gehen werde,
wird uns, die [Seligen]1, sie
  wieder einen
inmitten dieser sonnenatmenden
  Erde . . .

And tomorrow the sun will shine
  again,
and on the path I will take,
it will unite us again, we happy
  ones,
upon this sun-breathing earth. . .

They would remain happily married until his death in 1949; Pauline outlived Richard by just eight months. I listen to this song, surely one of the most beautiful ways imaginable in which to spend three-and-a-half minutes of your life, and I can't help but think this may not be a coincidence.

12 June

~

Mi Teresita (Little Waltz)
by Teresa Carreño (1853–1917)

Well. If Pauline and Richard Strauss yesterday epitomized the ideal of lifelong marital bliss, here's Teresa Carreño to bring us back down to earth – and the complicated, messy vicissitudes of the human heart. The virtuoso Venezuelan pianist and composer got married three times, was in a common-law partnership with the brother of her final husband, and had children with three of her men. Of her son and four surviving daughters, her daughter Teresita also became a famous pianist, like her mother, and it's after her that this little waltz is named.

Born in Caracas, Carreño later moved to New York and toured Europe, where she was a sensation. Henry Wood, the conductor and all-round musical legend who founded the summer promenade concerts in London known as 'The Proms', once observed: *'It is difficult to express adequately what all musicians felt about this great woman who looked like a queen among pianists – and played like a goddess. The instant she walked onto the platform her steady dignity held her audience who watched with riveted attention while she arranged the long train she habitually wore. Her masculine vigour of tone and touch and her marvellous precision on executing octave passages carried everyone completely away.'*

(Okay, so it's highly regrettable that he had to shoehorn the word 'masculine' into his praise, but I think we get the picture.)

As a composer Carreño was also highly regarded: she wrote at least forty works for piano as well as chamber music, orchestral works and songs including the smash-hit 'Tendeur'. She died on this day in 1917, and like Lili Boulanger with her asteroid (see 11 February), Carreño also has a celestial body named after her: a crater on Venus. Frankly, no other planet would have done.

13 June

The Salley Gardens
by Benjamin Britten (1913–1976)

In his collection *The Wanderings of Oisin and Other Poems* in 1889, the poet William Butler Yeats, who was born on this day in 1865, noted that one of the poems was a deliberate attempt to '*reconstruct an old song from three lines imperfectly remembered by an old peasant woman in the village of Ballisodare, Sligo, who often sings them to herself*'. He initially called the poem in question 'An Old Song Resung' (a title that, in some ways, could stand for the whole history of classical music). When he reprinted it in 1895, he renamed it 'Down by the Salley Gardens':

> *Down by the salley gardens my love and I did meet;*
> *She passed the salley gardens with little snow-white feet.*
> *She bid me take love easy, as the leaves grow on the tree;*
> *But I, being young and foolish, with her would not agree . . .*

The quietly moving poem was set by a number of twentieth-century composers. My favourite is this yearningly simple setting by Benjamin Britten, written during the Second World War, when he and his partner Peter Pears were on a self-imposed exile to the USA (they were both ardent pacifists).

Perhaps it was homesickness or nostalgia that had turned Britten's fierce musical intellect – elsewhere concentrated on highly complex, large-scale operatic, orchestral and choral works – towards these artless and sincere folk songs. Either way, they provided a rich vein of inspiration. He continued to set folk song for the next thirty-odd years, long after he and Pears had moved back to the UK and settled in Aldeburgh; indeed right up until his death.

14 June

The Lark Ascending
by Ralph Vaughan Williams (1872–1958)

Speaking of folk songs and their influence on some of our greatest composers, it's time to meet Englishman Ralph Vaughan Williams. Do you remember how, back in March, Béla Bartók talked of assimilating the peasant music of his homeland so deeply that it became inextricable from his own musical language? Vaughan Williams was similarly immersed in the song tradition of his country: this is a perfect example of how, although he never quotes directly from them, the vast amount of work he had done to collect and arrange traditional English songs had somehow altered his musical DNA. This was written in 1914 but, because of the outbreak of war, only premiered in 1920. It is based on a poem by George Meredith about the song of the skylark, which seemingly effortlessly – although with masterful technical skill – echoes its subject matter through verse. Vaughan Williams' soaring melodic line manages something similarly rhapsodic.

> *He rises and begins to round,*
> *He drops the silver chain of sound . . .*
>
> *For singing till his heaven fills,*
> *Tis love of earth that he instils,*
> *And ever winging up and up,*
> *Our valley is his golden cup*
> *And he the wine which overflows*
> *to lift us with him as he goes . . .*

A music critic from *The Times* who attended the London premiere, given by soloist Marie Hall on this day in 1921, memorably observed that the piece, standing outside time, *'dreamed itself along'*. What a way to put it.

15 June

8 Concert Études, op. 40
Prelude: Allegro assai
by Nikolai Kapustin (b. 1937)

Nominally at least, the étude is a short study used by pianists to develop and refine a particular aspect of their keyboard technique. In reality, as we've already seen with Chopin (2 January) and Scriabin (16 January), composers have used études as a way to peacock their own technical inventiveness and compositional flair. In 1852, for example, Franz Liszt published a set of twelve études so fiendish, their execution was specifically described as *'transcendental'*. In his set of twelve from 1915, Claude Debussy, issuing *'a warning to pianists not to take up the musical profession unless they have remarkable hands'*, specified what each one was targeting – for example, *'chromatic degrees'* or *'arpeggios'* – then unleashed sequences of notes that were both personally and musically revolutionary. (It's said he could hear the German bombs falling on his beloved France as he wrote them; they are considered his late masterpieces.)

It takes chutzpah, then, for any modern pianist to get in on the étude act, but I think it's safe to say the jazz-influenced Russian composer Nikolai Kapustin smashes it.

Aaaaand breathe.

16 June

~

The Frog Galliard
by John Dowland (1563–1626)

Renaissance lute music really does it for me.

I know it sounds unlikely, but if you don't trust me, just ask Sting, whose 2006 album *Songs from the Labyrinth* was one big old love letter to Dowland's music.

He may be relatively unknown now, but in his day Dowland was hugely successful. Lavishly well paid for a court musician, he was something of a one-man hit-factory, churning out dozens upon dozens of what we'd now recognize as pop songs – instantly relatable ballads about love, heartbreak, and so on.

It's in Dowland's unaccompanied lute music that I find the real magic, though: it exudes a meditative clarity that I often crave when I'm frazzled, or struggling to concentrate, or badly in need of a mental break. And it's really beautiful. Dowland's contemporary, the poet Richard Barnfield, put it well in his poem *The Passionate Pilgrim* of 1598 when he wrote that Dowland's *'heavenly touch upon the lute doth ravish human sense'*.

(A galliard, by the way, was an instrumental dance form that was all the rage in the Elizabethan era. Nobody seems to be able to account for this one's curious epithet, although it's been suggested that it may have something to do with one of Queen Elizabeth's suitors, the French duc d'Alençon, whom she called her 'frog'. I'll say no more.)

17 June

I Lie
by David Lang (b. 1957)

First performed on this day in 2001, this unusual work was commissioned by the female California vocal ensemble Kitka, who have a particular interest in the folk traditions of Eastern Europe. When they asked the New York-based, Grammy- and Pulitzer-winning composer to write them a 'modern folk song', Lang turned to the words of an old Yiddish ditty and furnished it with some extraordinary new music.

The text, he says, has a *'darkly expectant'* feeling about it. *'It isn't about being happy or sad or miserable or redeemed; rather, it is about waiting for happiness or sadness or misery or redemption. As is the case in many Yiddish songs, something as ordinary as a girl waiting for her lover can cast many darker, more deeply beautiful shadows.'*

> *I lie down in bed alone and snuff out my candle.*
> *Today he will come to me who is my treasure.*
> *The trains run twice a day. One comes at night.*
> *I hear them clanging – glin, glin, glon.*
> *Yes, now he is near.*
> *The night is full of hours, each one sadder than the last.*
> *Only one is happy: when my beloved comes.*
> *I hear someone coming, someone raps on the door.*
> *Someone calls me by name. I run out barefoot.*
> *Yes! He has come!*

(Lang, by the way, co-founded the contemporary music collective Bang on a Can. Among other cool initiatives, they host informal 'Marathon concerts', in which an eclectic programme is performed over many hours while audience members are encouraged to come and go as they please.)

18 June

Violin Sonata in A major
4: Allegretto poco mosso
by César Franck (1822–1890)

Mid-June already, and we are hurtling towards peak wedding season. This glorious violin sonata – later appropriated by cellists too – was written as a wedding present for César Franck's great friend, fellow Belgian and '*ideal interpreter*', the thirty-one-year-old violinist Eugène Ysaÿe.

The story goes that Franck gave the work to Ysaÿe on the morning of his nuptials and later that same day, after a very speedy rehearsal, Ysaÿe and another wedding guest, pianist Léontine Bordes-Pène, played the sonata at the ceremony. That must have been pretty special for all involved.

It's certainly a work shot through with radiant passion. Some music historians believe Franck composed this while in the grip of his love for the beautiful Irish piano student and composer Augusta Holmès (7 November). Holmès, however, had also captured the heart of Liszt and Saint-Saëns so it was all about to get a bit messy (see 8 November). In any case, the sonata is wistful, yearning, occasionally unbridled in its intensity – and makes the most romantic of musical statements.

19 June

'Der Fischerknabe' – 'The Fisher Boy'
from *Songs Based on Schiller's William Tell*
by Franz Liszt (1811–1886)

'Let me first of all tell you, best of all men on earth, how astounded I am at your enormous productiveness!' Richard Wagner wrote to Franz Liszt in the 1850s. *'When I look back over your activities during the past years, you seem to me simply superhuman. I marvel how you can create so much . . . you are the greatest musician of all times!'*

Wagner was not exactly known for his self-effacing modesty or his generous support of others, so we should take this as the highest praise indeed. And Liszt really was a marvel, no question: the most famous pianist of his day – indeed the first musical 'celebrity' – he was so revered as a pianist and composer of music for the piano that it's easy to forget what a superb songwriter he was.

In the world of 'lieder' (songs), Liszt tends to be overlooked for the likes of Schubert, Schumann, Hugo Wolf, Richard Strauss et al. And yet, in his development of the art song as a vehicle not just for direct emotional expression but for narrative drama, he can actually be seen as the connective tissue between them all. He endlessly rewrote his songs, tinkering away and reissuing them with a dedication that suggests he was just as emotionally invested in these tiny, intimate gems as he was in his blockbuster piano works.

This one, depicting Friedrich Schiller's fisher boy, transports us to the fresh air of the Alpine highlands. It's sheer joy.

20 June

27 Pieces for Viola da Gamba
Prelude
by Carl Friedrich Abel (1723–1787)

A two-minute interlude in the key of life, this.

With some pieces of music, the primary effect on us is emotional; with some, it's intellectual; with others still, it's physical. It may sound fanciful, and I can't explain it in rational terms, but this piece works on me in a way that is instantly physically grounding. From the very first bar I can feel the gently arpeggiated (broken) chords of the viola da gamba start to act on me like a sort of benign musical gravity, guiding my hunched shoulders down towards the floor, releasing tension in my spine, allowing me to breathe deeper. It's nuts. I imagine this is what happens to people who do regular yoga, or something. I don't do regular yoga but I listen to this and I feel that the music is doing something *active* to me, that it's not just '*sonorous air*', as Busoni once memorably described music.

Abel died on this day, in 1787. We know that he was a student of J. S. Bach and became great friends with Bach's son Johann Christian, even setting up a popular and long-running concert series with him in London. But he's largely out of the canon now: if he's known at all, it's for an unfortunate misattribution of one of his symphonies, thought for years to have been written by Mozart when in fact young Wolfgang Amadeus had simply copied it out in an act of fandom as an enthusiastic teenager.

Abel's music is rarely heard, then – but you may well notice that his intoxicating chord progressions have been emulated (whether consciously or not) by all manner of twentieth-century pop artists. He lives on.

21 June

~~~~~~~

Mercy
by Max Richter (b. 1966)

The American violinist Hilary Hahn commissioned this piece as part of her groundbreaking 2013 project '27 Encores', which called upon some of today's leading composers to produce short 'encore' works for Hahn – or any violinist – to play at the end of a concert (should the audience still be demanding more after the main programme).

Richter takes as his starting point Portia's famous lines from Shakespeare's *The Merchant of Venice*:

> *The quality of mercy is not strain'd,*
> *It droppeth as the gentle rain from heaven*
> *Upon the place beneath: it is twice blest;*
> *It blesseth him that gives and him that takes:*
> *'Tis mightiest in the mightiest: it becomes*
> *The throned monarch better than his crown . . .*

It's a beautiful piece, yet also plaintive and mournful, so I was going to say: please skip this track and come back to it another day if by any chance you're feeling blue; I don't want to bring you any further down. But then I listened again and I realized it was working on me in that magical way that only music can: amplifying a feeling, and by some alchemical process transforming it. Blues, in other words, redeemed. Have mercy.

22 June

Scaramouche for two pianos, op. 165b
3: 'Brazileira' (Mouvement de samba)
by Darius Milhaud (1892–1974)

A very different musical mood today as Darius Milhaud, born on this day, brings a little samba to proceedings.

He wrote this on commission from the Scaramouche Theatre Company in Paris, but it was surely influenced by his time spent in Rio de Janeiro between 1917 and 1919, where he worked as secretary to the poet Paul Claudel, who was French Ambassador to Brazil at the time. (I know, my mind spins: poets and composers as top civil servants? Amazing.)

It was in Rio that Milhaud met the composer Heitor Villa-Lobos (7 September, 17 November), who introduced him to local street music, including the ubiquitous samba. The omnivorously curious Frenchman soaked up all these new sounds and later infused Brazilian-style vibes into much of his music, including this cheeky little caper.

Caipirinha optional.

23 June

~~~

The Seasons, op. 37b
6: 'June: Barcarolle'
by Pyotr Ilyich Tchaikovsky (1840–1893)

If yesterday was a day to dream of sipping cachaça-based cocktails on Copacabana beach, today's musical offering serves a somewhat different summer mood. Do you ever get melancholy in June? I know I do. And perhaps Tchaikovsky did too; for me this piece is the quintessence of a certain languid summer restlessness.

Tchaikovsky was a composer capable of communicating great joy, but whenever I hear him in this mode I can't help but think of the many struggles he had to contend with in his life. Prodigiously talented, he yet suffered from cycles of what he described as '*wearying, maddening*' depression, profound insecurity, and mental crises. Almost certainly gay, he once wrote wretchedly to his brother Modeste, also a homosexual, that '*our dispositions are the greatest and most insuperable obstacle to happiness, and we must fight our natures to the best of our ability*'. His subsequent marriage at the age of thirty-seven, to a former student who had been showering him with fan mail, was a disaster. It lasted just over two months and caused, in an already emotionally overwrought Tchaikovsky, a period of crippling writer's block.

And yet – and yet. Tchaikovsky was a great one for seeking out beauty and redemption in the world. '*Life is beautiful in spite of everything!*' he once wrote. '*There are many thorns, but the roses are there too.*' This short piece, written as part of a monthly twelve-part commission from a music magazine, manages to look in both directions at once.

Tchaikovsky died at fifty-three, but whether from cholera caused by drinking unboiled water in a café, or by suicide, is not clear.

24 June

~~~

The Silver Swan
by Orlando Gibbons (1583–1625)

When asked about his favourite composer in an interview, the legendary twentieth-century Canadian pianist Glenn Gould did not name, as we might have expected, the composer with which he is synonymous, J. S. Bach – nor did he mention the other composers with whom he is closely associated – Beethoven, say, or Berg, Schoenberg, Webern.

Oh no. Gould named as his favourite composer a relatively obscure early Jacobean Englishman called Orlando Gibbons. '*Ever since my teenage years, this music . . . has moved me more deeply than any other sound experience I can think of*', Gould said, going on to enthuse about Gibbons' '*supreme beauty*'.

It's an unlikely choice, but Gibbons was certainly a precociously talented and versatile composer. In 1611, he became the youngest contributor to *Parthenia*, the first ever printed collection of keyboard music in England. The following year, he published his *First Set of Madrigals and Motets* which opens with this stunner:

> *The silver Swan, who, living, had no Note,*
> *when Death approached, unlocked her silent throat.*
> *Leaning her breast upon the reedy shore,*
> *thus sang her first and last, and sang no more . . .*

Over the next decade or so, he would go on to write dozens more madrigals and verse anthems, all to English texts. Gibbons was at the peak of his compositional powers when he died an extremely grisly death, probably from the plague, aged just forty-one.

25 June

Sicilienne
by Maria Theresia von Paradis (1759–1824)

After the gigues, the tarantellas and the chaconnes we've already heard, another hugely popular Baroque and Classical dance form today. Loosely associated with Sicily, the 'sicilienne' was sometimes inserted as an interlude during operas, concertos and instrumental works; this is one of its loveliest stand-alone examples.

One of Vienna's most celebrated pianists of the day, Maria Theresia von Paradis had a superhuman memory and more than sixty concertos at her fingertips. She wowed Viennese musical society with her concerts and was held in such high esteem that she could commission composers as eminent as Haydn, Salieri and Mozart (who supposedly wrote his Piano Concerto no. 18 in B flat for her; see 11 December). As a composer, we know that she wrote operas, songs and chamber music, but alas hardly anything beyond this piece survives.

However, there is one contribution Maria Theresia von Paradis made to history that has not been lost – and is arguably even more important than her music. Blind since early childhood, in the late eighteenth century she developed a tactile alphabet which she used to read and write, and later showed this to the calligrapher Valentin Haüy. He was greatly inspired to discover that von Paradis had been using this method to communicate with a blind German man called Johann-Ludwig Weissenburg, who was subsequently teaching other blind students her finger alphabet. Encouraged by this proof that the blind could learn by reading with their fingers, in 1784 Haüy opened the first school for the blind in Paris. It used a comprehensive raised alphabet system based on Maria Theresia's version; this became the model employed by educators of the blind for the next fifty years.

26 June

Sinfonietta
1: Allegretto – Allegro – Maestoso
by Leoš Janáček (1854–1928)

Janáček had some lofty ambitions for this electrifying mini-symphony, which he wrote for a local 'gymnastic' festival, part of a national and Slavic-wide movement called *Sokol* which promoted a *'strong mind in a sound body'* and celebrated independent nationhood through youth, sport and festivities (the word *sokol* comes from the Czech for 'falcon').

The piece, which was premiered on this day in Prague in 1926, was dedicated to the Czechoslovak Army. Nearing the end of his own life – he would be dead in two years – Janáček approached it with splendid vim and vigour, right from the sparkling opening fanfare. He said he wanted it to express *'contemporary free man, his spiritual beauty and joy, his strength, courage and determination to fight for victory'* – and he scored it accordingly. The piece requires epic instrumental forces, including twenty-five brass players, a vast number compared to most orchestral performances.

Bemusing as it would probably have been to Janáček himself, the Sinfonietta has become one of the few works from the modern era to transcend the classical bubble and be embraced by the mainstream – including prog-rock group Emerson, Lake and Palmer, who used it in their 1970 song 'Knife Edge'. More recently, after the novelist Haruki Murakami referenced it throughout his dystopian trilogy *1Q84*, sales of Janáček shot up in the author's native Japan.

27 June

〜〜〜〜

Bring us, O Lord God
by William Henry Harris (1883–1973)

A dose of divine choral music today from late 1950s England, this is the much-loved choirmaster and organist William Henry Harris setting immortal words by John Donne. It's so beautiful, my advice is simply to try and find three and a half minutes to yourself – and temporarily switch the rest of the world off.

> *Bring us, O Lord God, at our last awakening into the house and gate of heaven, to enter into that gate and dwell in that house, where there shall be no darkness nor dazzling, but one equal light; no noise nor silence, but one equal music; no fears nor hopes, but one equal possession; no ends nor beginnings, but one equal eternity: in the habitations of thy majesty and glory, world without end.*

28 June

Lavender Field
by Karen Tanaka (b. 1961)

Karen Tanaka was born in Tokyo but moved to France in 1986 to take up an internship at Pierre Boulez's institute IRCAM in Paris (see 26 March). She has a really eclectic style, as befitting someone working across multiple different cultures in modern classical music, but if her work is unified by anything, it's by her love of nature and concern for the environment. That has manifested itself in a number of her pieces, including *Questions of Nature*, *Silent Ocean*, and this one, composed in the year 2000.

Late June is lavender season – in Japan, in France – and hearing this piece at this time of year, I cannot help but imagine vast fields of fragrant, purple flowers.

Long may they flourish.

29 June

~~~~~~

Eclogue for piano and strings, op. 10
by Gerald Finzi (1901–1956)

Music and literature have long made for harmonious bedfellows. While literature is often described – albeit not always with great precision – in musical terms, composers in turn have also been drawn to emulate literary forms. Glazunov, for example, composed curiosities called 'novelettes', Britten was drawn to the seven sonnets of Michelangelo, and so on.

Not many musicians of the modern era, however, have been tempted to try their hand at the 'eclogue' – an archaic form of literary pastoral exemplified in Virgil in which shepherds – yep, shepherds – converse. But the English composer Gerald Finzi, who was born on this day, had niche tastes: he was also an expert on English apple varietals and saved a number of them from extinction. (For real.)

His timeless musical take on an eclogue, in which the piano and string orchestra take on the role of those conversing shepherds, is a thing of introspective beauty, an intense and lyrical pastoral that unfolds with great gentleness, even where Finzi introduces strains of tension and dissonance. It's eleven minutes long, so, not a hop, but in some ways it has the effect of suspending time. This piece for me is a great example of music that you take in perhaps superficially as you go about your life, while meanwhile it quietly does its work without you even being conscious of it. It may sound far-fetched, but I feel cleansed, somehow, after I've listened to this piece.

It was half-written in the late 1920s, originally as a slow movement for a piano concerto, but Finzi revised and revisited it in later life. It was only published the year after his death; sadly he never got to see it performed.

30 June

~⁓

Song of June
by Jonathan Harvey (1939–2012)

On the face of it, Jonathan Harvey was an upstanding member of the English musical establishment – PhD from Cambridge, resident with the BBC Scottish Symphony Orchestra, composer of string quartets, operas, choral and orchestral works, and so on. But underneath that veneer of conventionality lay a creatively fearless musical maverick, who once worked at Boulez's IRCAM; provoked the wrath of his peers by suggesting classical concerts needed a good shake-up to attract new audiences; and let his imagination run wild in the more unconventional fields of electronics and the spoken word.

Song of June is Harvey's sensuous 2010 take on Wilfred Owen's 1914 poem about young lovers on a hot June day:

> *Leaves*
> *Murmuring by myriads in the shimmering trees.*
> *Lives*
> *Wakening with wonder in the Pyrenees.*
> *Birds*
> *Cheerily chirping in the early day.*
> *Bards*
> *Singing of summer, scything thro' the hay . . .*
> *Bees*
> *Shaking the heavy dews from bloom and frond.*
> *Boys*
> *Bursting the surface of the ebony pond . . .*

Harvey believed great music could express *'freedom, light and love'*. Far too humble to make those claims for his own work, I think that's exactly what he achieves.

JULY

1 July

Gymnopédie no. 1
by Erik Satie (1866–1925)

The musical eccentric Erik Satie, who died on this day, was twenty-one when he began self-styling himself a *'gymnopédist'*.

It may sound like a made-up thing, but *gymnopédie* had its roots in ancient Sparta. According to Herodotus and Plato, at the 'Gymnopedia' festival every year Greek youths would pay tribute to the god Apollo by doing a bit of naked war dancing to show off their athletic and martial skills. In 1775, the Enlightenment philosopher-composer Jean-Jacques Rousseau included the word in his *Dictionary of Music* to denote *'an air or chant to which young female Lacedaemonians danced nude'*. But it's fair to say the term was not exactly common parlance, and by 1887 had fallen sufficiently out of use that it definitely felt like a Satie original.

What Satie did with the trilogy of *Gymnopédies* from 1888 was in any case all-new, each note a precisely placed distillation of mood; chords never quite resolving; harmonies oscillating; yet with this great sense of stillness at its core. Although the *Gymnopédies* predate Satie's 1917 gloriously unpretentious concept of *'musique d'ameublement'* – literally 'furniture music', pieces that could be played in bistros or in homes amid the clamour of everyday life, with no need for the reverent ritual that normally surrounds classical music – the seeds of this philosophy are very much there. (The idea was later taken up by John Cage in his theory of 'minimalist' background music; see 12 August.)

2 July

Trio for piano, violin and cello in D minor
1: Allegro non troppo
by Ethel Smyth (1858–1944)

On this day in 1928 the Representation of the People (Equal Franchise) Act became UK law. Expanding on a 1918 Act which had allowed women over thirty who met minimum property qualifications to vote, this one gave women electoral equality with men: now all women over twenty-one, regardless of property ownership, could vote in parliamentary elections. Adding five million more women to the electoral roll, the Act created a majority female electorate, 52.7%, in the general election the following year.

This landmark in women's rights had been tirelessly campaigned for by the Suffragettes – including today's composer Ethel Smyth, who joined the Women's Social and Political Union in 1910 and, like her friend Mrs Pankhurst, was sent to Holloway Prison. Smyth had composed the suffragettes' signature rallying tune, *The March of the Women*, and there exist eyewitness reports of her conducting it in the prison yard at Holloway in 1912, vigorously beating time with her toothbrush.

As a composer, Smyth was single-minded. (She had to be: her aristocratic father had been appalled when his daughter announced she wanted to be a composer.) Resorting to tactics that would come in useful later – hunger strikes, locking herself in her room, and so on – aged nineteen she eventually got her way and went to study in Leipzig – where she befriended Brahms, Tchaikovsky, Grieg, Dvořák and Clara Schumann. Throughout her life Smyth had friends in high places, but none of that helped secure the professional recognition she so deserved. Her frustratingly neglected output includes six operas and large orchestral and choral works, alongside vocal pieces and wonderfully fresh chamber music – such as this engaging, conversational piano trio.

3 July

Rhapsody on a Theme of Paganini, op. 43
Variation no. 18: Andante cantabile
by Sergei Rachmaninov (1873–1943)

To one of the heroes of the Romantic piano movement today.

By the time he wrote this, Rachmaninov had had a rocky ride. In 1917, with Russia in turmoil after the October Revolution, he and his family had left on an open sled, with nothing but a bit of cash, some sketches of compositions and two opera scores: Rachmaninov's own unfinished *Monna Vanna* and Rimsky-Korsakov's *The Golden Cockerel*. Travelling north through Finland, they made it safely to Stockholm, moved to Copenhagen the following year, later decamped for New York, and finally, the year before his death, settled in Los Angeles. Rachmaninov never returned to Russia, but he missed it all his life, and his later music is riven with nostalgia.

Not that Rachmaninov managed to compose much in his years of exile. With Modernism in full swing, there was little taste among music critics for his unashamedly ripe, overtly Romantic pianism: in 1926, for example, his fourth concerto was a flop. Due to financial pressures, he was forced to undertake a punishing schedule as concert pianist and conductor; there wasn't much time to write.

It was only when he finished building a villa in Switzerland that reminded him of his old family home that he was able to begin composing again with any relish. It was in this villa, near Lake Lucerne, on this day in 1934, that he first put pen to paper on what would be one of his most enduringly beloved works, *Rhapsody on a Theme of Paganini*. (We heard the original earlier this year; see 26 April.)

Formally ingenious, the piece is studded with magic – but there's one movement in particular that has captured people's imaginations and never let go. Rachmaninov was well aware that Variation no. 18 would be the smash hit. '*This one,*' he apparently quipped, '*is for my agent.*'

4 July

Short Ride in a Fast Machine
by John Adams (b. 1947)

It's the Fourth of July – US independence day. I was so spoiled for choice when it came to picking music for today that I have scattered the rest of this month with American musical legends (oh hey, Scott Joplin, George Gershwin, Duke Ellington!) as well as including the ultimate music love-letter to America, Dvořák's String Quartet no. 12 (21 July).

In the end, amid some stiff competition and having already heard from major American composers such as Steve Reich, Philip Glass, Aaron Copland, Leonard Bernstein and John Williams, I decided it was about time we heard from the contemporary master John Adams. His 1986 orchestral fanfare *Short Ride in a Fast Machine* very much does what it says on the tin.

In other words, hold on to your hats!

5 July

Beati quorum via
by Charles Villiers Stanford (1852–1924)

In some ways, given the constant exchange of musical ideas flowing back and forth across time and space, every classical composer might be considered both student and teacher. But then there are the many fine composers in history who made it their mission to guide the next generation, running the risk that their students might go on to surpass them in greatness and reputation. These days you don't see so many leading contemporary composers who also teach on a regular basis, although there are of course some shining exceptions.

The Dublin-born, Leipzig-educated Stanford is a prime example of a composer who dedicated his life to teaching, and whose own reputation was duly eclipsed in the process. Aged twenty-nine, he became one of the founding professors of London's Royal College of Music, where he would work for the rest of his life, and where his starry students included Gustav Holst (27 November), Ralph Vaughan Williams (14 June), Frank Bridge (6 October), Samuel Coleridge-Taylor (27 August), and so on.

Defiantly anti-modernist – the increasingly unfashionable Johannes Brahms was his idea of genius – Stanford loved opera and produced at least nine, none of which ever made it into the repertory. He also composed seven symphonies and other orchestral works that are largely ignored. But in the field of choral music, he is held in high regard; some even consider him responsible for the twentieth-century renaissance in British choral music which has borne such beautiful fruit.

His setting of words from Psalm 119 is a thing of beauty.

> *Blessed are the undefiled in the way,*
> *who walk in the law of the Lord.*

6 July

'My Ship'
from *Lady in the Dark*
by Kurt Weill (1900–1950)

On that note, here's an example of a composer who vastly benefitted from being taught by a teacher who was himself a bit of a superstar. It was in December 1920 that Kurt Weill – who, like Satie with his Montmartre clubs, was largely supporting himself by playing the piano in bierkellers and taverns – went to play for the Italian pianist and composer Ferrucio Busoni, whom we'll meet later in the month (27 July).

Busoni was so bowled over by the twenty-year-old German's talents that he accepted him as one of just five master students in composition, and helped shape Weill's early language into something far more interesting than what could have been a mere emulation of his heroes Mahler, Schoenberg and Stravinsky. Weill went on to become one of the most distinctive and significant figures in his field, collaborating with the German writer Bertolt Brecht and contributing to the canon such iconic works as *The Threepenny Opera*.

Weill always said he believed in writing music that served a socially useful purpose; thankfully he also believed in writing music that was hugely entertaining. He was married (twice) to the great actress and singer Lotte Lenya, and his cabaret songs are unparalleled in the genre.

Weill's music was admired by composers such as Alban Berg, Alexander von Zemlinsky, Darius Milhaud and Igor Stravinsky, but as a prominent Jew he was officially denounced by the Nazis. Like so many other Jewish composers, he was forced to flee Germany, in March 1933. He settled in America, where he wrote songs, operas and Broadway musicals – including, in 1941, *Lady in the Dark*, from which this timeless number comes.

7 July

Symphony no. 5 in C sharp minor
4: Adagietto: Sehr langsam – very slowly
by Gustav Mahler (1860–1911)

On the anniversary of Mahler's birth, the wrenchingly beautiful love-letter he encoded into his monumental Fifth Symphony.

Before we launch in, a little background. In February 1901, he suffered a near-fatal brain haemorrhage and it took him a while to recover. That July, he started work on what would become this symphony at his summer house in the Austrian lakeside village of Maiernigg. With the piece half-finished, he returned to Vienna that autumn, where he met Alma Schindler (13 August), the former girlfriend of Alexander von Zemlinsky (6 May). It was a coup de foudre: by the time Mahler returned to Maiernigg to complete his symphony the following summer they were married and Alma was expecting their first child (their beloved Maria Anna, who would die in childhood; see 18 May).

This hyper-romantic fourth movement is a lavish declaration of love. Opening with a whisper, it blooms with longing, building to an almost excruciating rapture and then subsiding, with the utmost tenderness, to a place of serenity and peace. Mahler went to town with the marking, peppering his score with directions such as *'expressive'*, *'soulful'* and *'with the most heartfelt sentiment'*. And yet, as ever – he was obsessed all his life with death – shadows hover perilously close to the surface.

The conductor Willem Mengelberg, who was a friend of the Mahlers, wrote on his own score at this movement: *'Love! A smile enters his life.'* Which may be just about the best definition of falling in love ever.

It would not, alas, be there for long.

8 July

Gladiolus Rag
by Scott Joplin (c. 1867–1917)

To the King of Ragtime today, the Texas-born genius who, in pieces such as *Maple Leaf Rag* and *The Entertainer*, created the phenomenally successful archetypes from which practically all later ragtime and swing derive. Joplin was to have an inestimable influence on twentieth-century American music – from jazz to rock to classical music.

Not unlike James P. Johnson, whom we met a few months back (11 May), for all his success Joplin struggled to be taken seriously beyond the form for which he was famed, and his experiments in opera, such as *Treemonisha*, were failures in his own lifetime. But he always had a conviction that his time would come: two years before he died, he proclaimed, '*Fifty years after I'm dead, my music will be appreciated.*' He wasn't far off. Thrust back into the American limelight in 1970 by the pianist Joshua Rifkin on classical label Nonesuch, Joplin's music became world-famous due to its inclusion in the Oscar-winning 1974 movie *The Sting*. Joplin was posthumously awarded the Pulitzer Prize, and *Treemonisha*, as it happens, was produced to great acclaim in 1972.

I've long had a soft spot for Joplin rags, with their looping sixteen-bar phrases, their teasing melodies, cheekily misbehaving right hands and giddy syncopations. There are so many to choose from you can practically pick by mood, and as July is gladioli season, this one feels particularly appropriate.

9 July

Cello Concerto in E minor, op. 85
3: Adagio
by Edward Elgar (1857–1934)

Elegiac and fierce and with moments of such blisteringly raw emotion that you emerge from a performance somewhat shredded (in a good way), this concerto, made iconic by the young British cellist Jacqueline du Pré in 1965, should dispel once and for all the notion of Elgar being an uptight Edwardian who busied himself with a bit of English pastoral here, a spot of nationalist bombast there, and not much else. Right from its ferocious opening chord, and without wasting a single precious second, this concerto has more soul in its little finger than many composers can hope to summon in a lifetime.

The cello concerto was the last major work that Elgar wrote, and it carries in its DNA the long, bleak shadow cast by the Great War. The main theme of the electrifying first movement had announced itself to Elgar – allegedly after he came around from an operation to remove a septic tonsil – in 1918. He started writing it in earnest the following summer of 1919 at his cottage in Sussex. Peace was less than a year old; only the previous summer he would have been able to hear, from this very cottage, the sound of artillery across the English Channel at night. To add to that, his beloved wife, Alice, was fading away before his eyes; this would be their last summer together.

The work was a disaster at its premiere, the orchestra and soloist critically under-rehearsed and the audience perhaps wrong-footed by a public work that felt so intensely and ragingly private. Its reputation was restored, however, by the singular artistry of du Pré, and it has stood as one of the greatest of twentieth-century musical statements ever since.

10 July

Song without Words in E major, op. 19 no. 1
by Felix Mendelssohn (1809–1847)

Some music historians believe it was actually Fanny Mendelssohn (2 February, 14 May, 14 November) who first came up with the inspired concept of a 'song without words', but we have to give credit where credit is due. Felix, born on this day in 1809, perfected the form, producing eight volumes of the things between 1829 and 1845. Given how intensely lyrical they are, it is perhaps not surprising that right from the beginning, people kept trying to furnish them with words. But Mendelssohn always rejected the idea of taking too literally their being 'songs'. When a close friend actively sought to set text to them – slightly missing the point – the composer hit back with a statement that has long added spice to the debate around whether music can actually 'mean' anything.

'*What the music I love expresses to me*', he said, '*is not thought too* indefinite *to put into words, but on the contrary, too* definite' (Mendelssohn's own emphases). This sentiment very much flies in the face of those who have declared that music is too abstract to have actual meaning. What I take from it is that, if a piece moves you in a certain way, brings to mind certain images or stories, it doesn't matter if what you're interpreting is what Mendelssohn *intended*. If it gives you what the internet might call many feels, it means what it means.

11 July

'Bess, you is my woman now'
from *Porgy and Bess*
by George Gershwin (1898–1937)

Apparently Gershwin, who died on this day, used to bash out four songs each morning in order to get the bad ones out of his system. If that's correct, it was a damn good strategy because almost every bar of music that he left behind in his short life *'S Wonderful!*

(Sorry, but, true.)

By his mid-thirties, Gershwin was already a sensation in the worlds of musical theatre, symphonic and instrumental classical music and jazz, but he'd never written an opera. After a few false starts, he found his ideal material in DuBose Heyward's 1925 novel, *Porgy*.

It tells the tale of a crippled street-beggar, Porgy, and the beautiful Bess, whom he loves, but who can't escape the toxic clutches of two other men: her drug dealer, Sportin' Life, and her jealous, abusive lover, Crown. In Gershwin's mind, *Porgy and Bess* would be a 'folk opera'; not because he would quote directly from traditional folk sources, but because the spirit of African-American music and spirituals would infuse his own score, Bartók- or Vaughan Williams-style. He temporarily relocated from New York to South Carolina to soak up the authentic sounds of the slums in which the action takes place. Being Gershwin, he absorbed all he'd heard and combined it with the myriad other sounds that were buzzing away in that singular brain of his: the Jewish, the Afro-American, the blues, the jazz; he could intuitively hear what connected them all and synthesize them into something of a masterpiece.

The opera shocked audiences when it opened in 1935, not least because its cast was made up almost entirely of African-American singers. This was unprecedented at the time (and would still be a rarity in most Western opera houses). It closed after a few months, but was later hailed as a classic.

12 July

Nocturno, op. 7
by Franz Strauss (1822–1905)

We've already heard twice from the wildly talented Richard Strauss; time now to meet his old man, Franz (he, if you recall, of the anti-Wagner revolt during rehearsals for *The Mastersingers*; see 6 February).

Although Franz Strauss played the guitar, clarinet and viola, it was for his French horn-playing that he was renowned. (For his part, Wagner apparently said: '*Strauss is a detestable fellow but when he blows his horn one cannot sulk with him.*') He was principal horn in the Bavarian Court Opera for four decades and taught the instrument to students at Munich's leading music conservatoire.

He'd also been writing music since his mid-teens, and although his efforts as a composer would later be vastly eclipsed by his genius son, Strauss produced a handful of fine music over the course of his long career. Not surprisingly, he was especially good at writing for the French horn – which did not boast a large solo repertoire then (or even now: horn players often have to transcribe works originally written for other instruments).

Contrary to the musical direction of the day, Strauss's musical tastes were firmly rooted in the Classical: his heroes were Mozart and Haydn (certainly *not* Wagner and other contemporary giants). You can hear those preoccupations, I think, in this richly textured concert piece, which was published in 1864 and has been beloved of horn players ever since. It's a slice of mellow horn gold; I recommend putting your feet up and relaxing with a nice glass of something, if you can.

13 July

String Quartet in G major, op. 76 no. 1
1: Allegro con spirito
by Joseph Haydn (1732–1809)

To the godfather of the string quartet today, 'Papa Haydn', as he was affectionately nicknamed by the musicians working under him at the court of Prince Esterházy as well as by Mozart and successive generations of string quartet composers.

The string quartet did already exist as a form by the time Haydn got stuck in, but through the sixty-eight that he wrote during the course of his life it's fair to say he reinvented, reinvigorated and reimagined what it could possibly do. Structurally and musically, he set the benchmarks that nobody writing in this form subsequently could ignore, and from which much of the quartet ingenuity of the next generation (Beethoven, Mendelssohn & co.) would derive.

This work, from his last completed set, was written at the peak of Haydn's career when he was probably the most famous composer in the world – more famous even than Mozart. For me it's a distillation of what makes him *Haydn*: his wit, his inventiveness, his intelligence, and a certain jaunty joie de vivre that is communicated with such uncomplicated emotional directness. I'm obsessed with the way he develops things shortly after the three-minute mark, but it goes without saying there's a Haydn string quartet to suit pretty much every mood, so I hope you'll think of this one as a mere jumping-off point to explore further.

14 July

Sonatine
2: Mouvement de minuet
by Maurice Ravel (1874–1937)

The history of classical music is full of examples of freelance composers hustling for extra income. Maurice Ravel was no exception. Keen to find ways to make a few extra francs, he composed the first movement of what was to become his charming sonatine on the encouragement of a friend who'd seen news of a competition posted in a 1903 edition of the *Weekly Critical Review* of Paris.

Okay, first of all, let's take a moment to consider how amazing it is that local rags once thought nothing of running *classical music* competitions in their weekly editions.

Second of all, how extraordinary that the applicants could include someone of the talent of *Maurice Ravel*, who, as we have already seen, is one of the twentieth century's all-time greats.

In fact, Ravel was the only applicant. He was also disqualified because his piece was slightly longer than the specified seventy-five bars. And it all turned out to be academic anyway, as the newspaper soon went bankrupt and decided to cancel the competition.

However, all was not lost: two years later Ravel submitted the Sonatine, now with two further movements and exhibiting an almost Classical elegance of form, to the Paris publisher Durand. It's been a favourite among pianists and audiences ever since. A nice choice, I hope you'll agree, for Bastille Day.

15 July

Three Latin Motets from *The Last Supper*
3: 'In supremae nocte cenae' –
'On the night of the last supper'
by Harrison Birtwistle (b. 1934)

Sir Harrison Birtwistle, who was born on this day, has a reputation for being one of the enfants terribles of English contemporary music, a bracingly intelligent provocateur who, along with his Manchester-based pals Peter Maxwell Davies (5 May) and Alexander Goehr, smashed the complacency and sentimentality of a 1950s English musical scene which thought it had escaped the worst of the century's atonal and amorphous excesses.

The atmospheric Latin Motets are, I think, a good place to start with Birtwistle's music. They were composed for inclusion in his 1999 opera *The Last Supper*, but occupy a discrete role within the piece. Unlike the rest of the work, which has a contemporary libretto, the texts are drawn from a fourteenth-century prayer and a hymn by Thomas Aquinas. Despite being written on the cusp of the year 2000, to me they feel far more Renaissance than Millennial.

This is not so surprising given that Birtwistle has always plundered voraciously from the ancient world. For all he has been shaped by the torrential musical energy of, say, Pierre Boulez (26 March), 'Harry', as he is affectionately known among musicians, has been equally lured by the plangent dissonances of medieval plainchant and old-school polyphony. Moreover, many of his meatiest subjects for opera have come from the past, including *Gawain, The Minotaur,* and, here, the Gospels.

16 July

Canarios
Traditional improvisation
Version by Jordi Savall (b. 1941)

Are you in the mood for a *'fiery wooing dance'*? I sure hope so.

To add to our collection of Renaissance and Baroque dances, today, I give you . . . the 'canario', or canary, a dance craze that spread all over Europe in the late sixteenth and early seventeenth century (an equivalent of dabbing, I guess, or whatever centennial dance meme is currently blowing up the internet).

The canary is not only referenced in French and Spanish dance manuals of the day, such as those by Fabritio Caroso, Cesare Negri and Thoinot Arbeau, but even has its moment in Shakespeare. In Act 3 of *Love's Labour's Lost*, for example, Moth speaks of *'jigging off a tune at the tongue's end, and canarying to it with the feet'*, while in Act 2 of *All's Well That Ends Well*, Lafeu tells the king that he has seen a medicine:

> *That's able to breathe life into a stone,*
> *Quicken a rock, and make you dance canary*
> *With spritely fire and motion.*

'*Sprightly fire and motion*', eh? To be honest, the canary does sound like a pretty intense move, if the instructions in the manuals are anything to go by. There are those *'rapid heel-and-toe stamps'*, for example; or the *'energetic jumps'*, the scissor-kicks that give it its alternative nickname: *'frog's legs'*. Maybe don't try this one at home.

17 July

Nocturne
by Dobrinka Tabakova (b. 1980)

Disclaimer: I got to know this fabulously talented, Grammy-nominated and multi-award-winning composer personally when she joined the team of BBC Young Musician 2016, which I was presenting, as head of the jury. Before we met, I'd never heard any of her music, but after the first time we were introduced I went off and immersed myself in her sound world – and was fully bewitched. Bulgarian-born and London-based, Tabakova has taken lessons with the likes of John Adams (4 July) and many other bright lights from contemporary music, but what I heard that night, and what I hear every time I listen, is a woman wholly in control of her own gifts, her own compositional voice.

Orchestral, choral, vocal, chamber, it doesn't seem to matter what she turns her fierce attention to: she nails it. Tabakova has won awards around the world and is often commissioned by leading soloists. Beyond her formal craftsmanship she's unashamedly emotional: she feels things deeply and it shows in her music, with which, she says, she always wants to have '*something to say*'. Perhaps most tellingly, she admits: '*I never place boundaries on my listening.*'

This seems to be a sensible mantra to have in life – for composers, especially, but for all of us.

From Tabakova's output, which is considerable, especially for someone still in her mid-thirties, I have chosen this beautiful piano nocturne because I love how that form, pretty much devised by John Field (17 March), gets reinvented and refashioned for every generation.

18 July

Requiem in D Minor, K. 626
1: Introitus: Requiem
by Wolfgang Amadeus Mozart (1756–1791)

Mozart's Requiem begins with you walking towards a huge pit. The pit is on the other side of a precipice, which you cannot see over until you are right at its edge. Your death is awaiting you in that pit. You don't know what it looks like or sounds like or smells like. You don't know whether it will be good or bad. You just walk towards it. Your will is a clarinet and your footsteps are attended by all the violins. The closer you get to the pit, the more you begin to have the sense that what awaits you there will be terrifying. Yet you experience this terror as a kind of blessing, a gift. Your long walk would have no meaning were it not for this pit at the end of it. You peer over the precipice: a burst of ethereal noise crashes over you. In the pit is a great choir . . . This choir is the heavenly host and simultaneously the devil's army. It is also every person who has changed you during your time on this earth: your many lovers; your family; your enemies, the nameless, faceless woman who slept with your husband; the man you thought you were going to marry; the man you did. The job of this choir is judgement. The men sing first, and their judgement is very severe. And when the women join in there is no respite, the debate only grows louder and sterner. For it is a debate – you realize that now. The judgement is not yet decided. It is surprising how dramatic the fight for your measly soul turns out to be.

Zadie Smith, *On Beauty*

And that, my friends, is all.

19 July

Three Black Kings
1: 'King of the Magi'
by Duke Ellington (1899–1974)

'*I don't believe in categories of any kind,*' Edward 'Duke' Ellington once said, and he composed accordingly. Although immortalized for his contribution to American jazz in all its variant forms, Ellington's harmonic, melodic and formal inventiveness make him so much more than just a jazzman. Among some two thousand works, he produced concertos, oratorios, orchestral suites, symphonic tone poems, instrumental solos, ballets, ballads, operas, movie and show scores, a television musical and arrangements by core classical composers (21 December).

Unlike his hero James P. Johnson (11 May), in his day Ellington was much admired by leading classical figures. Percy Grainger, then head of music at New York University, was a fan, as was Basil Cameron of the Seattle Symphony Orchestra, and Leopold Stokowski of the Philadelphia Orchestra. In January 1943, his ensemble became the first ever African-American swing band to appear at Carnegie Hall, performing his landmark symphonic suite *Black, Brown and Beige*, a musical history of black Americans.

Right up until his dying day, Ellington championed the cause of the black man through music. *Three Black Kings* was the last thing he wrote, composed on his deathbed in 1974 with the aid of his son, Mercer. Each movement of the three-parter depicts a black 'king': Ellington's close friend Martin Luther King, for whom the whole work can be seen as a tribute; King Solomon in the middle; and in this opener, with its invigorating African drum calls, Balthazar, the King of the Magi.

On the day of Ellington's funeral, US President Richard Nixon described him as 'America's foremost composer'. No doubt that didn't go down so well with the classical purists, but it was probably true.

20 July

Piano Concerto no. 1 in E Minor, op. 11
2: Romance: Larghetto
by Frédéric Chopin (1810–1849)

History was made on this day in 1969 when Neil Armstrong and Buzz Aldrin became the first human beings to walk on the moon. The classical canon is full of musical moonlight – Debussy's *Clair de lune* and Beethoven's Sonata no. 14 spring to mind – but to celebrate that giant leap I wanted to look a little askance at our loyal lunar satellite.

Remember back in the spring (15 April) we encountered a love-struck Chopin in 1829 pouring his unrequited feelings for his classmate Constantia Gladkowska into his first piano concerto? Fast-forward to the spring of 1830 and he was still smitten: his next piano concerto (confusingly published as no. 1 despite being written subsequently) is similarly laced with longing. He writes to his friend Titus that he *'often tells his pianoforte'* what he can't put into words, and describes this piece as *'a romance, quiet, melancholic; it should give the impression of gazing tenderly at a place which brings to mind a thousand dear memories. It's a sort of meditation . . . by moonlight'*.

No number of heavenly moonlit larghettos, alas, were sufficient to win Constantia's heart. Her later verdict on the composer was that he was *'temperamental, full of fantasies, and unreliable'*. Ouch.

21 July

String Quartet no. 12 in F major, op. 96 ('American')
4: Finale: Vivace ma non troppo
by Antonín Dvořák (1841–1904)

A close contender for the 4 July spot, Antonín Dvořák (pronounced Dvor-zhack) composed this ebullient string quartet whilst on holiday in, of all places, Spillville, Iowa. The Czech composer was living in New York City at the time, running the National Conservatory of Music, and the long summer vacation offered an extended break not just from his busy teaching schedule but from the relentless momentum of the Big Apple.

We know from his letters to friends at this time that Dvořák was relaxed, happy, and in 'good spirits'. Surrounded by nature, fresh air, family and the support of a local expat Czech community, he was also creatively inspired: taking old 'Papa Haydn' as his model (see 13 July) but drinking in the world of African-American spirituals and folk traditions, Dvořák sketched out the basis of this melodiously splendid work in just three days – and finished the whole thing less than a fortnight later. '*Thank God!*' he commented. '*I am content. It was fast.*'

22 July

~~

The Homeless Wanderer
by Emahoy Tsegué-Maryam Guèbrou (b. 1923)

Classical music is often portrayed as a creaky old museum of dead white European males. I hope by now that this stereotype has been well and truly busted, but in case we are in need of further proof of this music's extraordinary range and vitality, here's a ninety-three-year-old Ethiopian nun to seal the deal. Emahoy Tsegué-Maryam Guèbrou has led a life less ordinary – from Ethiopian aristocracy to fancy Swiss finishing schools to singing for Emperor Haile Selassie to becoming one of her country's first female civil servants to finding her calling as a nun and ending up in a tiny room in the Ethiopian church in Jerusalem, where she still lives, alongside her beloved piano. Phew!

Although she is often grouped together with exponents of so-called 'Ethio-jazz', a loose musical movement from 1960s Addis Ababa, Emahoy's background is very much core classical; her language derives principally from the 'pentatonic' modal chants of the ancient Orthodox church – whose scales are built around five notes, rather than the traditional seven – and her favourite composers include Mozart and Strauss. You can hear touches of a Chopin-esque lilt here; a Lisztian flourish there. Yet truly her music sounds like nothing else on earth.

23 July

Symphony in G major, op. 11 no. 1
1: Allegro
by Joseph Boulogne, Chevalier de Saint-Georges (1745–1799)

Today's musical offering comes from the man generally regarded as the first classical composer of African ancestry. The son of a wealthy planter and his slave, Nanon, Joseph Boulogne was born on a plantation in Guadeloupe, moved to France at the age of seven, and, as the 'Chevalier de Saint-Georges', as he was later designated, went on to dazzle the most refined European Classical salons with music that can at times match Mozart and Haydn for formal elegance. (He is in fact sometimes dubbed 'The Black Mozart'.)

In addition to his vast achievements in music, which include instrumental concertos, chamber works, *sinfonie concertanti*, at least six comic operas and a pair of terrific symphonies, Boulogne was Colonel of the first all-black regiment in Europe during the French Revolution. He was also a champion fencer, renowned all over France for his phenomenal swordsmanship.

(As a student, he had beaten the famous fencing master Alexandre Picard, who had been mocking him publicly as a 'mulatto'. The match's heavy-betting spectators were divided into partisans and opponents of slavery; Boulogne's triumph was seen as a significant coup for the latter.)

24 July

Stabat Mater
by Alissa Firsova (b. 1986)

Happy birthday to the immensely talented pianist, composer and conductor Alissa Firsova. Where other millennial composers may feel they need to prove a point by continuing to shun tonality and focus on gritty modern subjects, Firsova's rigorously intelligent music tends toward an ethereal, otherworldly beauty: she writes a lot, she says, about 'paradise'.

Firsova moved to the UK from Russia in 1991 with her musician parents (who had been blacklisted by the authorities) and won her first big composition prize when she was just fifteen. Before she turned thirty, her work had been performed at the BBC Proms (where she's also appeared, twice, as a pianist) and she now receives commissions from all over the world. This luminous 2016 setting of the Stabat mater was part of a major international project to reconsider a text that has captured composers' imaginations since the thirteenth century (see also 18 April, 26 December).

25 July

Nocturne
by Maria Szymanowska (1789–1831)

Daughter of a pub landlord and brewer, the Polish composer Maria Szymanowska became one of the first professional virtuoso pianists of the nineteenth century, blazing a sensational trail around England, Italy, Germany, France, Belgium and Holland.

Back home in Warsaw, as well as being a single mother to three children (including a set of twins), she was considered a respected teacher, an influential *salonnière* and a composer of considerable gifts who contributed around a hundred attractive pieces to the repertoire – most of them, as we might expect, small-scale art songs, chamber works and piano pieces such as this one.

The nocturne may these days be most famously associated with another Polish composer, Frédéric Chopin (who was much influenced by the Irishman John Field), but here is Szymanowska a full generation before Chopin bringing her own compositional flair to the form.

She died on this day, felled by cholera during an outbreak in St Petersburg.

26 July

Déploration sur la mort de Jehan Ockeghem
by Josquin des Prez (c. 1450–1521)

Back in March, we met the great Franco-Flemish composer Johannes Ockeghem. He was so widely respected by his fellow musicians that his death inspired a number of heartfelt tributes, including this beauty from the man often considered Ockeghem's greatest successor. Using the technique known as 'cantus firmus', by which the voices weave around an instantly recognisable pre-existing chant, Josquin, as he is known, echoes Ockeghem's own style of counterpoint to moving effect.

Josquin's musical curiosity made him something of an experimentalist. In his sacred motets and masses and secular chansons he played around with different styles and polyphonic techniques that may sound a bit arcane on paper – paired imitations anyone? – but nonetheless pack a profound expressive punch, moving away from the sheerer sonic abstractions of the medieval era.

He also reached a greater level of fame than probably any musician before him because of his enthusiastic embrace of modern technology – in this case the newly invented printing press. Many of his masses were printed in his lifetime, picking up admirers including the seminal Reformation theologian Martin Luther. Josquin, said Luther, was *'master of the notes, which must do as he wishes; other composers must do as the notes wish'*.

27 July

Partita no. 2 in D Minor, BWV 1004
5. Chaconne
by Johann Sebastian Bach (1685–1750)
transcribed by Ferruccio Busoni (1866–1924)

The world in which the Italian composer and pianist Busoni grew up was one that dismissed the supposedly austere, 'mathematical' genius of Bach, preferring instead the warmth of bel canto Italian opera and folk songs. Yet, for reasons that remained mysterious to the young Ferruccio, his clarinettist father insisted that his son only study the music of Bach.

This decision was to shape the course of Busoni's life for ever: over a period of three decades, he arranged and transcribed for piano vast amounts of Bach's music, including, around 1892, a piece for unaccompanied violin known as the 'Bach Chaconne'. Many composers consider it the gold standard, the ultimate musical benchmark. As Brahms once said:

> On one stave, for a small instrument, Bach writes a whole world of
> the deepest thoughts and most powerful feelings. If I imagined that
> I could have created, even conceived the piece, I am quite certain
> that the excess of excitement and earth-shattering experience
> would have driven me out of my mind.

Busoni did much more than merely transcribe this 'whole world'. Instead, he reconceives it with his own bold, majestic vision; honouring and respecting the Bach original but teasing out new ideas, new arguments, new questions and, finally, new consolations. It's breathtaking.

28 July

Partita no. 2 in D Minor, BWV 1004
5: Chaconne
by Johann Sebastian Bach (1685–1750)

And today, on the anniversary of Bach's death, time to hear the original version.

This is everything.

29 July

Gran Vals
by Francisco Tárrega (1852–1909)

After the emotional tumult of back-to-back Bach Chaconnes, a sunny diversion from the man considered 'the father of the classical guitar', Francisco de Asís Tárrega y Eixea.

As a young child, Tárrega would often wait until his flamenco-playing father had gone out, then 'borrow' his dad's guitar and try to recreate the sounds he'd heard. It was also whilst a child that this spirited youngster ran away from his nanny – and fell into an irrigation canal, badly damaging his eyes. His father had the foresight to realize that Tárrega's interest in music could be the making of him if he never fully recovered his sight – which he didn't – and he moved the family to a place where his son could take lessons in piano and guitar. Tárrega's first two teachers were also blind.

Blindness turned out to be no barrier to success. Although he was a fine pianist, the guitar remained his first and deepest love, and soon he began to write his own music: he studied composition at the Madrid Conservatoire, did a number of transcriptions of composers such as Mendelssohn, Chopin and Beethoven, and developed his own, highly Romantic compositional style. His output includes some of the grandest guitar works of the canon, pieces that have become central to any classical guitarist's repertoire.

This piece, charming as it is, is not on that scale. I was about to write: 'This sweet little waltz is not exactly music that's going to change the world, unlike, say, the Bach Chaconne' – but then I remembered that it's almost certainly been heard by more humans than will ever listen to Bach.

With apologies if you have a certain Nokia ringtone earworming you for the rest of the day.

30 July

Eternal Source of Light Divine
(Ode for the Birthday of Queen Anne)
1: 'Eternal source of light divine'
by George Frideric Handel (1685–1759)

Britain has long held a tradition of celebrating the reigning monarch's birthday with court festivities, including dancing and new music. For the birthday of Queen Anne in 1713, Handel – who, although German-born, had settled in England the year before and whom we've proudly claimed as our own ever since – absolutely did the business.

Setting words by the poet Ambrose Philips, he lets rip across nine varied movements, from jolly bass solos to sprightly duets to lyrical pastoral echoes, plus plenty of sprightly chorus action thrown in for good measure. The real heart-stopper of the piece though is this opening movement. In its day, it was a vehicle for a legendary singer called Richard Elford alongside a court trumpeter who frankly must have had balls of steel (the music is hair-raisingly exposed, especially for a 'natural' trumpet with no valves). In modern times its soaring, radiant lines are often sung by a soprano.

31 July

Piano sonata in B minor, S. 178
Andante sostenuto
by Franz Liszt (1811–1886)

My heart always twists a little when I think of Franz Liszt lovingly dedicating this piece to Robert Schumann, sending it to the German composer in May 1854, and it arriving chez Schumann too late – Robert having already been admitted to the Endenich sanatorium for the mental health struggles that plagued him all his life.

The original reception of Liszt's sonata was disastrous: with its single-unfolding-movement structure, it was considered intolerably daring 'new' music, in which Liszt had messed with formal expectations and effectively inserted a sonata-within-a-sonata. (The impudence!) I'm sorry to say that even Clara Schumann was appalled by the work, finding it '*frightful*', and as for the hugely influential Viennese critic Eduard Hanslick, he reckoned:

Whoever has heard that and finds it beautiful is beyond help.

Yikes. I suppose this should give us pause every time we raise our eyebrows or close our ears to baffling new music of our own time. Because this enigmatic and dramatic sonata, now adored by pianists and audiences around the world, is probably considered Liszt's finest work, if not the very pinnacle of the Romantic piano repertoire in its entirety.

I have this crazy idea that poor old Schumann, if he'd been in a fit state to hear it, could have told us that all along.

AUGUST

1 August

Csárdás
by Vittorio Monti (1868–1922)

The history of classical music is scattered throughout with one-hit wonders, and I'm afraid today's piece falls very much into that category. Poor old Monti: we know the Neapolitan composer was also a talented conductor, violinist and mandolin player, but it's for this famous Hungarian-influenced, gypsy-inflected *Csárdás* – and this alone – that he is remembered.

Still, it's not a bad legacy . . .

2 August

To be Sung of a Summer Night on the Water
1: Slow but not dragging
by Frederick Delius (1862–1934)

We've already seen (30 March) that Bradford-boy Delius had no interest in following his father's footsteps into the family wool business, but was instead determined to forge his own path towards a life in music. He once described composing as an *'outburst of the soul'* and declared, *'It is only that which cannot be expressed otherwise that is worth expressing in music.'*

From orange-picking on a Florida plantation to European adventures where he soaked up the sounds of the continent and befriended the likes of Edvard Grieg and Percy Grainger, Delius collected experiences and influences and converted them into his own highly distinctive style.

This dreamy, textless choral idyll, written during the Great War but only premiered in 1920, conjures a particularly heady atmosphere. I find it the perfect soundtrack to a summer night.

3 August

Cello Sonata no. 1 in E minor, op. 38
1: Allegro non troppo
by Johannes Brahms (1833–1897)

Brahms started playing the cello as a young man and always adored its rich, mellow sound. In this sonata he creates one of the undeniably great Romantic vehicles for the instrument, but it's also a major achievement for the piano; in fact, he specified that the keyboard *'should be a partner – often a leading, often a watchful and considerate partner – but it should under no circumstances assume a purely accompanying role'*.

Drenched with soul, this was the first of seven duo sonatas by Brahms to survive his ruthless perfectionism and escape the rubbish bin (see e.g. 7 May). He was twenty-nine at the time he wrote it, spending the summer composing with a friend and fellow former student of Robert Schumann, Albert Dietrich. (We know from his letters that the house in which they were staying was not far from where Brahms's beloved Clara Schumann was summering at Münster am Stein. Longing pervades its every bar.)

A big-boned and muscular musical dialogue that also exudes a tender vulnerability, the sonata reminds us of the immensity of Brahms's musical imagination. Brimful of ideas, of conversational statements and counter-statements, it also pays tribute to his love of the music of Bach. The main theme of this first movement (as well as moments in the third) are based on passages from Bach's seminal unfinished masterpiece from towards the end of his life, *The Art of Fugue*.

4 August

'Beim Schlafengehen' – 'Going to Sleep'
from *Vier letzte Lieder – Four Last Songs*
by Richard Strauss (1864–1949)

Strauss was eighty-four and drawing towards the very end of his life when he composed this song, on this day in 1948. It was one of his 'four last songs', all of which address themes of death. Yet rather than raging against the dying of the light, as well they might, the songs radiate a mood of serene acceptance, their melodic lines soaring heavenward in a gesture of reconciliation.

Intimate and personal, I find it touching that Strauss wrote these final songs for a solo soprano voice, given his long and happy marriage to the singer Pauline de Ahna. The works also contain notably lovely horn parts – which may be a nod, whether conscious or not, to the significant influence that Strauss's father Franz had on his life (see 12 July).

As valedictory musical statements go, it's hard to imagine one more beautiful than this.

Hände, laßt von allem Tun,	*Hands, cease your activity,*
Stirn, vergiß du alles Denken,	*head, forget all of your thoughts;*
alle meine Sinne nun	*all my senses now*
wollen sich in Schlummer senken.	*will sink into slumber.*
Und die Seele unbewacht	*And my soul, unobserved,*
will in freien Flügen schweben,	*will float about on untrammeled*
um im Zauberkreis der Nacht	*wings*
tief und tausendfach zu leben.	*in the enchanted circle of the night,*
	living a thousandfold more deeply.

5 August

Clarinet Sonata in E flat major, op. 167
1: Allegretto
by Camille Saint-Saëns (1835–1921)

After yesterday's wonder from an octogenarian Richard Strauss, here's another composer writing towards the very end of a long and illustrious life. Not that this sounds anything like 'old man' music: right from its lyrical opening proposition, it bubbles along with charm and a clean, formal elegance that hearkens back to the Classical era.

With woodwind instruments drastically less well served for solo repertoire than their stringed counterparts, Saint-Saëns – who once declared that he, *'produced music as an apple tree produces apples'* – had nobly taken it upon himself in the last year of his existence to contribute one sonata apiece for oboe, clarinet, bassoon, flute and cor anglais (a gorgeous-sounding but much neglected instrument that sits somewhere between the oboe and bassoon).

Alas, he died before he could finish the project, leaving generations of flute and cor anglais players to wonder what might have been. With minimal fuss, Saint-Saëns here gives the clarinet a powerful calling card and takes the instrument forward into the twentieth century. It's a gem.

6 August

~~~

Ride Through
by Eleanor Alberga (b. 1949)

On Jamaica Independence Day, music from one of that country's most magnificent musical daughters. Born in Kingston, Alberga was just five when she decided she wanted to be a pianist. Later she came to the UK to study at the Royal Academy of Music, and her work as a composer has been heard everywhere from the soundtrack of *Snow White and the Seven Dwarves* to classical music's biggest knees-up, The Last Night of the Proms. She's also a conductor.

The mix of influences in Alberga's music makes it hard to pin down her style. There's music that directly reflects African and Caribbean traditions in its tonal and rhythmic palette, and there's stuff that's more reflective of twentieth-century European influences.

'I don't have a fixed style,' she has said. *'Every time I start a piece I like to feel as if I've wiped everything clean, with an approach of "Where on earth am I going to go from here?"'*

This piece came about after the Scottish cellist Robert Irvine read on UNICEF's website that a child dies as a result of violence every five minutes; as a result of malnutrition every fifteen seconds; and that 17,000 children under five die every day because they don't get the health care they need. Recognising that *'playing the cello will not end child suffering'*, Irvine nevertheless wanted to do something more *'useful'* than just giving concerts. He convinced a group of contemporary composers, including Alberga, to donate a work to an album, *Songs and Lullabies*. Every penny raised goes to UNICEF's work.

Alberga based her contribution on a traditional Jamaican nursery rhyme:

> *Ride through, ride through the rocky road. Any bwoy me no love me no chat to dem.*

7 August

If ye love me
by Thomas Tallis (c. 1505–1585)

Hats off to the undisputed greatest English composer of his generation, who somehow managed to serve four monarchs with vastly different religious practices, in one of the most turbulent periods of our history, without losing his head.

In other words, if you were ever wondering what impact the Reformation had on the soundtrack of English church music – no, really! – Tallis is your man. Rolling with the liturgical punches throughout a prolific forty-year career, he switched styles, languages and approaches with breathtaking fluency and speed, to the point that each new monarch could claim him proudly as their own. Under Henry VIII, Tallis initially doled out Latin Catholic church music; following the break with Rome between 1532 and 1534, it was all about Latin *Anglican* music. After Henry died in 1547 and his nine-year-old son Edward took the throne, it was suddenly mandated that church services must be sung in *English*; the new choral music – of which this anthem is a luminous example – must give '*to each syllable a plain and distinct note*'. Following Queen Mary's restoration of Roman Catholicism in 1553, Tallis once again returned to composing appropriately Latin Catholic music, until Mary's half-sister Elizabeth I came to the throne and it was back to English.

Phew.

God only knows what Tallis himself made of all this, or where his own religious convictions and personal sentiments lay. But the music he left behind contains some of the greatest treasures of the entire canon, and continues, as we will see, to exert a profound influence on contemporary composers (see e.g. 26 August).

8 August

Duet for two violins
by Steve Reich (b. 1936)

Contemporary musicians often get a bad rap when it comes to accessibility. Steve Reich is a good example of an avant-gardist who actively wants to connect. *'I write music, and I want people to listen to it and care about it and have it make some difference in their lives,'* he once said. *'When I'm fortunate for that to happen . . . I feel very, very good about it.'* Here he is reminding us that, while minimalism might give the impression of being a resolutely twentieth-century phenomenon, it has ancient roots.

This piece, which premiered on this day in 1994, was written for the greatest violinist of the past century, Yehudi Menuhin, and his dear friend Edna Michell. Reich explains that *'the music is built around simple unison canons between the two violins which, from time to time, slightly vary the rhythmic distance between their two voices'.* Reich is brilliant at synthesizing diverse influences into something unique. His highly distinctive sound world here owes a debt, for example, to the lean, neoclassical textures of Stravinsky; to the sublime mathematical pattern-making and conversational flow of J. S. Bach; and, even further back, to the transparently decorative part-writing and pulsing drones of the twelfth-century French composer Pérotin (16 November). And yet, it's wholly Steve Reich. The effect is mesmerizing.

Menuhin was a committed humanitarian, driven by a belief that musicians have a moral responsibility to society beyond providing mere entertainment and delight. As we saw back in June, he was global in his outlook. Reich pays tribute to this singular human by dedicating this piece to the spirit *'of international understanding which Lord Menuhin has practiced throughout his life'.*

9 August

~~~~~

Eyes Shut – *Nocturne* in C minor
by Ólafur Arnalds (b. 1986)
after Frédéric Chopin (1810–1849)

To be honest, there aren't many composers whom I could legitimately feature in a book about classical music who could also boast of being a drummer in hardcore/metal bands and releasing experimental techno albums. But the BAFTA-winning Icelandic musician Ólafur Arnalds (who scored the leading UK television drama *Broadchurch*, among many other things) is not your average classical composer. Like Nils Frahm, whom we encountered back in March, and Max Richter, arguably the unwitting architect of the whole scene, Arnalds is part of a handful of musicians having some amazing adventures at the borderlands of what might be described as classical, electronic, ambient minimalist and pop musics – and doing away with such labels full stop.

So-called classical music has always been at the heart of his practice, though, and his love and respect for Frédéric Chopin goes all the way back to his relationship with his grandmother. In his metal-head younger years, Arnalds would apparently sit with her and listen to Chopin's music whenever he went over to visit. He was there, too, on her deathbed. '*I sat with her and we listened to a Chopin sonata*', he explains. '*Then I kissed her goodbye and left. She passed away a few hours later.*'

In 2015 he turned his love of the composer into something unique: a groundbreaking, genre-busting initiative called *The Chopin Project* which combined a handful of original works with his own Chopin-inspired music for piano, string quintet and synthesizer. In collaboration with the German-Japanese pianist Alice Sara Ott and recorded in Reykjavik on various types of pianos using vintage recording equipment, the album spins an ethereally beautiful sound world; this casts the original nocturne into a new and meditative light.

10 August

Violin Concerto in A minor, op. 82
Andante
by Alexander Glazunov (1865–1936)

On the anniversary of Alexander Glazunov's birth, the glories of his Violin Concerto. Taking its inspiration from Liszt (31 July), this piece does away with the traditional three-movement concerto structure and creates a single free-flowing entity that bursts with juicy melodies and (occasionally schmaltzy) emotion.

As well as being a composer, Glazunov was a prominent Russian conductor, music professor and administrator. Living through some pretty turbulent times, both politically and culturally, he managed peacefully to reconcile competing forces of nationalism and cosmopolitanism, and as director of the St Petersburg Conservatory at a time when the students included Dmitri Shostakovich (22 January, 10 May, 12 November, 17 December), he was widely regarded as a figure of pragmatism and sanity in Russian music.

His own work is inspired by the rich musical poetry of Alexander Borodin (27 February), the virtuosity of Rimsky-Korsakov (14 September) and the dramatic lyricism of Tchaikovsky (1 April, 23 June, 4 December). The avant-gardists of successive generations may have viewed him as a touch old-fashioned, but he was acknowledged to be a stabilizing influence.

As well as his steady personal and professional temperament, Glazunov was famous in his day for his legendarily photographic memory, his sight-reading prowess and his superb talents as an orchestrator and melodist. These are in particularly luscious evidence in this melting middle section of the concerto.

11 August

Locus iste
by Anton Bruckner (1824–1896)

It was on this day in 1869 that the late Romantic Austrian composer Anton Bruckner composed this astonishingly beautiful motet for four unaccompanied voice parts (soprano, alto, tenor, bass). Although Bruckner had recently moved to Vienna, the piece was written for the dedication of the votive chapel at the New Cathedral in Linz, Austria, where he had previously been organist.

A man of devout faith and crippling self-doubt, Bruckner was captivated by the structural intricacies of Renaissance counterpoint. This three-minute motet makes a strong case for the argument that there is little more powerful in music – or indeed, in life – than the sound of intertwining human voices.

Locus iste a Deo factus est   *This place was made by God*

This music, too? I can't help but wonder . . .

12 August

In a Landscape
by John Cage (1912–1992)

John Cage was a Zen Buddhist who believed that '*Good music can act as a guide to good living*'. A student of Arnold Schoenberg and a devotee of Erik Satie, Cage is known for his theory about the equality of sounds, as well as for his pioneering work around concepts of silence, emptiness and time. Inspired by his friend Robert Rauschenberg's pure white paintings, Cage's iconic three-movement *4'33"* famously instructs the performer not to play throughout the duration of the piece: at its premiere in 1952 the pianist David Tudor duly walked on stage, sat down, lifted the piano lid, played nothing, closed the lid after the specified time; repeated this for each of the three 'movements'; then walked off stage.

This was no joke, no gimmick: Cage was positing a radical idea, namely that the act of listening is a fundamental part of musical performance. '*I wanted to mean it utterly and be able to live with it*', he emphasized, later describing *4'33"* as his most important work.

For all his work on the aesthetics of silence, Cage, who died on this day, had a raucous inner life. Relentlessly curious and inquisitive, he is one of the most influential composers of modern times, animating not just musicians but writers, artists, filmmakers and particularly dancers. His life partner was the choreographer Merce Cunningham, and this beautifully meandering, reflective piece was written in 1948 for the dancer Louise Lippold.

Cage described music as '*a purposeless play*' which is '*an affirmation of life . . . a way of waking up to the very life we're living*'. I love this. He also offered this timeless advice:

Look at everything. Don't close your eyes to the world around you.
Look and become curious and interested in what there is to see.

13 August

Laue Sommernacht – Balmy Summer Night
by Alma Mahler (1879–1964)

We've already encountered Alma Mahler through the prism of two of her menfolk: her boyfriend/teacher Alexander von Zemlinsky (6 May) and her first husband Gustav Mahler (18 May, 7 July). Time to meet the woman herself.

Do you remember Mahler's radiant love letter to Alma last month? That shimmering symphonic depiction of his new bride ('*A smile enters his life*')? Well. The bliss was not to last: within a few years the Mahlers had lost a child and Alma had been plunged into depression; shortly after, she started an affair with the architect and Bauhaus founder, Walter Gropius. (She went on to marry Gropius after Mahler's death; she was also later wife to the novelist Franz Werfel and a muse to many others, including Oskar Kokoschka, whose extraordinary expressionist painting *The Bride of the Wind* was based on their relationship.)

Before marrying Mahler (nineteen years her senior) in 1902, Alma had been a talented song composer. The 'terms' of their marriage, though, were that she would abandon all attempts to become a composer in her own right. Although she initially threw herself into the role of loving wife, supporting Gustav's music, none other than Sigmund Freud later concluded that the curtailing of her own career and stifling of her artistic expression contributed to her depression and her infidelity. (In case you wondered why they pay Freud the big bucks.)

After a distraught Mahler discovered the affair, he finally deigned to take Alma's musical ambitions seriously. He encouraged her work and edited a selection of songs – including this one, which she had written whilst a student of Zemlinsky's. A handful of her songs were eventually published but it was too little too late: she never composed with any regularity again, and fewer than twenty pieces survive.

14 August

Alt Wien
by Leopold Godowsky (1870–1938)
arr. Jascha Heifetz (1901–1987)

Sticking with the Viennese mood today: if the Mahlers represent an iconic moment in fin-de-siècle Vienna, this nostalgic little parlour piece – which bears the superscription '*Whose yesterdays look backwards with a smile through tears*' – shuttles us back still further to the previous century and the golden era of the *echt* Viennese waltz.

Godowsky was a Polish-American composer and hugely talented pianist who was almost entirely self-taught. He had eclectic musical tastes, often riffing in his own work on pieces by those who had gone before him, especially the Romantics (e.g. Schubert, Chopin) and French Baroque masters (e.g. Rameau, Lully). He had a penchant for the odd schmaltzy melody, but his intelligence invariably shines through and saves his music from pure sentimentality.

This piece was written in August 1919 as part of a collection of thirty piano pieces, but I think it works a treat in other arrangements, especially this one, which has become a favourite encore for concert violinists. Treating its subject with genuine affection, it never cloys, but rather has the pleasing effect of transporting us, for two charming minutes, to a different time and place. Spot of Sachertorte, anyone?

15 August

Sospiri, op. 70
by Edward Elgar (1857–1934)

Speaking of nostalgia, I think about the first performance of this piece, which took place at the Queen's Hall in London on this day in 1914, and it seems to freeze a moment in time. Scratch that: it seems to freeze a world in time. Six weeks previously, Archduke Franz Ferdinand had been assassinated. Eleven days previously, as Big Ben chimed midnight, war had been declared. Elgar couldn't have known, could he, what devastation would lie ahead? The war 'would all be over by Christmas', wouldn't it?

And yet – and yet. Having originally planned to write a companion piece to his straightforwardly romantic vignette *Salut d'amour*, he found himself, seemingly instinctively, drawn to an altogether bleaker and more heartrending tonal palette in this piece, whose title means 'Sighs'. Who knows what was in Elgar's head and heart at the time he was putting pen to manuscript paper. But as a listener, knowing what was to lie around the corner for Elgar's England, for everywhere, for everyone, it is hard not to hear in the wrenching musical upheavals that disrupt its mood of serene pastoral the very essence of a farewell.

16 August

Partita no. 3 in E major, BWV 1006
1: Prelude
by J. S. Bach (1685–1750)

This piece for solo violin always works on me like a shot of musical caffeine. (Bach did, as it happens, write a Coffee Cantata but that's for another year.) It opens the final work in his Six Sonatas and Partitas, that monumental and miraculous collection of solo violin works which Bach completed in 1720 but which was subsequently ignored until the violinist Joseph Joachim rediscovered it in the early twentieth century (see 27, 28 July).

In just a hundred seconds or so this piece has the effect of apparently rearranging the molecules around me, making me see and think more clearly. (I know! Sounds crazy. But: true. And cheaper than an espresso . . .) As we'll see tomorrow, I'm not the only one to find it deeply affecting.

17 August

Violin Sonata in A minor, op. 27 no. 2
1: 'Obsession' Prelude: Poco vivace
by Eugène Ysaÿe (1858–1931)

Remember a couple of months ago we were at the wedding of Belgian violinist Eugène Ysaÿe? He was presented with César Franck's gorgeous violin sonata (18 June) and later played it to his wedding guests? Well here's the man himself – wearing his Bach-obsessed heart on his sleeve.

This piece was, as it happens, also a gift for a fellow violinist, Ysaÿe's great friend Jacques Thibaud, who ritually began his daily practice with Bach's solo partita in E major (which we heard yesterday). Ysaÿe was fascinated to the point of obsession with this piece: he had been trying to write his own set of six unaccompanied violin sonatas, inspired by but not *based* on Bach, but admitted that his inability to escape the pervasive influence of Bach's music was threatening to derail the whole project.

And so he tames the beast, as it were, by inviting it in: he opens with a direct quote from the beginning of Bach's prelude, sotto voce, and then intertwines a freewheeling paraphrase on that with the Dies irae theme from the Requiem Mass (also referenced, as it happens, by innumerable other composers over the years, including Thomas Adès, Johannes Brahms, Hector Berlioz, Gustav Mahler, Wendy Carlos). Again and again, Ysaÿe tries to rid his piece of Bach's phrases; again and again they return – until the two themes are finally resolved in a coruscating, playful finale.

The piece was written in 1922, the year of James Joyce's *Ulysses* and T. S. Eliot's *The Waste Land* – twin peaks of literary modernism. Yet Ysaÿe remarked that the work was set in a *'consciously* postmodern *idiom'* (my emphasis); to my ears it still sounds, indeed, both thrillingly and bracingly new.

18 August

Symphony no. 35 in D major, K. 385 ('Haffner')
1: Allegro con spirito
by Wolfgang Amadeus Mozart (1756–1791)

Nobody knows why one of the most supernaturally talented humans in human history died so young (although contrary to the rumour, he definitely wasn't murdered by his supposed rival Antonio Salieri). It's probable that a toxic combination of mental strain, financial stress and being massively overworked all played their part. Mozart, like most freelancers, had clearly not learned the 'yes' of saying 'no': he took on commission after commission and, although his music always sounds effortless, we know from his letters that composing didn't *always* come easy to him.

The request in 1782 to write a piece for a member of a prominent Salzburg family, the Haffners, arrived while Mozart was up to his eyeballs. Teaching, writing and frantically arranging operas, he was also in the process of trying to move house and get married. Yet he did it: rewiring, reorchestrating and beefing up a serenade he'd written a few years earlier for the same family. Being Mozart, you can't hear any of that angst behind its transparent, gleaming surface. It's a knockout. Exuberant, elegant, life-affirming, the perfect musical mood-booster – and an excellent soundtrack, I find, to the dreariest of mundane tasks.

(An aside: a few years ago, I was living in New York. One day I wandered into the Morgan Library on Madison Avenue. They were exhibiting the autographed copy of this symphony. Staring at it, at the real thing, with Mozart's actual handwriting, his mistakes, his ink-blots, did something funny to my insides. Sometimes it can be hard to hold on to the fact that a real person wrote this stuff. A real over-worked, underpaid, frazzled, busy, brilliant person. I've never been able to listen to it in quite the same way since.)

19 August

Légende
by Georges Enescu (1881–1955)

Today we celebrate the birth of one of classical music's neglected giants. Georges Enescu's intensely personal and imaginative works remain largely unknown outside his native Romania – which is an outrage really, because this violinist, pianist, conductor, teacher and composer was arguably the greatest musical all-rounder of the twentieth century.

Enescu had a decisive experience at the age of three, when he heard a gypsy folk band playing near his village and became captivated by their sound. By five, he was dreaming of being a composer; at seven he became the youngest person ever to enter the famous Vienna Conservatoire. Later, he went to Paris, where he studied composition with the likes of Gabriel Fauré (30 January, 15 May). In 1927, Maurice Ravel (7 March, 14 July) turned up at Enescu's apartment with a new violin sonata for them to play together. After going through it once, Enescu set aside the music. He had memorized the whole thing. In one go! No wonder Pablo Casals (19 March) called him *'the greatest musical phenomenon since Mozart'.*

Shortly before his death Enescu admitted to a friend: *'If I could put down on paper all the music that I have in my head, it would take hundreds of years . . .'* A fierce perfectionist, he only left us thirty-three pieces, but his output is unique, reflecting his fantastically rich and varied musical heritage. As his protégé the great violinist Yehudi Menuhin put it, Enescu was a *'very special mixture of human being: early folk and gypsy roots from Romania and Hungary blended with the cultivated world of Western music'.* His music often has an improvisatory air, but he was meticulous in the way he marked his scores, giving minute instructions to inflect every nuance of technical and expressive colour. This fabulous trumpet piece from 1906 is an intoxicating example.

20 August

Piano Concerto no. 2 in C minor, op. 18
2: Adagio sostenuto
by Sergei Rachmaninov (1873–1943)

For all the enormity of his musical gifts, Rachmaninov was a composer crippled by bouts of mental illness and lacerating self-doubt. After his First Symphony had bombed in 1897, he was struck by writer's block and fell into a clinical depression so intense and unrelenting that it took a period of sustained hypnotherapy, administered by one Dr Nikolai Dahl, to bring Rachmaninov back to a state where he could compose anything again.

It's telling that Rachmaninov dedicated this piece, the first he wrote after his recovery, to his doctor. (It doesn't bear thinking about what would have happened if Dahl had not succeeded with his therapy: I wouldn't want to live in a world without this piece in it.) I deliberated hard over which movement to suggest but again and again I circled back, perhaps inevitably, to the iconic slow movement.

This is the sort of unashamedly wonderful piece that some classical music critics pride themselves on deriding – for being, I don't know, 'cheesy' or 'populist'. Whatever. (As far as I'm concerned, this is precisely why 'Classical Music' has such an image problem.) To these people I say: relax, guys! It's okay to get off on this music even though *everyone else in the rest of the world does too*! Being universally loved does not detract from the concerto's genius. Quite the opposite.

There's a great scene in the 1955 Billy Wilder movie *The Seven Year Itch* where Marilyn Monroe's character goes: *'This is what they call classical music, isn't it?'*

Call it whatever you want, love. This piece is *it*.

21 August

G-Spot Tornado
by Frank Zappa (1940–1993)

I'll never forget being at the BBC Proms one night in the summer of 2013 and feeling as though the Royal Albert Hall might just lift off, such was the zany and flamboyant exuberance of this work by the experimental American musician, filmmaker and activist Frank Zappa.

I'd never heard it before, and had certainly never expected to experience Zappa in one of the great temples to classical music. (In 1971, he'd actually been banned by the Royal Albert Hall on grounds of obscenity: the 2013 performance by Aurora Orchestra was the first time his music had been heard there since.) But the self-taught maverick had begun doodling around with classical forms whilst still in high school. His raft of diverse musical influences included Igor Stravinsky (29 May), Anton Webern (15 September) and, most critically, the *'weird jumble of drums'* of Edgard Varèse (6 November), whose music he'd chanced upon while reading a magazine aged thirteen and about which he once declared *'I love very much'*.

Having fallen hard for the infectious rhythms of this piece, I went hunting for more and was tickled to discover that Zappa was much admired, from a classical standpoint, by none other than Mr Twentieth-Century Music himself, Pierre Boulez (26 March). Boulez was such a fan, in fact, that he conducted a whole album of Zappa's music back in 1984. That too is a sonic riot.

22 August

‹La fleur que tu m'avais jetée› – 'The flower that you threw to me'
from *Carmen*
by Georges Bizet (1838–1875)

We've already seen that Bizet suffered from crushing disappointment and lack of critical appreciation in his all too brief life (3 March) and how his thirtieth attempt at an opera, *Carmen*, was a spectacular failure at its premiere, which took place just three months before he died.

This sensational aria from Act 2 is my favourite moment in the whole opera. We are at a local tavern, after hours. Carmen is with her friends – and suddenly there is Don José, singing in the street. A signal announces that he should return to the barracks; he ignores it. She dances for him; and from his suit he pulls the flower that she had in a moment of caprice thrown to him in Act 1 – before he went to prison for allowing her to escape.

At this point you might hear an ominous, creeping 'fate motive' played by a cor anglais cutting through the shimmering, luminous strings. Don José obviously ignores that too, instead launching into this passionate admission to Carmen that this innocuous bloom has been the one thing that kept him going throughout his time behind bars.

La fleur que tu m'avais jetée,	*The flower that you threw to me*
Dans ma prison m'était restée . . .	*Stayed with me in prison . . .*
Et je ne sentais en moi-même,	*And I felt inside myself,*
Je ne sentais qu'un seul désir,	*I felt but a single desire,*
Un seul désir, un seul espoir:	*A single desire, a single hope:*
Te revoir, ô Carmen, oui, te revoir!	*To see you again, O Carmen, yes to see you again!*

It's one of opera's most splendid love songs, but naturally, this *being* opera, it won't be long before it all ends in tears . . .

23 August

Beau soir – Beautiful Evening
by Claude Debussy (1862–1918)

The son of a seamstress and china shop owner, Claude Debussy was one of the great musical innovators of his age. One listener, after hearing a concert of his music in 1916, wrote to a friend to say: '*I know of no sensation more delicious: I felt I was listening to music for the first time.*' High praise indeed.

Debussy was influenced by the likes of Borodin (27 February) and Wagner (6 February, 13 April, 10 June, 24 December), but he developed his own distinctive style, full of novel harmonies that deliquesce, forms that dissolve, melodies that slip and slide and don't stay still, all painted in a lush, chromatic palette. As such, his music tends to be described as 'impressionistic' for its shared preoccupation with what his counterparts such as Claude Monet and Edgar Degas were doing in painting: namely to evoke a certain mood and emotion through art rather than depict something precise. Debussy, however, loathed the term 'impressionism' when applied to music, decrying its use as 'imbecilic'. (Fair play: given how versatile he was, it does seem rather limiting to try and label him as anything.)

As well as solo piano works, orchestral pieces, chamber music and an opera, Debussy wrote some eighty-seven songs over the course of his career. His earliest date from when he was still a teenager at the Paris Conservatoire, where his teachers included César Franck (18 June, 8 November). He'd lately become enchanted by the voice (and perhaps more) of a talented amateur soprano called Marie-Blanche Vasnier. She inspired in him a flood of songs, including this one, which takes place in the rose-gold light of a setting sun, on a particularly beautiful evening.

24 August

Partita no. 1 in B flat major, BWV 825
2: Allemande
by J. S. Bach (1685–1750)

It may seem a bit irreverent to describe the mighty J. S. Bach as a 'palate cleanser', but among the many services into which I have pressed his music over the years (commute companion, grief counsellor, baby wrangler, and so on) the role of life-clarifier and head-clearer is right up there. Whenever I'm stuck, whenever I need to quiet my raging mind, whenever I require what I imagine is the sonic equivalent of yoga or meditation, it's to this sort of music I turn, and submit myself, and go still, and recover.

(It goes without saying, I hope, that Bach's music also rewards more active listening, if you're in the mood for that instead.)

This entire partita, written supposedly as a keyboard exercise but containing multitudes, is simply outstanding. Choosing a favourite movement was like choosing a favourite child – impossible. I eventually plumped for the second movement, but the whole work only lasts about ten minutes. If you can, do yourself a favour: stick it on, and see what happens.

25 August

'Somewhere'
from *West Side Story*
by Leonard Bernstein (1918–1990)

This year we've met a few creative geniuses who had the confidence to quote from all over the canon whilst staying true to their own brilliant selves. One of the greatest is the American Leonard Bernstein, who was born on this day. As well as composing some of the finest works in musical theatre history, Bernstein wrote symphonies, masses and chamber works. He was a superstar conductor, associated with such world-class bands as the New York and Vienna philharmonics and the London Symphony Orchestra. He was also a skilled pianist, a writer and lecturer of considerable intellectual depth, and an outstanding communicator, making programmes in the new medium of television that sought to open up the wonders of classical music and educate people, young and old, in a refreshing, unpatronising way. He is one of my all-time musical heroes.

Here Bernstein borrows from both Beethoven (a phrase from the Adagio of his 'Emperor' piano concerto, the first movement of which we heard back in May) and Tchaikovsky (his ballet *Swan Lake*). It is during a ballet sequence that this song is first heard; later reprised by a distraught Maria as her beloved Tony dies in her arms. Bernstein, together with his lyricist Stephen Sondheim, takes the simplest yet most gut-wrenching of scenarios – not now, my love, but *someday*, *somewhere*, we will be able to be together – and enshrines it in music that is so direct and relatable it just takes you apart.

Little wonder this song has enjoyed life outside the theatre and concert hall: it has been covered by everyone from The Supremes (who interpreted it as a civil rights anthem) to the one and only Barbra Streisand.

26 August

Set Me as a Seal
by Nico Muhly (b. 1981)

Happy birthday to the outrageously talented, madly prolific and eclectically inspired Nico Muhly.

The *New Yorker* critic Alex Ross recalls meeting Muhly early on and asking about his philosophy of engaging with the outside world. Muhly summed it up as *'not being an asshole'*. (*'Among American composers'*, noted Ross, *'this tactic is not as unremarkable as it should be.'*)

This protégé of Philip Glass writes instrumental music, cantatas, film scores, operas, you name it, and has collaborated with everyone from Grizzly Bear to Björk, Sufjan Stevens to Antony Hegarty (now Anohni). He was the youngest composer to be commissioned by the Metropolitan Opera for *Two Boys*, which takes place in an internet chat room. And he communicates, via social media and his blog, like a regular millennial – albeit one whose brain is capacious enough to contain interests as diverse as particle physics, computing and Norse code. (He's also a terrific cook.)

Muhly was steeped in Anglican church music growing up and credits Renaissance composers such as Tallis (7 August) and Byrd (24 January) as major influences. Such music, he reckons, is *'slow food for the soul'*.

This early choral piece sets words from the Old Testament text *Song of Solomon*, also known as the *Song of Songs*, whose sensuous, mysterious, at times even ecstatic language has inspired composers through the ages. Muhly describes it as an early example of his interest in taking a text set by the great composers (in this case, William Walton) and making something 'as radically different to theirs as possible'. Unlike most previous settings, Muhly sets the text in a 'macaronic' way, using both Hebrew words and their English translation. The result, he says, *'is meant to be hypnotically calm in the choral parts, with little anxious interjections from the piano'*. It delivers – to unforgettable effect.

27 August

'Deep River'
from *24 Negro Melodies*, op. 59 no. 10
by Samuel Coleridge-Taylor (1875–1912)

We've met a few classical composers this year who sought to reflect their heritage through music. Born in London to a Sierra Leonean father and English mother, Samuel Coleridge-Taylor (whom Edward Elgar once described as *'far and away the cleverest'* of the new generation of composers) placed himself firmly in this tradition. About this work, he noted: *'What Brahms has done for the Hungarian folk music, Dvořák for the Bohemian, and Grieg for the Norwegian, I have tried to do for these negro melodies.'*

Although Coleridge-Taylor (named in homage to the poet) never made it to Africa, he was riveted by the rhythms and melodies of his father's continent. His works include a set of *Symphonic Variations on an African Air*; an *Africa Suite*; and an opera collaboration with the African-American poet Paul Laurence Dunbar. He also worked with spirituals: the work for which he is best known, *Hiawatha's Wedding Feast*, incorporates the famous *'Nobody Knows the Trouble I've Seen'* into its overture.

As one of only a few black classical composers to attain even a modicum of renown (a situation that persists, depressingly, to this day), Coleridge-Taylor was an icon among pan-Africanists in the early twentieth century. He was greeted as a hero in the USA, where President Theodore Roosevelt invited him to the White House, and he hung out with the educator and civil rights activist Booker T. Washington. Back home, despite the support he received from leading composers, the situation was somewhat different. Nicknamed 'Coaley' as a child, in adulthood he remained subject to racial abuse.

28 August

～◦～

Guaracha: Ay que mes abraso – I'm ablaze with love
by Juan García de Zéspedes (c. 1619–1678)

From yesterday's spiritual, which originated among African slaves, to the day on which, in 1833, the UK Abolition of Slavery Act got its royal assent.

I came to the Mexican composer, singer, viol player and teacher Juan García de Zéspedes through the remarkable Catalan polymath that is Jordi Savall. In one of his many diverse musical projects, Savall decided to explore the history of the European slave trade from 1444, the year of the first mass Portuguese slaving expedition, to 1888, when slavery was abolished in Brazil. Savall describes slavery as *'the most monstrous of all the man-made institutions created throughout history'*, and for this ambitious project he collaborated not just with his usual European ensembles but with a group of African and Latin American performers who are directly connected to this musical heritage. This charges the performances with an extra piquancy and makes for an urgent, thought-provoking, at times electrifying listen.

Zéspedes' compositions ranged from sacred pieces to secular pieces inspired by folk music. This is an old-style Spanish *guaracha*, early street peasant music that was popular in Caribbean colonies. It's full of swagger and defiance. I love it.

29 August

Serenade for strings in E major, op. 22
3: Scherzo: Vivace
by Antonín Dvořák (1841–1904)

By the late nineteenth and early twentieth century, orchestras were expanding all the time, and composers, giddy with the new forces at their disposal, began writing larger and longer symphonies (see e.g. 11 October, 15 November). Dvořák was no exception, and his contribution to the symphonic genre is considerable, including his Symphony no. 9 'From the New World' (otherwise known as the music from the iconic Hovis bread ad). But in the interests of shaking things up a bit, from time to time composers would rebel against these epic orchestral canvases and turn to a more intimate configuration, such as the string orchestra, which had been the height of fashion in the Classical era and for which composers wrote all manner of elegant serenades and divertimenti.

This piece fits very much into that tradition. Dvořák dashed it off in just a couple of weeks during 1875, whilst in the first golden flush of marriage and fatherhood. There is a certain cloudlessness to proceedings, and although the whole thing is beautiful I'm particularly fond of this lively scherzo, which is by turns witty, yearning and dramatic.

Dvořák was one of the most influential composers of his time, especially among the next generation of composers in his Czech homeland. Tomorrow we'll hear how his serenade directly influenced his future son-in-law . . .

30 August

Serenade for Strings in E flat major, op. 6
3. Adagio – Piu andante – Tempo 1
by Josef Suk (1874–1935)

Before he married Dvořák's daughter Ottilie, Suk was the great Czech composer's star pupil. His own Serenade for Strings, composed when he was eighteen and about to graduate from the Prague Conservatory, bears in its lush melodies and sophisticated orchestration many hallmarks of his mentor and future father-in-law's style.

As close as they were both personally and musically, in their innate character Dvořák and Suk were fundamentally different. Even as a young man, years before the tragedies that would befall him (he lost his beloved wife prematurely), Suk had a tendency to the blues. His musical language was often underscored by introspective darkness; this piece apparently came about because Dvořák instructed Suk to write *something cheerful for a change*.

Suk didn't quite nail the brief. 'Cheerful' the serenade is not. But there is a certain romantic radiance at its heart, and I find this Adagio, with its lyrical opening cello melody and intensely emotional passages, a particularly rich and gratifying listen. It would be extraordinary music for anybody to have written, let alone a moody teenage boy.

31 August

Goyescas
Suite 1: 'Los requiebros' – 'Compliments'
by Enrique Granados (1867–1916)

A compelling example, today, of how one art form can directly inform another, as a major Spanish composer pays tribute to perhaps the greatest Spanish painter of all time. Enrique Granados was a leading figure in the Spanish nationalism movement, and his piano suite *Goyescas* – 'The Gallants in Love' – is inspired by the paintings and etchings of Francisco de Goya (1746–1828).

On this day in 1910, Granados wrote that he was composing *'great flights of imagination and difficulty'*; by the following March the first book from the suite was ready and he himself gave the premiere. This opening movement is a *jota*, a popular form of song and dance from Aragón, in northern Spain (see also 23 November). From its sultry, languorous opening it soon takes off in a more energetic and highly ornamented direction, with passages that require dazzling technical virtuosity. Painted in vivid musical colours, the piece was once described by a critic as *'a gorgeous treat for the fingers'*. It's a treat for the ears, too.

The success of *Goyescas* was such that an opera version was later commissioned by the Paris Opéra. Due to the outbreak of war, it was premiered not in Europe but at the Metropolitan in New York. Granados and his wife journeyed to America to see it – and during that trip he also took up an impromptu invitation to perform at the White House for President Woodrow Wilson. This turned out to be a fateful decision. In March 1916, as they were travelling across the Channel on their way back to Spain, their ship, the *Sussex*, was torpedoed by a German submarine. Thrown into the water, Granados managed to clamber into a lifeboat, then dived back into the water to try and rescue his wife. They both drowned, leaving their six children as orphans.

SEPTEMBER

1 September

The Blue Bird, op. 119 no. 3
by Charles Villiers Stanford (1852–1924)

This is the month when eastern bluebirds begin to flock, and we shall begin our own musical journey this September with one of them immortalized in notes. Just as Ralph Vaughan Williams took a poem about a skylark and turned it into a transcendent piece for solo violin (14 June), so his teacher Charles Villiers Stanford took a relatively unknown piece of verse on an avian subject (by Mary Coleridge) and created a gleaming choral treasure that delivers an effect of profound stillness, even as it soars.

> The lake lay blue below the hill,
> O'er it as I looked, there flew
> Across the waters, cold and still,
> A bird whose wings were palest blue.
> The sky above was blue at last,
> The sky beneath me blue in blue
> A moment, 'ere the bird had passed,
> It caught its image as it flew.

2 September

Violin Concerto in D major, op. 35
2: Romanze: Andante
by Erich Wolfgang Korngold (1897–1957)

The Austrian-born Erich Korngold was a child prodigy whose compositional genius was spotted early in childhood by Gustav Mahler (18 May, 7 July, 15 November). He went on to study with Alexander von Zemlinsky (6 May), had his first ballet produced aged eleven, was forced to flee the Nazis in 1934, wound up in California and became the godfather of classy Hollywood film music.

Who knows what might have happened had Korngold been able to stay in Europe, with its prevailing modernist winds of atonality and jagged rhythms – his own musical language looks naturally back to an era of lush and lyrical Romanticism. But in mid-century America, and particularly in the world of the movies, Korngold could give his full-bodied, heart-on-sleeve musical expression full voice.

Korngold scored over sixteen Hollywood films and picked up a handful of Oscars and other major awards in the process. He is a useful reminder, then, that the assumption among some classical purists that film composers are somehow inferior to core classical composers is nonsense. The son of an influential film critic, he wrote for the movie screen and the concert hall side by side, and the two genres were evidently mutually enriching in his work. He said he approached film scenarios like opera libretti, and it worked the other way, too: there's an air of cinematic mystique to many of his classical works, not least his terrific violin concerto, which was first composed in the late 1930s at the same time he was writing some of his finest film scores (he then revised it in 1945). I particularly love the sweeping, filmic brush strokes of this bittersweet slow movement.

3 September

Gnossienne no. 1
by Erik Satie (1866–1925)

Like the *Gymnopédies* with which he made his name (see 1 July), a *gnossienne* was a form that Satie pretty much invented – perhaps inspired by his involvement with Gnostic sects; perhaps by a passage in John Dryden's 1697 translation of Virgil's *Aeneid*:

> *Let us the land which Heav'n appoints, explore;*
> *Appease the winds, and seek the Gnossian shore.*

Who knows. Wherever he got the inspiration from, Satie did something characteristically novel with the music. First published in September 1893, the *Gnossiennes* are unencumbered by the usual restraints of time signatures and bar divisions, and they take the sort of radical ideas about form, harmony and rhythm that he had already been playing with in the *Gymnopédies* to new extremes.

Satie counted among his collaborators Pablo Picasso, Jean Cocteau and Sergei Diaghilev, and was friends with many more avant-garde icons, including the artists Man Ray, Constantin Brâncusi and Marcel Duchamp. He remains one of the most iconoclastic yet influential figures in modern art, prefiguring, in his spare textures and meditative sense of detachment, many of the minimalist revolutions that were to come. In the words of one of his most ardent devotees, John Cage (12 August): *'It's not a question of Satie's relevance. He's indispensable.'*

4 September

It seems inconceivable now, given the marginalization of opera and classical music in our own society, but back in the day composers such as Verdi were the pop stars of their time. Verdi was such an icon, in fact, that when he died, half a million Italians lined the streets singing the chorus of Hebrew slaves from his opera *Nabucco*; a piece that was considered instrumental in the reunification of Italy and an unofficial anthem among Italian nationalists (in the intervening years it has been recommended as a replacement for the *actual* national anthem).

Nabucco was just one of twenty-five operas that Verdi composed in his long career. This sparkling quartet is from *Rigoletto* (1851) and in it Verdi displays his peerless gifts for combining gorgeous melody with human high jinks and scintillating drama. Set in sixteenth-century Mantua, the opera tells the tale of a shameless Duke, his court jester Rigoletto, and Rigoletto's daughter Gilda, who falls for the Duke and ultimately surrenders her life to save him.

At this moment in Act 3, Verdi conjures what are essentially two parallel and completely contrasting conversations – one an attempted seduction of a prostitute by the Duke; the other a fraught exchange between Rigoletto and Gilda – and intertwines them into a sensational whole, extracting the utmost psychological and dramatic potency from the four different humans on stage (soprano, contralto, tenor and baritone), each with their own agenda and personality.

It's as brilliant as it is beautiful: a complex and intricate confection that in Verdi's hands comes across as apparently effortless.

5 September

Clarinet Quintet in A major, K. 581
2: Larghetto
by Wolfgang Amadeus Mozart (1756–1791)

Remember last month we encountered Mozart juggling commissions and scrabbling to meet deadlines while also trying to move house and plan a wedding? Fast forward a few years to 1789 and frankly that would have seemed an ideal scenario. The composer's reputation among the fickle Viennese public had tanked; many of his teaching posts and commissions had dried up; and the bulk of his modest income now derived from churning out opera arias, unattributed, for mediocre artists who were held (for some baffling reason) in much higher esteem than he was.

Meanwhile, he and his wife Constanze were both suffering health-wise; that year they lost another daughter within an hour of her birth (only two of the couple's six babies survived infancy); medical bills were piling up – as were gambling debts; and Mozart was forced to send begging letters to friends for financial assistance. *'I must entreat you,'* he would write, *'to show your friendship and brotherly love for me by supporting me with whatever funds you can spare at once . . .'* Many such letters exist among Mozart's correspondence; they break my heart.

Yet somehow, from the depths of despair, Mozart creates this wondrous piece of music. Like the 'Kegelstatt' trio we heard back in May, this was written for his pal, the virtuoso clarinettist Anton Stadler. Exemplifying ideals of friendship and human connection throughout, the piece combines Mozart's inestimable gifts, somehow taking the best of his opera, his chamber music and his instrumental concertos and weaving them into something whose emotional impact feels disproportionate to what it is: a few pages of manuscript paper, covered in dots of ink, written in a hurry.

6 September

Sonata duodecima
by Isabella Leonarda (1620–1704)

In 1693 a group of instrumental sonatas were published that are generally regarded to be the first ever written by a woman. The groundbreaking female in question was an Ursuline nun called Isabella Leonarda. Born on this day, she entered the convent Collegio di Sant'Orsola, in Novara, north-west Italy, as a teenager. Rising through the ranks to the highest order, *superiora*, Leonarda nevertheless found time to write over two hundred pieces of music, of which this eerie, atmospheric sonata is particularly ambitious and unusual.

I find it incredible, thinking of this woman, cloistered away in that convent, coming up with such music as this. We have no way of knowing what sort of things Leonarda may or may not have been able to hear in her lifetime, but we can be pretty certain she and her fellow nuns were not popping out to gigs every Friday night to sample the latest developments in sonata form. It's worth restating: for the vast majority of history, *the only way for people to experience music was to hear it performed live.* For many of the composers in these pages, especially the women, opportunities to do that were scarce.

If Leonarda was being regularly exposed to music at all, it would presumably have been of the sacred choral variety. That makes her focus on instrumental music even more remarkable. One of only two Italian women (that we know of) who wrote instrumental rather than vocal music at the time, her achievement did not go unacknowledged. Twenty years after her death, an eminent French critic declared: '*All of the works of this illustrious and incomparable composer are so beautiful, so gracious, so brilliant and at the same time so knowledgeable and so wise, that my great regret is in not having them all.*'

7 September

Suite popular brasileira
4: 'Gavotta-choro' (1949 version)
by Heitor Villa-Lobos (1887–1959)

On Brazil National Day, time to meet the one and only Heitor Villa-Lobos, the man who once declared, rather brilliantly, that his first harmony teacher was '*a map of Brazil*'. In music that does its best to reflect the extraordinary cultural diversity of his country, its people and landscapes, topographies and traditions, he worked in every conceivable musical genre and his output makes even Bach look a slouch. Villa-Lobos produced thousands of works during the course of his life.

Although he was curious about trends in European classical music, Villa-Lobos was repeatedly drawn back to the folk and popular music of his homeland: his unique genius lies in the way he was able to combine both. As a young man, he found himself temperamentally unsuited to the strictures of formal music education and quit his studies, supporting himself by playing in the cinemas, nightclubs, and cafés of Rio de Janeiro. Here he met and jammed with the street musicians and chorus bands that would have as much of an impact on the development of his musical language as would the avant-garde European modernism that he soaked up in Paris in the early 1920s.

That multivalent set of influences working on Villa-Lobos's imagination is evident in this early suite, each of whose titles combine a European form – such as, here, a gavotte – with a traditional Brazilian dance, the chôro, which originated in nineteenth-century Rio and could be heard on street corners up and down the country.

8 September

Piano Quartet no. 2 in E flat major, op. 87
2: Lento
by Antonín Dvořák (1841–1904)

On Dvořák's birthday, a beautiful, passionate and virtuosic take on the relatively unusual format of piano quartet. Mozart – surprise – had been the one to come up with the idea of writing for this distinctive combination, producing a gem apiece in E flat major and G minor, and the idea was later picked up by Beethoven, Schumann (16 February), Brahms and Fauré. But it's fair to say that relatively few composers had the requisite skills to write effectively for this particular blend – which could so easily pose problems of texture and balance in a lesser hand.

Back in 1880, Dvořák had had a first stab at the form, but almost another decade went by before he revisited it. He eventually caved after pressure from his publisher Simrock, who (freelancers, look away) used to send him notes like: *'I'd like to receive a piano quartet from you, at last – you promised me this a long time ago! Well? How is it faring?'*

By the time Dvořák focused his full attention on it, in the summer of 1889, it was thankfully faring pretty well. This was the prime of his life, and he wrote to a friend to say: *'My head is full of it . . . I already have three movements of a new piano quartet completely ready, and the finale will be finished in a few days. It's going unexpectedly easily and the melodies are coming to me in droves . . .'*

Those melodies are certainly gorgeous things, especially in this hyper-lyrical second movement. (Soon after he finished this, by the way, he took up a position as professor of composition at the Prague Conservatory. There, as we know, his students included a young Josef Suk – later to become his son-in-law – who would take a cue from Dvořák in writing his very own piano quartet – his symbolic 'opus 1'.)

9 September

Che si può fare – What am I to do?
by Barbara Strozzi (1619–1677)

We don't hear much these days about Barbara Strozzi, despite the fact that she was said to be the most prolific composer – man or woman – of printed secular vocal music in Venice in the mid-seventeenth century. She published eight collections of cantatas, comprising more than a hundred works, and her music travelled far beyond her native Italy – to England, Austria and Germany at least. She was also celebrated for her literary talents and was a fine poet and word-setter.

Poetry perhaps ran in her blood: Strozzi was likely the illegitimate offspring of a wordsmith named Giulio Strozzi and his servant. He recognized her as his legitimate daughter and encouraged her own creative efforts, finding her teachers and publicly promoting her music and verse. Her musical idols were figures such as Claudio Monteverdi (20 March, 29 November), who with his new style or 'seconda pratica' – second practice – had revolutionized what music could do, laying the foundation, in his operas and madrigals, for the beginning of modern music.

This haunting song is written on a passacaglia (variations over a bass line) that consists of the first four notes of a descending D minor scale. As it happens, it's a bass line that crops up again and again in twentieth-century jazz and blues (see for example 'Hit the Road Jack').

Che si può fare?	*What am I to do,*
Le stelle ribelle non hanno pietà;	*If those rebel stars take no pity,*
se 'l cielo non dà un influsso	*If heaven does not use its influence*
di pace al mio penare,	*To soothe my sorrows with peace;*
che si può fare?	*What am I to do?*

10 September

Impromptu in B flat major, op. 32b
by Dora Pejačević (1885–1923)

Speaking of pioneering women, one of Croatia's finest composers, Dora Pejačević, was born on this day. She came from a noble family but rebelled against the trappings and strictures of the aristocratic lifestyle. During the First World War Pejačević volunteered as a nurse, and her political views later led to a breach with her family and her being labelled a 'socialist'.

Pejačević's mother was a glamorous Hungarian countess who had given her daughter piano lessons as a child, but beyond this, Pejačević was largely self-taught. Polyglot and fiercely curious, she started composing at the age of twelve and left behind over a hundred pieces in a late-Romantic idiom, including piano works such as this lovely impromptu; songs; chamber music; and large-scale orchestral works. She is generally regarded as the first modern symphonist in Croatia and the first Croatian composer to write a concerto – yet most of her music has yet to be published or recorded. She died shortly after giving birth to her son Theo, a result of complications in childbirth.

Heartbreakingly, just a few months before Theo was born, Pejačević had written to her husband in such a way that not only reveals her innately feminist principles but suggests she had a premonition she might not be around to see her baby grow up:

> I hope that our child should become a true, open and great human being . . . Let it develop like a plant . . . if it has talent, encourage it . . . give it freedom when it seeks it . . . so act this way if it is a boy or girl; every talent, every genius, requires equal consideration, and sex cannot be allowed to come into the matter.

11 September

'In Paradisum'
from *Trinity Requiem*
by Robert Moran (b. 1937)

The chapel of St Paul at Trinity Church, Wall Street, sits across the street from the former World Trade Center in downtown Manhattan.

On the morning of 11 September 2001, after al-Qaeda terrorists ploughed two airliners into the twin towers, the chapel, miraculously untouched, became a hub and a haven. People started stopping by to rest, wash, eat, sleep, pray, reflect; in the coming days volunteers of all stripes arrived to give food and succour to those who needed it. In the first twelve weeks after 9/11, more than three thousand workers passed through the chapel's gates: rescue workers, police officers, Port Authority workers, firefighters, National Guardsmen, construction and sanitation crews and engineers. Trinity Church became a focal point for the stunned, grieving community at Ground Zero.

In 2011, to commemorate the tenth anniversary of the attacks, American composer Robert Moran was commissioned to write a Requiem for Trinity Church's Youth Chorus. A former student of Darius Milhaud (8 April, 22 June), Moran has worked in many musical styles over his long and varied career, but here opts for simplicity, setting the sweet, pure voices of the children against an accompaniment of cellos, organ and harp.

In the western Requiem Mass, the In Paradisum – 'in paradise' – is sung as the body is taken out of the church. The composer, who has no affiliation with any organized religion, has described his *Trinity Requiem* as '*a reflection upon those thousands of children throughout the world with no future and little if any hope*', adding, '*We all hope that this work will be of some comfort to those listeners who have lost beloved friends.*'

12 September

Adagio and Allegro for cello and piano, op. 70
by Robert Schumann (1810–1856)

On Robert and Clara Schumann's wedding anniversary (they married on this day in 1840), we'll hear Schumann in full-on love-song mode. He began writing this work on Valentine's day in 1849 (and it was finished in just three days); later that year he declared, '*I have never been busier or happier with my work.*' Darkness would engulf his stricken mind again before too long, but for now, it's simply a joy to hear Schumann writing from such a place of unalloyed happiness.

As a young man, Schumann had learned to play the cello and adored it. Although he later prioritized the piano, he never lost his affinity for the instrument: in his chamber music, in a fabulous solo concerto, and in works such as this (which he also wrote to be played on the French horn) he found ways to explore the cello's rich and expressive range. Here, the long, sustained lines of the Adagio yield to the fizzing energy of the Allegro to truly splendid effect.

13 September

Presto in C major
by Arnold Schoenberg (1874–1951)

Arnold Schoenberg, born this day, is known for being the bad-boy of tonality: the man who rocked up at the end of the nineteenth century and basically tore up the rule book on a thousand years of Western harmony. Like Pablo Picasso with painting, though, or James Joyce with literature, Schoenberg was only in a position to do that because he was so rigorously and intelligently engaged in what had gone before. (In other words, no, your three-year-old could *not* have done that.)

As a young man, Schoenberg used the money he earned from teaching German to buy as many scores as he could get his hands on. He was especially fascinated by Beethoven, poring over manuscripts of the symphonies and the early and late string quartets (see e.g. 4 January). These triggered a significant reaction in the budding composer. *'From then on'*, Schoenberg admitted, *'I had a desire to write string quartets.'* From Beethoven, he said, he learned *'the art of developing themes and movements'*. You can hear that influence shining through in this rich and rewarding early work, which I find throws up new things every time I hear it.

14 September

'Kogda volnuyetsya zhelteyushchaya niva' –
'When the golden cornfield waves'
from 4 Songs, op. 40 no. 1
by Nikolai Rimsky-Korsakov (1844–1908)

Rimsky-Korsakov was part of the group of Russian composers known as the 'Mighty Handful', whose other members included Alexander Borodin (27 February) and Modest Mussorgsky (21 April). You may remember that the objective of this idealistic young gang – who were much inspired by Mikhail Glinka (4 June) – was to develop the musical independence of Russia from Europe.

Rimsky-Korsakov, who enjoyed a parallel career as a naval officer, played a particularly critical role in this regard: he became the editor of a publishing enterprise, financed by a local industrialist, that was dedicated exclusively to the publication and promotion of music by Russian composers. His contribution to twentieth-century classical music was further immortalized by the fact that he was the first person to see and encourage the early compositions of a young Igor Stravinsky (29 May); he went on to teach Stravinsky privately for many years. Outside Russia, Rimsky-Korsakov also had a considerable influence on European composers such as Maurice Ravel (7 March, 14 July) and Claude Debussy (1 May, 23 August).

As a composer, he is probably most celebrated for his operas and his epic, narrative orchestral canvases such as *Scheherazade*, a vivid depiction of the legendary storyteller from the *The Thousand and One Nights*. For me, his music is just as appealing in miniature, such as in this evocative and transporting part-song.

15 September

Langsamer Satz – Slow Movement
by Anton Webern (1883–1945)

Two days ago, we met Arnold Schoenberg. Today we meet his student Anton Webern. Together with Alban Berg (9 February) these three musical mavericks were collectively known as the Second Viennese School, and would be responsible for a ruthless and systematic overhaul of Western harmony.

Webern had started studying with Schoenberg the autumn before he wrote this piece, which predates the radical innovations in harmony, pitch, rhythm, dynamics and melody which would have such a profound impact on composers in the second half of the twentieth century, including Pierre Boulez (26 March) and György Ligeti (18 November). It was inspired by a hiking trip he took in Lower Austria with the woman who later became his wife, Wilhelmine Mörtl. Still clinging to the vestiges of Western tonality – and bearing a debt in its 'chromaticism' to Liszt and Wagner – this is a work drenched in love.

As twenty-one-year-old Webern noted rhapsodically in his diary: *'to walk forever like this among the flowers, with my dearest one beside me, to feel oneself so entirely at one with the Universe, without care, free as the lark in the sky above. Oh what splendour . . . When night fell (after the rain) the sky shed bitter tears but I wandered with her along a road . . . Our love rose to infinite heights and filled the Universe. Two souls were enraptured.'*

Webern's music was denounced as *'cultural Bolshevism'* and *'degenerate art'* by the Nazis, and after the Anschluss in 1938 it was forbidden to perform or publish it. On this day in 1945, during the Allied occupation of Austria, Webern was shot and killed by a US soldier. He had stepped outside his house, forty-five minutes before curfew, reportedly so as not to disturb his grandchildren, to smoke the cigar that his son-in-law had likely procured on the black market and given him that evening.

16 September

Danzón no. 2
by Arturo Márquez (b. 1950)

Although the *danzón* as a dance form has its origins in eighteenth-century Europe and was refined in nineteenth-century Cuba, it has become synonymous with parts of Mexico. What the tango is to Buenos Aires, for example, the *danzón* is to Veracruz. And so, on Mexico's Independence Day, let us jump on this magic sonic carpet and be conveyed back to the 1940s and the golden age of the *danzón*. And here were are: a smoky local dance hall, a *charanga* band, couples gathering to dance together, just as their parents would have done, their grandparents, their great-grandparents . . .

Arturo Márquez is a contemporary Mexican classical composer steeped in local musical forms and idioms – his father was a Mexican mariachi musician and his grandfather a folk musician. It was whilst on a trip to Veracruz in 1993 with friends who took him round such local dance halls that Márquez fell under the spell of the *danzón*, with its equal parts fiery passion and formal elegance. He was inspired to write his set of eight concert *danzónes* as a gesture of admiration and respect for his heritage; this one is a particularly sensuous and alluring orchestral take on music that has shaped the folklore, the culture, the very social fabric of urban Mexican life.

17 September

'Goldberg' Variation no. 5 , BWV 988
by Johann Sebastian Bach (1685–1750)

In 1741, Bach published the fourth and final volume of his *Clavier-Übung* (literally, 'piano practice'), consisting, as he put it, *'of an Aria with diverse variations for the harpsichord with two manuals'*.

The story goes that Bach wrote these astonishing variations as an insomnia cure after Count Hermann Karl von Keyserling, Russian ambassador to the Saxon court, commissioned them in order that his young harpsichordist, Johann Gottlieb Goldberg, might play them through the night to soothe his sleep-deprived soul. (The story is likely apocryphal, but I have been known to press play in the wee small hours with a similar purpose in mind.)

Whatever their purpose, the 'Goldberg' Variations are the sort of music that sends numerologically inclined folk into raptures. After the opening aria Bach does indeed unleash the promised array of diverse variations, and they are mathematically perfect: the thirty-two movements of the set are built on a thirty-two-note bass-line; each is in binary form; all the phrases are of two, four or eight bars in length. The entire work is divided in half, but the variations are also divisible into groups of three. Bach adds to his crystalline structure a set of canons, that most mathematically precise of musical forms. And so on, and so on. Numbers geeks could spend a lifetime uncovering and analysing the dazzling numerological patterns the Goldbergs reveal.

Tellingly, though, on Bach's manuscript he also noted that the work was *'prepared for the soul's delight of lovers of music'*. For me it's a brilliant example of how music can work its magical effect on you, even if you know not the cause. So me, I'm going with 'soul's delight'. No further math qualifications required.

18 September

'Sovente il sole' – 'Oftentimes the sun'
from *Andromeda Liberata* ('*Serenata Veneziana*')
by Antonio Vivaldi (1678–1741)

When you've been in the classical music game for as long as I have, it can be easy to fall into the trap of assuming there are few surprises left, especially when it comes to the best-known composers like Vivaldi. Surely, you think, you've heard it all?

And then something like this comes along and just fells you.

I only discovered this piece recently, while researching a documentary about Vivaldi, and I'm not exaggerating when I say I cannot physically listen to it without my eyes starting to sting, my nose prickle. It is just So. Insanely. Beautiful.

The manuscript of the serenata from which it comes ('serenata' being a sort of costumed concert-opera designed to celebrate a specific event) dates from this day in 1726. It's a matter of fierce academic dispute as to whether the whole thing was written by Vivaldi or is rather a 'pasticcio', a pastiche put together by a group of composers. What we do know is that this particular aria is the only piece of music in Vivaldi's own hand that survives in all of Venice (goosebumps!)

And what a piece it is. It's sung by the character of Perseus, who has rescued Andromeda from a sea-monster and is now in love with her. Vivaldi intertwines the plangent voice of a lovesick human with the devastating purity of a solo violin. The effect is astounding:

Sovente il sole	*Oftentimes the sun*
risplende in cielo	*Shines in the sky*
più bello e vago (caro)	*With more beauty and clarity*
se oscura nube	*If dark clouds*
giá l'offuscò	*Were previously obscuring it . . .*

19 September

Ave Maria
by Paweł Łukaszewski (b. 1968)

The new millennium is witnessing an exciting, if unlikely, renaissance in sacred choral music.

I say 'unlikely' because the prevailing narrative in Western societies is that religious faith, especially as expressed through the established church, is in precipitous decline. But for whatever reason – frazzled lives, a hunger for spiritual purpose, increased focus on the benefits of taking time out of each day for mental reflection – the market for sacred choral music is booming, and not just for the old stuff. A thrillingly diverse range of contemporary composers are turning their minds (and perhaps souls) to religious themes and liturgical texts: see, for example Nico Muhly (26 August), James MacMillan (30 November), Charlotte Bray (10 February), Alissa Firsova (24 July) and Eric Whitacre (6 December), to name but a handful from these pages alone.

A particularly vibrant choral scene is emerging in Poland, and one of the composers at the forefront of that new wave is Paweł Łukaszewski, whose birthday it is today. His music bears the imprint of his Polish forebears Henryk Górecki (4 April) and Wojciech Kilar (29 December) as well as the influence of John Tavener (2 May, 18 December) and Arvo Pärt (24 February). But the profound spirituality that Łukaszewski wrings from a complex yet uncluttered tonal language is very much his own.

I think this luminous setting of the timeless Ave Maria prayer can proudly take its place alongside more established settings (see e.g. 3 June, 10 December).

20 September

Violin Concerto in D minor, op. 47
2: Adagio di molto
by Jean Sibelius (1865–1957)

If you're only going to write one concerto in life, it may as well be this one. Now viewed as one of the repertoire's towering peaks, Sibelius's Violin Concerto nevertheless takes its place in that honoured club of masterpieces that were initially considered failures. After a disastrous premiere in 1904, Sibelius revised it considerably. The new version was conducted by Richard Strauss the following year and has been beloved of audiences and fiddlers ever since.

Sibelius passionately loved the violin. It *'took me by storm'*, he recalled in his diary of his first encounter with the instrument in his early teens. *'For the next ten years it was my dearest wish, my overriding ambition, to become a great virtuoso.'* But Finland at that time was lacking in good violin teachers (unlike today, when it punches well above its weight in all aspects of music education); he was probably also hampered by starting comparatively late. And so, while he may have dreamed of being able to play this himself, like Ravel with his piano concerto (7 March), his technique wasn't up to the task. (He also suffered from acute stage fright, which would not have helped.)

We know that as a student Sibelius played the great violin concertos of Mendelssohn and Tchaikovsky (see 30 April, 4 December). To that ultra-Romantic canvas he brought his own signature sound, inflected as always by the dramatic landscapes of his icy Nordic homeland. It's very special. My mum has always loved this concerto and she would often stick it on at home. Even as a child it spoke to me profoundly; one of my 'before-and-after' pieces. The second movement in particular is extraordinary: a mercilessly beautiful, eight-minute benediction.

21 September

Autumn Crocus
by Billy Mayerl (1902–1959)

Billy Mayerl was born on the Tottenham Court Road, in the heart of London's theatre and musical district, so perhaps it was written in his stars that he would become one of twentieth-century England's great entertainers. A prodigious pianist, he was accepted by London's celebrated Trinity College of Music at the age of seven, and gave his first public performance at the age of nine – playing Edvard Grieg's fiendish piano concerto (4 November).

It was whilst he was a student at Trinity (and supplementing his income by playing in silent movie theatres and dance halls) that Mayerl reportedly began frequenting a local music arcade known as 'Gayland'. That was where he first encountered American 'ragtime' (see e.g. 8 July), which blew his mind – and soon prompted him to try his own hand at something similar. His composition teachers at Trinity were not impressed, however: he was threatened with expulsion if he ever sullied his hand with such lowly forms again.

Uncowed by the pretensions of the purist classical class, Mayerl's career focused on music hall and musical theatre and he became something of a local celebrity as a member of the Savoy hotel's legendary Havana Band. Later dubbed the 'King of Syncopation' for his correspondence school, which specialized in ragtime stride piano and was said to have over thirty thousand students, he was also much in demand as a piano soloist. He gave the London premiere in 1925, for example, of Gershwin's iconic *Rhapsody in Blue*.

As a composer, Mayerl produced over three hundred piano pieces. Usually classed as 'light music' (which does a disservice to his considerable inventiveness), many of them were named after trees and flowers, such as today's charming autumnal crocus.

22 September

Wer Dank opfert, der preiset mich – *He who gives thanks,
praises Me*, Cantata BWV 17
Part 2, no. 7 Chorale: 'Wie sich ein Vater erbarmet' –
'As a father has mercy'
by Johann Sebastian Bach (1685–1750)

Today we journey to the very heart of the sacred choral tradition, and the miraculous world of Bach's cantatas – that series of two hundred (surviving) compact choral works that adorn the liturgical calendar like so many glittering jewels.

Bach never wrote an opera, alas, but in these cantatas he demonstrates just what a phenomenal grasp on the human condition he had – and how instinctive was his knack for dramatizing it. Bach signed off each cantata with the flourish 'for the glory of God alone' but I believe that for people of any faith or none, they contain music that is so fresh, so alive, so direct and so immediately affecting that a commitment to the Lutheran theology without which they would not exist is no condition for entry. I've had long conversations with Christian priests, conductors, singers and others about this – sometimes wondering if I am 'allowed' to love the cantatas as much as I do when I'm truthfully quite wary of organized religion; an agnostic at best. I've been reassured that they can be enjoyed and appreciated by anyone; they work on so many levels.

So I may as well just admit that I'm obsessed with the Bach cantatas. *Obsessed*. I honestly could have picked almost any movement from any one at random, such is the treasury of wonders at our disposal. I find in this tiny, calming chorus – which was first performed on this day in 1726 – such a beguiling mix of peace and profundity. I love its box-fresh dissonances; its crunchy harmonic resolutions (listen out around 1'20"!) I love it. I love them all.

23 September

'Casta diva' – chaste goddess
from *Norma*
by Vincenzo Bellini (1801–1835)

Happy birthday to the composer known as the 'Swan of Catania'. Bellini's nickname reflects the graceful, flowing curves of his tunes, the *'broad curves'* and *'long, long, long melodies as no one else had ever made before'*, as Giuseppe Verdi later described them.

Bellini was apparently singing opera arias at eighteen months. He started studying music theory at two, and the piano at three. One of the leading practitioners (along with Rossini and Donizetti; see 29 February, 12 May) of the Italian bel canto style, he packed a lot into a tragically short life. 'Casta diva', from the 1831 opera *Norma*, is not just a bel canto classic, but a fine example of Bellini's superb ability to match those extended melodic lines to text, with potent dramatic effect.

This beautiful aria takes place in Act 1, not long after the eponymous Norma first appears. A high-priestess of the druids in Gaul, she is in love with the Roman proconsul Pollione, the leader of the occupying force suppressing her people. They have two children together, but Pollione has fallen in love with Norma's fellow priestess Adalgisa – which Norma will soon discover. Meanwhile, the people are looking urgently to Norma to lead their rebellion. *'The time is not ripe for our revenge'*, she declares, predicting that Rome will perish one day. Then she sings this timeless hymn to the moon:

Casta diva . . .	*Chaste goddess . . .*
A noi volgi il bel sembiante	*Turn thy beautiful face upon us,*
senza nube e senza vel . . .	*unclouded and unveiled . . .*

Norma goes on to plead that the goddess might cast upon earth the peace she has created in heaven. It's an electrifying moment.

24 September

Les baricades mistérieuses
by François Couperin (1668–1733)
arr. Thomas Adès (b. 1971)

What's your ideal day?

For the British composer Thomas Adès, it would apparently be *'staying at home and playing the harpsichord works of Couperin – new inspiration on every page'*. Niche it may be, but if it results in musical gems like this, frankly Tom: *you do you*.

Couperin, who came from a family of musicians, was a sensation in his day. By the time his first book of pieces for harpsichord came out in 1713, the Versailles harpsichordist and organist was known as 'Couperin the Great'. His music is characterized by an easy, almost improvisational elegance and an intelligence that never feels over-wrought. And he was a real musician's musician. Brahms helped edit the first complete edition of his keyboard works for piano and per-formed them in public; Richard Strauss took Couperin's music as the basis for several of his orchestral works; Ravel named his celebrated wartime memorial suite *Le Tombeau de Couperin*.

Les baricades mistérieuses comes from a book of pieces for harpsi-chord, and its title – literally 'The Mysterious Barricades' – has foxed musicologists for centuries. Some of the more outlandish suggestions as to what these 'barricades' might be include women's virginity (for real), women's underwear or chastity belts, and women's eyelashes. Others wonder if it wasn't perhaps a technical in-joke on Couperin's part; the continuous chain of suspensions and resolutions he constructs being a 'barricade' to the fundamental harmony. I think we can safely say none of these is particularly edifying; just enjoy instead this kaleido-scopically intricate yet deliciously direct music, which is blessed with even more wit and sophistication in Adès's prodigious hands.

25 September

Les Boréades
Act 4, scene 4: Entry of the muses, zephyrs, seasons, hours and arts
by Jean-Philippe Rameau (1683–1764)

Staying in the world of French Baroque, Jean-Philippe Rameau should give any late starters in life hope. He was fifty when his first opera was produced, yet went on to become the most important French opera composer of his day.

He was also a music theorist with a nose – or rather, ear – for radical harmonic invention. His 1722 *Treatise on Harmony* proposed a *'fundamental law'* that underpins all Western music and called upon science and mathematics to illuminate supposedly universal harmonic principles. It led to his being nicknamed the *'Isaac Newton of music'*. The treatise was a bestseller throughout Europe; its theories have endured.

Rameau was baptized on this day in Dijon, but little else is known about his early life, other than that he was taught music before he could read or write. Music remained his abiding passion: he was monomaniacally focused (although he did find time to get married and have kids). *'His heart and soul,'* the playwright Alexis Piron, a collaborator, remarked, *'were in his harpsichord; once he had shut its lid, there was no one home.'*

Les Boréades was his last opera. The setting is ancient Bactria, where Queen Alphise has fallen for a mysterious foreigner, Abaris, but is required to wed a descendant of Boreas, the god of the north wind. It all seems doomed, until Apollo reveals that Abaris is actually his *own* son. Offspring of gods naturally trump the mere Boreads, so the marriage – phew – can go ahead.

It was never produced in Rameau's lifetime and wasn't staged properly until the late twentieth century, despite containing some fabulous music – including this dreamy orchestral interlude from Act 4.

26 September

Du bist die Ruh – You are peace, D. 776
by Franz Schubert (1797–1828)

Schubert, who died from syphilis at the age of thirty-one, never married or had a long-term relationship. This rapturous hymn to enduring love offers a glimpse into the heart of a highly emotional human who would surely have aspired to a lasting romantic union had he not been wrenched from the world by such a cruel disease.

As we have already seen, Schubert not only established the German 'lied' (song) as a significant art form, but produced more than six hundred of the things, many of them individual melodic masterpieces that set a gold standard for composers of the future – including the greatest pop songwriters of the past century. Schubert was so prodigious, so prolific, so *focused*, that he was sometimes dashing off five of these songs in a single day. '*I compose every morning*', he once explained, '*and when one piece is done, I begin another.*' (As well as all the songs, he left behind 8 symphonies, 22 piano sonatas, 35 chamber works, various piano miniatures, 6 masses and 15 attempted operas. It's as though he always knew he was living on borrowed time.)

The songs cover a vast emotional range. This one from 1823 sets an untitled poem by Friedrich Rückert, an expert on Eastern and Oriental literature. Sensuality is fused with idealism as words about love, longing and devotion are combined with a melody of exquisite simplicity.

What a thing, though, to be able to sing *this* to somebody you love:

Du bist die Ruh,	*You are peace,*
Der Friede mild,	*The mild peace,*
Die Sehnsucht du	*You are longing*
Und was sie stillt.	*And what stills it.*

27 September

Romance in E flat major, op. 11
by Gerald Finzi (1901–1956)

Finzi's music teacher Ernest Farrar (11 November) once described him as being '*very shy, but full of poetry*', which I find a pretty good description of much of the music itself. Being of the generation he was, Finzi saw tragedy first hand, losing all three of his brothers (as well as Farrar) in the First World War. His father, meanwhile, had died shortly before his eighth birthday.

Right from the outset, his music was tinged with elegy: a sense of loss shimmers always on the horizon. But he sought and found solace in verse, setting the poetry of Thomas Traherne, Thomas Hardy, Christina Rossetti and William Wordsworth. Again and again in his music, he returns to a motif of innocence disrupted, and the occasionally ecstatic textures of his orchestration and vocal writing go some way to redeem the melancholy.

There's also something about Finzi's music which feels quintessentially English – despite the fact his family roots were Italian, German and Sephardic Jewish. His music bears an obvious debt to Edward Elgar (28 February, 9 July, 15 August) and he was friends with Gustav Holst (27 November) and Vaughan Williams (14 June), although he never achieved anything like the critical acclaim they did.

He wrote this pensive but stirring romance for string orchestra in his late twenties (1928) but sat on it, later revising it a number of times. It wasn't published until 1951, the same year he was diagnosed with Hodgkin's Disease – and five years before he died, on this day.

28 September

Membra Jesu nostri
2: 'Ad genua'
by Dietrich Buxtehude (c. 1637/9–1707)

I've said it before: I find it mightily humbling, as I press play on my phone, accessing a digital streaming platform containing millions of instantly available songs, to consider that for most of human history people could not experience music unless they could find a way to hear it performed *live*. It's such an obvious point but worth repeating; for me it heightens the miraculous thing these composers do.

As a young man, J. S. Bach was such a fan of the Danish-German organist and composer Dietrich Buxtehude that he once walked 250 *miles*, uphill, in the snow, in winter, from his home town of Arnstadt to Lübeck to meet the older composer in person and hear his music in concert. (He'd had to apply for a leave of absence from his church post in order to make the trip: he outstayed the permission by some months, which got him into all sorts of trouble when he finally walked home.)

Only a hundred or so pieces from Buxtehude's output survive, but what we have makes it clear why Bach was such an admirer. His organ music is contrapuntally inventive; his choral music fresh, urgent, compelling. His seven-part cantata cycle, *Membra Jesu*, the first Lutheran oratorio, is full of the sort of vivid humanity and narrative drama that Bach will later take to the highest heights in his own choral writing (see e.g. 22 September, 13 October).

The complete Latin title translates as '*The most holy limbs of our suffering Jesus*'. Each movement is addressed to a different part of the crucified body of Christ. This one, '*To the knees*', sets words from Isaiah that portray Jerusalem as a mother.

29 September

And the Bridge is Love
by Howard Goodall (b. 1958)

Howard Goodall is one of British music's busiest bees, as likely to be found penning smash hit musicals (*Love Story, Bend It Like Beckham*) and TV shows (*Blackadder, Mr Bean, The Vicar of Dibley*) as he is making documentaries about the Beatles or composing orchestral and choral music for the concert hall.

This powerfully elegiac piece has a tragic context: it was composed in 2008 in memory of a young cellist, the daughter of family friends of Goodall's, who had died aged seventeen the previous September. Goodall is a musical chameleon, but in its searching yet ultimately redemptive mood this piece continues in a tradition of twentieth-century English string music that includes the Finzi we heard two days ago, as well as Elgar (28 February, 9 July, 15 August), Vaughan Williams (14 June), Frank Bridge (6 October), Michael Tippett (2 June) and Benjamin Britten (13 June, 22 November).

The inspiration, however, comes from somewhat further afield. '*And the bridge is love*' is a quotation from the American writer Thornton Wilder's novel, *The Bridge of San Luis Rey*, which won the Pulitzer Prize in 1928 and tells the tale of the collapse, in 1714, of a bridge in Peru which resulted in the deaths of five people. Goodall says he finds in the book a '*parable of the struggle to find meaning in chance and in inexplicable tragedy*'.

'*But soon we will die*', the novel concludes, '*and all memories of those five will have left Earth, and we ourselves shall be loved for a while and forgotten. But the love will have been enough; all those impulses of love return to the love that made them. Even memory is not necessary for love. There is a land of the living and a land of the dead, and the bridge is love.*'

30 September

'Au fond du temple saint' – 'At the back of the holy temple' from *The Pearl Fishers* by Georges Bizet (1838–1875)

I was listening to this on the tube recently and a fellow passenger actually touched me on the arm and asked if I was okay. 'Yes!' I gasped, 'I'm fine!' but in truth I was practically expiring due to the beauty of this piece of music. We're talking *crazy-beautiful*. Seriously. I don't know how anyone could possibly listen to it impassively: it's insane.

It comes from Bizet's opera *The Pearl Fishers,* which premiered on this day in Paris in 1863, when Bizet was twenty-four. Set in ancient-day Ceylon, now Sri Lanka, its story is the basis of many a Hollywood romcom. In a nutshell: how a vow of eternal friendship between two guys is jeopardized by their love for the same girl. (She faces her own dilemma: the conflict between secular love and her sacred oath as a priestess of Brahma.)

This duet comes at the peak of the bromance in Act 1, sung by the two pearl fishermen Zurga and Nadir, who are about to be newly caught in a love triangle with Leïla, the priestess.

De nos cœurs l'amour s'empare,	*Love takes our hearts by storm*
Et nous change en ennemis!	*and turns us into enemies!*
Non, que rien ne nous sépare! . . .	*No, let nothing part us! . . .*

As with *Carmen*, written a decade later, critics were largely hostile. Although the audience at the premiere was enthusiastic, even clamouring for Bizet to come to the stage, it ran for only sixteen performances and was never revived in his short lifetime.

This duet, though!

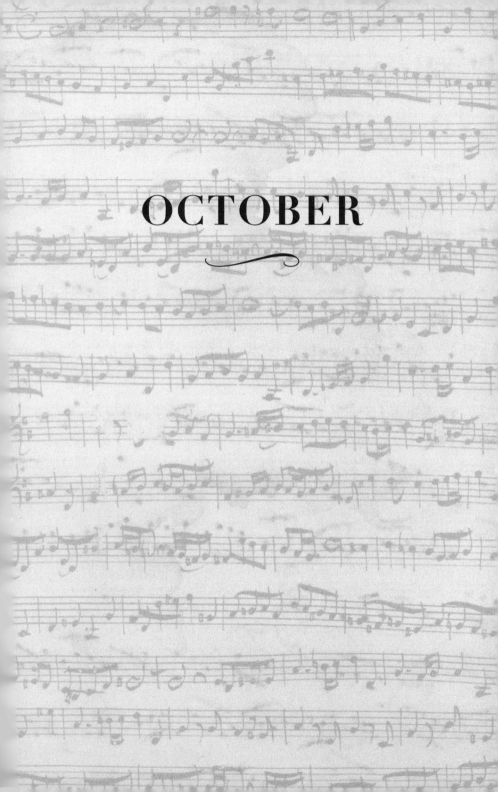

OCTOBER

1 October

6 *Études de concert*, op. 35
2: 'Autumn'
by Cécile Chaminade (1857–1944)

'*My little Mozart*' is how yesterday's composer Bizet reportedly described an eight-year-old Cécile Chaminade, daughter of family friends in Paris. He was so impressed with her compositions that he suggested formal music studies, but this did not go down so well chez Chaminade. '*Bourgeois girls*', her insurance-salesman father apparently fulminated, '*are predestined to become wives and mothers!*'

Yikes. Chaminade, nonetheless, had different ideas. '*Women have not been considered a working force in the world*', she once said. Prefiguring her fourth-wave feminist successors with their mantra to 'live your best life' by about a century, she added: '*The work that their sex and conditions impose upon them has not been so adjusted as to give them . . . scope for the development of their best self. They have been handicapped, and only a few, through force of circumstances or inherent strength, have been able to get the better of that handicap.*'

The heroic Chaminade got the better of it as best she could, inspiring fellow composer Ambroise Thomas to declare: '*This is not a woman who composes, but a composer who is a woman.*' She produced about 350 works, including opera, ballet, a choral symphony, chamber music and a hundred songs. Above all Chaminade was adept at the short, salon-style piano piece – such as this autumnal delight. In Britain, Queen Victoria was a fan and Chaminade performed for the royal family at Windsor. In the US, hundreds of 'Chaminade clubs' were formed after her debut with the Philadelphia Orchestra in 1908. Five years later, France made her a member of the Légion d'Honneur.

And yet, Chaminade's music was largely neglected after her death. It's only recently that her reputation has begun to be revived.

2 October

Kol nidrei, op. 47
by Max Bruch (1838–1920)

Back in January I mentioned that, despite his rich and varied output, Max Bruch tends to be celebrated for a certain violin concerto alone. Of his other music, it's this impassioned *Kol nidrei*, based on two Hebrew melodies, for which he is probably best known – but which has had the unintended consequence of leading people to assume he must be Jewish. Bruch, who died on this day, was actually a Lutheran Protestant, descended from a long line of Christian clerics.

He was, though, curious about all sorts of traditional music. (His *Scottish Fantasy* for violin, for example, makes use of Gaelic folk tunes; weirdly he was never mistaken for a Scot.) As a young man he had, in his words, *'enthusiastically studied folk songs of all nations, because the folk song is the source of all true melodies: the wellspring at which one must repeatedly renew and refresh oneself . . .'*

Bruch wrote his meditative *Kol nidrei*, in which a solo cello acts almost as Jewish cantor, around the same time he took up his post as Principal Conductor of the Liverpool Philharmonic, in 1880; Liverpool has had a thriving Jewish community going back to the 1700s. In a letter to a German cantor and musicologist, he explained: *'Although I am a Protestant, as an artist I felt profoundly the outstanding beauty of these melodies, and therefore gladly incorporated them into my arrangement.'*

I love Bruch's insistence on the universality of this stuff: his polite take-down of the idea that only Jews might legitimately respond to Jewish music. The *Kol nidrei*, sung on the eve of Yom Kippur, is a mournful, ancient synagogue chant which in Aramaic means 'all vows'. Bruch would likely have encountered its affecting melody through the cantor-in-chief of Berlin, Abraham Jacob Lichtenstein, who actively encouraged his interest in Jewish folk songs.

3 October

An den Schlaf – To Sleep
by Hugo Wolf (1860–1903)

Hugo Wolf was a late-Romantic Austrian composer and lieder writer, much influenced by Richard Wagner, whose copious gifts have long been underappreciated. Although he had a tremendous intellectual curiosity and was enthusiastic about music, poetry, literature and art, he battled depression and mental illness, once admitting: '*I appear at times merry and in good heart, talk, too, before others quite reasonably, and it looks as if I felt, too, God knows how well within my skin. Yet the soul maintains its deathly sleep and the heart bleeds from a thousand wounds.*' Before his death he would suffer a complete mental collapse, triggered by syphilis.

In happier – if manic – times Wolf would often write in a Schubert-like compositional frenzy, producing two, three or more songs per day. He had a particular genius for word-setting, describing himself as an '*objective lyricist*', following a '*duty to the poet*'. Unlike many Romantic composers who believed their music came first, Wolf felt it was his responsibility to reveal the '*true content*' of a poetic text to a listener by the most expressive musical means.

This is one of many luminously effective songs by Wolf. It comes from his so-called *Mörike-Lieder* collection from 1888, which set poems by the German writer Eduard Mörike:

Schlaf! süßer Schlaf!	*Sleep! Sweet Sleep!*
obwohl dem Tod wie du nichts gleicht,	*Although, next to death, there is nothing that so much resembles you,*
auf diesem Lager doch willkommen heiß' ich dich!	*on this couch I proclaim you welcome!*

4 October

String Quartet No. 3 ('Mishima')
1. '1957 Award Montage'
by Philip Glass (b. 1937)

Philip Glass is musical Marmite. I'm a lover (on which, more below)* but haters, you might want to skip a track, because this is vintage Glass. He assembled this string quartet from music he'd written for a Paul Schrader film about the Japanese author Yukio Mishima, who committed suicide after a failed coup d'état. The film was released on this day in 1985.

Viola player Nicolas Cords of the ensemble Brooklyn Rider talks of the *'glowing sonorities'* of Glass' string quartets and, intriguingly, describes Glass's 'minimalist' notation of interlocking patterns and elemental harmonies as *'a kind of Rosetta Stone [which] it was our job to decode'*. Reading Glass's music in this way, says Cords, opens up all sorts of intriguing connections *'whether it be the gossamer-like inner voices of Schubert, the urban landscape of New York, or the drone-infused textures of Persian music'*.

* On a personal note: I was introduced to the music of Philip Glass by a beloved parent, Robert, who was not my biological father but the closest thing I had to a 'dad' growing up (and from whom I get the Hill bit of my name). He died, suddenly and years too soon, shortly before I embarked on this *Year of Wonder* project, and his generous, unpretentious spirit is everywhere in its pages. Among the musical heroes he ushered into my life were Leonard Cohen, Bob Dylan and Nick Drake, but above all, Bobby adored Glass. A working-class boy from Birmingham, Bobby was a giant force of love in my life, an inspiration on many levels, and proof to me that any music might connect to anyone, from any background, anywhere. Before he died, we went to see a Glass concert at the Barbican together, and I'll always cherish that.

5 October

Mélodie
from *Orfeo ed Euridice*
by Christoph Willibald Gluck (1714–1787)
arr. Giovanni Sgambati (1841–1914)

Born in what is now modern-day Bavaria, Christoph Willibald Gluck ran away to Prague when he was in his early teens and then somehow hustled his way into working at the Hapsburg Court in Vienna. He became a central figure in the European musical scene, a man responsible for radically reforming opera by purifying the obscure plots and overly florid arias of conventional eighteenth-century productions, and imbuing both the music and the narrative with a 'noble simplicity' redolent of ancient Greek drama.

Indeed, Gluck set many Greek tragedies, including Euripides' *Iphigenia in Aulis*, *Iphigenia in Tauris* and *Alcestis*. But it was his first such 'reform' opera that was to prove his most popular. Based on the Orpheus myth, in which the master musician Orpheus must appease the Furies to rescue his beloved, *Orfeo ed Euridice* was first performed in Vienna's Burgtheater on this day in 1762, in the presence of Empress Maria Theresa. It was to have a significant impact on later German opera, including Mozart's *The Magic Flute*, Beethoven's *Fidelio* and Wagner's *Das Rheingold* – as well as on Rossini, Berlioz and scores of other leading opera composers in the following centuries.

Orfeo is ultimately an opera about the power of love. Gluck's melody – here arranged by the Italian pianist Giovanni Sgambati in a version that was beloved of Sergei Rachmaninov, no less – is a terrific example of how this newly spare, even chaste operatic language can nonetheless deliver overpowering emotion.

6 October

Autumn
by Frank Bridge (1879–1941)

These days, Frank Bridge is probably best known for being the adored teacher and mentor of Benjamin Britten (see 13 June, 22 November). But having been a student of the legendary Royal College of Music professor Charles Villiers Stanford (5 July, 1 September), Bridge was also a fine, if neglected, composer in his own right.

When Britten first heard Bridge's music he said he was '*knocked sideways*', and this captivating little choral number, composed when Bridge was in his early twenties, had a similar effect on me.

It sets music to Percy Bysshe Shelley's 1820 seasonally appropriate dirge from *The Seasons*:

The warm sun is failing, the bleak wind is wailing,
The bare boughs are sighing, the pale flowers are dying,
And the Year
On the earth her death-bed, in a shroud of leaves dead,
Is lying . . .

7 October

'Air, Deux insulaires'
from *Roland*
by Jean-Baptiste Lully (1632–1687)

Lully was an energetic and dynamic figure at the heart of the development of French opera who developed an array of forms, including novel theatrical spectacles such as comedy-ballets and music-tragedies. His ardent fans – known as the 'Lullyistes' – could give today's most devoted pop audiences a run for their money.

Although Lully was born in Tuscany, the son of poor Italian millers, a chance encounter with a French chevalier at Mardi Gras led to his being conveyed to work in France as a teenager. The multi-talented singer, violinist, guitarist and dancer soon found himself an indispensable member of the court of Louis XIV, and became a French subject in 1661. Entertaining, ruthless and flamboyant (he had many homosexual liaisons; he also had a wife, a mistress and a number of children), Lully collaborated with some of the leading lights of the time, including the playwright Molière.

For all he led a glittering life, he died a grisly death. Before conductors used batons, they kept the orchestra in time with a long, pointed staff, which they banged rhythmically up and down. During a performance of his *Te Deum,* Lully pierced his own foot and contracted gangrene. He must have been in agony, but refused to have his leg amputated. The gangrene spread through his body and infected his brain.

Roland was first performed in 1685 at Versailles. It's Lully's lavish take on Ariosto's epic poem *Orlando Furioso,* which provided rich pickings for opera composers – as we've already seen in Handel's *Alcina* (16 April) and Francesca Caccini's *La liberazione di Ruggiero* (3 February).

8 October

Folías criollas: Gallarda Napolitana
by Antonio Valente (dates unknown; *fl.* 1565–1580)

From the current standpoint, globalization as the handmaid of neo-liberalist orthodoxy has surely seen better days. But for all the criticisms being levelled against it in the late teens of the new millennium, it's hard not to raise a little cheer to the cultural cross-pollination that has been enabled as different peoples, resources and ideas have come into contact over the course of many centuries.

Today's musical offering reminds us of the effects that early globalization had on the development of the history of music. Once again, I have the genius that is Jordi Savall to thank for bringing it to my attention (see 28 August). Very little is known about the Renaissance keyboardist and composer Antonio Valente, other than that he was blind from childhood and worked as organist at the church of Sant' Angelo a Nilo in Naples between 1565 and 1580. We do know that he contributed significantly to the development of keyboard music of the day and was regarded as a founder of the early Neapolitan school. And that he was capable of writing a fantastic tune.

This intoxicating, up-tempo 'galliard' – an athletic form of Renaissance dance characterized by its vigorous leaps, jumps and hops (see also 16 June) – reminds us that European music was completely transformed by indigenous Mexican forms and other imports, especially African and Afro-Cuban music. Consider it an example, then, almost *half a millennium* old, of the early effects of multiculturalism.

9 October

Cantus arcticus
2: 'Melankolia'
by Einojuhani Rautavaara (1928–2016)

To the Arctic Circle today, to celebrate the birth on this day of the great Finnish composer Einojuhani Rautavaara (pronounced Row as in *now*-ta-vara). He was a protégé of his countryman Jean Sibelius, studied in the USA with Aaron Copland (5 April, 30 October), and once rather wittily declared: *'If an artist is not a modernist when he is young, he has no heart. And if he is a modernist when he is old, he has no brain.'*

Rautavaara's youthful modernist tendencies led him towards experimenting with electronic music in the 1960s, and in 1972, on commission from Finland's largest university, Oulu, he produced this unique work, subtitled a 'Concerto for Birds and Orchestra'. Birdsong has long had a grip on the imaginations of classical composers: from Rameau to Saint-Saëns to Messiaen, many have tried to capture the natural miracle of avian melody on manuscript paper. But Rautavaara's bold use of new technology took the notion of 'musical birdsong' to a new level. He incorporates actual recordings of birds captured on tape near the Arctic Circle and on the bogs of Liminka in northern Finland, then manipulates the sounds of the birds to blend with the orchestra to goosebump-inducing effect.

This evanescent second movement, titled 'Melancholy', features a slowed-down recording of the shore lark – whose song has been lowered by two octaves. Once heard, never forgotten.

10 October

'Touch her soft lips'
from *Henry V* Suite
by William Walton (1902–1983)
arr. Bob Chilcott (b. 1955)

Directed by, produced by and starring Laurence Olivier, the 1944 film *Henry V* is considered the first Shakespeare-based film to have achieved both critical and commercial success, scooping a handful of Academy Award nominations and bagging Olivier a special Oscar for his outstanding triple achievement in bringing *Henry V* to the screen.

As we've already seen with the likes of John Williams (18 February) and Ennio Morricone (23 February), the finest scores can make a film. William Walton's sensational music for *Henry V* surely played a part in the film's international triumph.

Walton went on to collaborate with Olivier on his *Hamlet* in 1948 and his *Richard III* in 1955. In 1963, the music for *Henry V* was assembled into a five-part concert suite. This exquisite fourth movement sets Shakespeare's words from Act 2, scene 3, and I find Bob Chilcott's dreamy modern update quite enchanting.

Come, come, let's away . . .

11 October

Symphony no. 9 in D minor
3: Adagio: Langsam, feierlich – slowly, solemnly
by Anton Bruckner (1824–1896)

This was the final symphony Bruckner would compose. '*I dedicate my last work to the Majesty of all Majesties, to the dear Lord*', he wrote, '*and hope that He will grant me sufficient time to complete it.*' God, alas, was deaf to such entreaties: when Bruckner died on this day, he left it unfinished.

The piece is extraordinary: a colossal, kitchen-sink bid for eternity, and this third movement, which Bruckner called his '*farewell to life*', is its shattering emotional heart. Mired in tonal ambiguity from the outset, we are thrust in on an immediately dissonant interval, a ninth – he starts the strings off on a low 'B' and wrenches them up, up, up beyond the natural octave, to an unnaturally higher 'C'. What then unfold are alternating episodes of devotion and rapture, humility and might, sorrow and farewell. It's awe-inspiring.

This is one of the longest pieces I've suggested this year, lasting around twenty-four minutes, but it's a work of such metaphysical magnitude, such transcendental scope, such preposterous humanity and such grace that if you can eke out the time, on this day or another, to give yourself over to the music completely, I would *urge* you to do so. Grab a glass of something, run a bath and lock yourself in; stick an eye-mask on and close the bedroom door; download it onto your phone and take it for a walk; hell, wait until you're on a train commute that's long enough to contain the whole thing undisrupted. Do whatever you need to, but if you can immerse yourself in it, if you can listen actively, without distraction, I *swear* it will be worth it.

In other words, unlike many of the pieces here, maybe don't try and do the ironing to this one.

12 October

Suite española, op. 47
1: 'Granada' (Serenata)
by Isaac Albéniz (1860–1909)

On Spanish National Day, here is Isaac Albéniz: a child prodigy with a taste for high adventure. The story goes that at the age of twelve, the gifted young pianist stowed away in a ship bound for Buenos Aires, and over the next three years made his way to Cuba; then the US, where he gave concerts in New York and San Francisco; then Liverpool, London and Leipzig – dazzling audiences along the way.

The tale has been somewhat exaggerated: Albéniz did indeed travel the world, and gave major public concerts whilst still a teenager. But, in a somewhat less rock'n'roll spin, he was always accompanied by his father, a customs officer.

No matter. Albéniz was still a Spanish musical hero. As a composer, he was influenced by the likes of Bach, Beethoven, Chopin and Liszt, but he was also captivated by the folk music of his native land, and sought to assimilate certain traits into his music by engaging and inventive means. Albéniz authority Pola Beytelman identifies the main ways in which he does this: his use of traditional Spanish dance rhythms and the gypsy/flamenco singing known as *cante jondo*; his extensive borrowing from the exotic scales and unusual 'modes' of flamenco music (Phrygian, Aeolian and Mixolydian if you want to get technical); and his application of guitar idioms to piano writing – which is ironic given that much of his piano music was subsequently arranged for guitar.

His 1886 *Suite española*, written in honour of the Queen of Spain, depicts different regions and musical styles. It has been immortalized in the version for guitar: this, the opening movement, might even be something of a cliché of 'Spanishness', were it not such undeniably fantastic music.

13 October

St Matthew Passion, BWV 244
1. Chorus: 'Come, ye daughters, help me lament'
by Johann Sebastian Bach (1685–1750)

Along with the cantatas (22 September), Bach's two complete Passion settings lay bare his beating heart. For my money, they are among the greatest artistic monuments we have. Written for the Good Friday vespers service and first performed in St Thomas Church in Leipzig, where Bach was based at the time, probably in 1727, this one sets chapters 26 and 27 of the Gospel of St Matthew. It portrays the events leading up to Jesus' crucifixion with engrossing drama, raw emotion and some of the most moving music ever written.

Bach focuses very much on Christ 'the man' – and here too is *Bach* the man, in all his flawed and messy humanity; his capacity for feeling all the feels; his gift for consolation – whoever you are, whatever you may or may not believe. Bach faces up to the overwhelming questions of life – and death – with unflinching rigour and generosity.

What's more extraordinary to contemplate than the work itself is the fact that we *so nearly didn't have it.* Bach, as I have previously mentioned, was not held in high esteem after his death; he slipped into relative obscurity during the Classical and early Romantic era, his music dismissed as cold and mathematical. If it had not been for the determination of a twenty-year-old Felix Mendelssohn, who mounted a historic revival performance in Berlin in 1829, the *St Matthew Passion* might have been lost to us for ever.

I could have chosen almost any moment, but this opening chorus is a marvel. Over the top of an interlocking double choir Bach sends a children's chorus, sweeping us helplessly into a tsunami of sound and emotion. Away we go.

14 October

∽

Crisantemi
by Giacomo Puccini (1858–1924)

Over the course of this year, we've encountered some composers writing at breakneck speed (see e.g. 21 January, 21 July); now here's Puccini, speedily conjuring an elegiac bouquet of musical 'chrysanthemums' for string quartet over the course of a single night in 1890.

The speed with which he produced this is even more remarkable given that Puccini was likely grief-stricken at the time. He was writing the piece overnight as a response to the death of his friend Amedeo, Duke of Savoy; the chrysanthemum, in Latin cultures, is the flower associated with funerals and remembrance rites.

It's perhaps surprising that Puccini opted for the genre of string quartet, given he hardly ever composed outside the opera house. (Puccini himself acknowledged that his talent lay here alone. In 1920 he remarked: *'Almighty God touched me with his little finger and said "write for the theatre – mind, only for the theatre". And I have obeyed the supreme command.'*) He was obviously sufficiently satisfied, however, to recycle its limpid melodies three years later in the opera *Manon Lescaut*, where the *Crisantemi* theme serves as the poignant signature music for the lead character Manon's death.

15 October

Love bade me welcome
by Judith Weir (b. 1954)

The position of Master of the Queen's Music – the musical equivalent of the poet laureate – has existed since 1625, when Charles I appointed a Huguenot court musician called Nicholas Lanier as head of the private band that conveniently accompanied him wherever he went, providing music for his every whim, on demand.

We've met a couple of subsequent Masters on these pages – see Edward Elgar (28 February, 9 July, 15 August) and Peter Maxwell Davies (5 May). It only took 388 years for a woman to be appointed to the post, but she got there in the end. Judith Weir writes music of intelligence and wit: she's unpretentious, full of integrity and deeply thoughtful about music's place in the world.

A former student of John Tavener (2 May, 18 December), Weir is a natural musical storyteller, with a gift for distilling musical and dramatic ideas. Drawn to the human voice, she has composed numerous operas, large-canvas works for orchestra and chorus, and smaller vocal pieces such as this lovely, fresh setting of verse by the metaphysical poet George Herbert (1593–1633).

This piece was written to celebrate the 500th anniversary of Aberdeen University.

> *Love bade me welcome. Yet my soul drew back*
> *Guilty of dust and sin.*
> *But quick-eyed Love, observing me grow slack*
> *From my first entrance in,*
> *Drew nearer to me, sweetly questioning*
> *If I lacked any thing . . .*

16 October

~~

Légende, op. 17
by Henryk Wieniawski (1835–1880)

Remember earlier this year we met the Polish composer and violinist Henryk Wieniawski (18 March) and I mentioned that his girlfriend Isabella's parents, who'd initially rejected his request for permission to take their daughter's hand in marriage, only came around to the prospect after they'd heard his *Légende?*

Well, here it is: the ultimate future-parents-in-law impresser. Enjoy.

17 October

Elevazione
by Domenico Zipoli (1688–1726)

The Baroque composer Domenico Zipoli was born in Italy on this day, but spent the best part of his life in Latin America, where he worked as a Jesuit priest and taught music to the Guaraní people. He died young, in Argentina, possibly from tuberculosis, but left behind books of keyboard works and sacred choral music that were embraced among music communities from Bolivia to Peru.

Hardly any of Zipoli's instrumental music survives, so little is known about the context of this achingly lovely work featuring the magical combination of solo oboe and cello – but it delivers what it promises in the title: this is music to elevate the spirit.

18 October

⌒

Liturgy of St John Chrysostom
13: 'Tebe poyem' – 'We hymn thee'
by Sergei Rachmaninov (1873–1943)

There's a certain ritual among British choirs that in order to hit the really, really low bass notes of Rachmaninov's two a cappella choral works, the *All-Night Vigil* (1915) and this one, you have to drink at least a shot of vodka before each performance. I have no idea if this is physiologically viable – it sounds like an excellent excuse to get drunk to me, something British musicians are really, really good at. But it's certainly the case that Rachmaninov writes *extremely* low notes for the basses, and that regular singers may not be able to go that deep. Apparently, when Rachmaninov first showed his score for the *All-Night Vigil* to a friend, the friend exclaimed: '*Now where on earth are we to find such basses? They are as rare as asparagus at Christmas!*'

(I'm totally stealing that image, by the way – and its timely reminder, ahem, that vegetables should only be available seasonally.) Back to the music, though, and this is *such* radiant writing for an unaccompanied choir: so far away, in its spare and luminous textures, from the ripe Romanticism of the piano works we've heard already from Rachmaninov this year. Hearing it was another 'before-and-after' moment for me: I simply could not believe my ears.

Rachmaninov was a man of profound but private faith, and had apparently been contemplating setting this liturgy – which is the primary worship service of the Eastern Orthodox church – for years before he embarked upon it in 1910. Unlike with many of his compositions, divine inspiration seemed to flow from the outset. '*I started to work on it somehow by chance*', he wrote to a friend . . . *and then I finished it very quickly. Not for a long time have I written anything with such pleasure.*'

19 October

Kehaar's Theme from *Watership Down* by Angela Morley (1924–2009)

The Emmy-winning composer Angela Morley was hugely versatile. As well as writing light classical music, she scored numerous movies, wrote for episodes of *Dallas*, *Dynasty* and *Wonder Woman*, and delivered pop hits for the likes of Frankie Vaughan, Shirley Bassey and Scott Walker. Morley also became an invaluable collaborator for John Williams (18 February), arranging his epic scores for films including *Star Wars* (1977), *Superman* (1978) and *The Empire Strikes Back* (1980).

Born Walter Stott in Leeds in 1924, in the mid-1970s the composer withdrew from the music industry altogether, only later to emerge, to the shock of her peers, as Angela Morley. She had undergone what was then described as a 'sex-rectifying operation' and, facing prejudice in a male-dominated musical world, preferred to stay under the radar.

And then in 1977 came an intriguing offer. The bestselling book *Watership Down* was being made into an animated film. The then Master of the Queen's Music, Malcolm Williamson, had been hired as composer. Three days before recordings were due to begin, he had written only seven minutes of music and had to pull out. Morley was asked to look at Williamson's sketches and score the rest of the film on very short notice. According to Sarah Wooley, who wrote a radio drama, *1977*, based on the events, '*She watched the* Watership Down *footage and read the book. It's a quest story, about finding a new home. There was something she saw in it. She went and composed a fantastic score inside two weeks.*'

Morley was the first openly transgender person to be nominated for an Academy Award (in 1975 and 1978). It would take until 2016 for another trans artist – also a musician, Anonhi, previously known as Antony Hegarty – to get another Oscar nod.

20 October

Homages
1: 'Contemplation'
by Cheryl Frances-Hoad (b. 1980)

Time to meet another of the wonderfully distinctive voices currently lighting up contemporary British classical music – see also e.g. Charlotte Bray (10 February), Anna Meredith (23 March) and Alissa Firsova (24 July).

Essex-born Cheryl Frances-Hoad has been composing since she was fifteen and draws from a wide array of inspirations, including literature, poetry, painting, dance and pop music. (She once wrote a piece called *Pay Close Attention* in tribute to big-beat electronic pioneers The Prodigy.) Her music has featured at the BBC Proms and in leading festivals around the world, as well as at local outreach workshops where it connects to young audiences who wouldn't ordinarily go anywhere near a concert hall.

Brimful of ideas and artistry, Frances-Hoad also boasts some seriously impressive discipline, joking that she can only work full-time as a composer thanks to '*obsessive dedication, imperviousness to rejection, inherent thriftiness and an endless stamina for filling in funding applications*'. She has composed across many classical genres, from opera, ballet and instrumental concertos to vocal, chamber and solo music – such as these expressive, mercurial, inventive *Homages* for piano.

21 October

Songs of the Auvergne
2: 'Baïlèro' – 'The Shepherd's Song'
by Joseph Canteloube (1879–1957)

Joseph Canteloube was born on this day into a family with a long and deep connection to the Auvergne region of France, so it's perhaps not surprising that the best part of his life's work was collecting, arranging, transcribing and orchestrating the folk music of his beloved local area. Canteloube, like Bartók et al., believed fervently that *'peasant songs often rise to the level of purest art in terms of feeling and expression'*, and he put his money where his mouth was, promoting their inherent value and unique beauty wherever he went.

In 1941, for example, during the Nazi occupation, Canteloube joined the Vichy government and made numerous radio broadcasts of national folk music, alongside tenor Christian Selva. The radio proved the perfect platform for disseminating popular music of the French regions and boosting public morale.

Meanwhile, Canteloube was busy compiling his great passion project: a comprehensive collection of Auvergne songs. Put together between 1924 and 1955, they lovingly paint the natural landscapes and traditions of the Auvergne in hyper-romantic orchestral colours and texts in the local dialect, Occitan. The collection brought the sound of rustic French melodies and folklore to the ears of millions.

This one, a pastoral song to a shepherd, is possibly the dreamiest of them all. If you can find six or so minutes to yourself today, close your eyes and let yourself be transported. If you can't, it still makes for a pretty idyllic soundtrack to modern life.

22 October

3 Pieces for cello and piano
1: Modéré
by Nadia Boulanger (1887–1979)

We've already encountered some of Boulanger's starry pupils in Philip Glass, Aaron Copland and Astor Piazzolla, as well as her protégé Igor Stravinsky and her sister Lili. Nadia herself was a force of nature. A fierce believer that you need to know the rules to break the rules, she had a rigour and respect for the past that helped shape the sound of the future.

The Boulanger sisters grew up in a household of music: their father Ernest was a composer, and friends such as Charles Gounod (3 June) and Gabriel Fauré (30 January, 15 May) would often pop round for a jam. At first, so the story goes, Nadia hated music, leaving the room whenever it was being played. Then, aged five, something switched: a melodious fire bell compelled her towards the family piano, where she attempted an imitation of its sound. She was hooked.

Nadia became a student at the Paris Conservatoire at ten and longed for success as a composer, entering the storied Prix de Rome – France's top composition prize – no fewer than four times, to no avail. It must have stung, then, when Lili won it in 1913, aged nineteen – the first woman ever to do so. Nadia gamely kept composing for a few more years – these lush cello pieces date from 1914 – but later committed herself to teaching, conducting and, after Lili's premature death, promoting her sister's music.

'Mademoiselle', as she was known, was indefatigable. Right up until she died – at ninety-two, on this day – she taught in her apartment on the rue Ballu, wearing thin bow ties, pince-nez, a long black dress, and her hair in a bun. She dished out *'advice on the good life'* and once told Quincy Jones *'your music can never be more, or less, than you are as a human being'*. My hero.

23 October

Canon and Gigue in D major
1: Canon
by Johann Pachelbel (1653–1706)

We've heard from quite a few one-hit wonders this year (oh hey, Vittorio Monti, Gregorio Allegri, Domenico Zipoli!) But arguably no classical composer fits so decisively into this category as poor old Johann Pachelbel. In his day, the German composer, organist and teacher was revered as one of the most important figures of the middle Baroque period: he wrote vast amounts of sacred and secular music, and was instrumental in developing the chorale prelude and fugue – with which Bach & co. would go on to do amazing things.

These days, though, you're unlikely to hear anything Pachelbel wrote except for this canon. And then, you're likely to hear it *all the blinking time* – on phone lines, piped through shopping centres, as background muzak everywhere from random elevators to the dentist. It's thought that it might have been written for the wedding of his student, J. S. Bach's brother Johann Christoph, on this day in 1694. Just imagine if Pachelbel had known of all the weddings it would later be played at, for time immemorial, everywhere? Truly, the mind boggles.

Truth be told, I deliberated hard over whether to include this or not: it's one of the best known pieces in all classical music, so familiar and so ubiquitous that its effect has been somewhat worn down with misuse. You certainly don't need me to bring it back into your life. Or do you? Listen again. It's actually so, so brilliant: a complex, circular conversation between three violins, a cello, and eight bars of music repeated twenty-eight times. And how's about that *bass-line?* So good it's been pilfered by musicians through the centuries ever since. (Yes, Jackson Five, I am looking at you – see e.g. 'I want you back'). Definitely worthy of another hearing, I hope you agree.

24 October

Rataplan
by Maria Malibran (1808–1836)

Maria Malibran was one of the most celebrated divas of her day: a singing sensation in Italy, France, the UK and US, as well as in her native Spain. Her many admirers included Rossini, Bellini, Donizetti, Liszt and Mendelssohn – who once wrote a special aria accompanied by solo violin for her and her partner, the Belgian violinist Charles de Bériot.

Malibran was legendary for her fiery personality, and was invariably described (by men) in excessive terms: an *'angel'* one day; an *'enchanting siren, setting her spectators on fire'* the next. Rossini, in whose operas her father Manuel García often appeared, and whose music she was also closely associated with, once declared:

> *Ah! That wonderful creature! With her disconcerting musical genius she surpassed all who sought to emulate her, and with her superior mind, her breadth of knowledge and unimaginable fieriness of temperament she outshone all other women I have known . . .*

(I love Rossini here for the fact he focuses on her 'superior mind', not her other attractions.) Because Malibran clearly was super-talented: as well as being a star singer, a mum and a common-law wife, she wrote her own music, producing around forty works for solo voice or duet before her untimely death after a horse-riding accident at the age of twenty-eight.

This effervescent little number means 'drumming sound'; in other words, *rat-ta-tat* . . .

25 October

Gala Water
by Sally Beamish (b. 1956)

It was a personal disaster that led to the British musician Sally Beamish becoming a composer: the theft, in 1989, of her beloved, irreplaceable viola.

She'd been composing ever since she was little. *'My mother gave me a little blue manuscript book, and showed me how to mark the staves'*, she recalls. *'The marks I made were flowers, faces – and I learned how their exact position on those five lines, or between them, translated miraculously into different notes from her violin.'* Between a busy freelance viola career and motherhood, however, composing fell by the wayside.

The loss of her viola changed all that. *'I made a conscious decision that something positive had to come out of this'*, she says. *'I wanted to be able to look back and say: "If my viola hadn't been stolen, then I would never have . . ." And what I wanted most of all was to become a full-time composer.'*

She moved from London to Scotland with her two young sons and husband, cellist Robert Irvine – whom we previously encountered through Eleanor Alberga (6 August). Inspired by her mentor, Peter Maxwell Davies (5 May), Beamish threw herself into composition, writing chamber, vocal, choral and orchestral music.

This deeply personal piece was written in 1994, Beamish explains, *'as an expression of our grief at the loss of a baby through miscarriage'*. Based on a local folk tune, 'Braw, braw lads of Gala Water', it exposes a range of raw emotions.

The couple later had a daughter. And in the cheering way that life can sometimes come full circle, aged eighteen Stephanie decided to become a professional luthier – a stringed-instrument maker. And guess what: she made her mother a viola.

26 October

Sonata in A major, Kk 208
by Domenico Scarlatti (1685–1757)

Domenico Scarlatti, whose father Alessandro was also an influential composer, represents a critical bridge between the Baroque and Classical periods. On the anniversary of his birth, I wanted you to hear one of the most gorgeous of the 555(!) keyboard sonatas that this prolifically talented Italian composer produced.

I'm an amazingly mediocre pianist, but even I can just about pick my way through this one – and I always find it an immensely meditative and nourishing experience when I do. It's four little minutes or so of clean, clarifying, music: balm for a frazzled mind and soul. I highly recommend you just stick it on wherever you are and let it do its lovely thing.

27 October

Cantabile in D major, op. 17
by Niccolò Paganini (1782–1840)

Back in April (and in July, via Rachmaninov) we encountered the Italian composer Niccolò Paganini, who had a reputation for being the king of virtuoso violin fireworks. And he was so protective over his technical trickery, in fact, so determined not to give away the violinistic secrets that made his name, that he allowed hardly any of his works to be published in his lifetime. Ten years after he died, a handful of pieces were printed, but it was not until the 1920s that authorities in his home town of Genoa, which had been sitting on stacks of manuscripts, finally released a comprehensive collection of his compositions.

What that collection revealed was that Paganini, who was born on this day, had so much more to him as a composer than the mere surface pyrotechnics for which he was internationally famous. Here was music with real heart and soul. It also seemed to indicate (a touch ironically?) that the music he preferred to play in private was generally a lot more chilled out than the stuff he produced for his awe-inspired public.

I love the aura of warmth and intimacy, for example, in this *Cantabile*, which means 'singing'. It was almost certainly written for Paganini to play at home, behind closed doors, with a friend.

28 October

Má vlast – My homeland
2. 'Vltava'
by Bedřich Smetana (1824–1884)

On Czech national day, may I present the ultimate Bohemian rhapsody.

In the way that we've seen Grieg become synonymous with Norwegian music, Sibelius with Finnish and Bartók with Hungarian, Bedřich Smetana promoted an innately Czech identity in his music. *Má vlast*, his suite of six 'symphonic poems' dedicated to the city of Prague, can be interpreted as an imaginative, ambitious and impassioned tribute to his homeland: its folklore, landscape, people and stories. In painting such a canvas, the fervently nationalist Smetana did something that had never been done before. It's even more remarkable that he wrote it while in the throes of going permanently deaf.

This spectacular movement traces, melodically, the course of the Vltava River from its source as it snakes majestically through Prague. The writer Václav Zelený, who worked on each movement's narrative with Smetana, explains that it sings *'of the first two springs, one warm the other cold, rising in the Bohemian forest; watches the streams as they join and follows the flow of the river through fields and woods [and] a meadow where the peasants are celebrating a wedding. In the silver moonlight the river nymphs frolic, castles and palaces float past, as well as ancient ruins growing out of the wild cliffs. The Vltava foams and surges in the Rapids of St John, then flows in a broad stream toward Prague. The high castle appears on its banks. The river strives on majestically, lost to view, finally yielding itself up to the Elbe'.*

A musical magic carpet if ever there was one!

29 October

Someone to Watch Over Me
by George Gershwin (1898–1937)
arr. Joseph Turrin (b. 1947)

We've already seen how George Gershwin (7 April, 11 July) was a singular musical synthesizer, intuitively able to combine elements of core classical music with emerging trends elsewhere in music, such as ragtime and jazz. He took as many cues from Milhaud, Satie and Stravinsky as he did from James P. Johnson and Duke Ellington, and was as ardently admired by the likes of Ravel and Prokofiev in Paris as he was by Alban Berg in Vienna. The great classical conductor Serge Koussevitzky once described seeing Gershwin in action at the keyboard: *'As I watched him, I caught myself thinking, in a dream state, that this was a delusion; the enchantment of this extraordinary being was too great to be real.'*

But is his music classical? Is it jazz? Who cares? Gershwin saw no virtue in restrictive labels on one side or the other. In 1933, he wrote: *'Jazz I regard as an American folk music; not the only one, but a very powerful one which is probably in the blood and feeling of the American people more than any other style of music. I believe that it can be made the basis of serious symphonic works of lasting value.'*

End of story.

This piece, originally written for the Broadway musical *Oh, Kay!*, was first recorded on this day in 1926. I love it with all my heart – especially in this version, arranged so lusciously by the contemporary American classical composer, Joseph Turrin.

30 October

Suite from *Appalachian Spring*
1: Very slowly
by Aaron Copland (1900–1990)

It was the wonderful American choreographer and dancer Martha Graham who commissioned Aaron Copland to write music for a ballet 'with an American theme'.

Copland turned to the traditional songs, dances and rituals of the American Shakers for inspiration. *Appalachian Spring* – originally just called 'Ballet for Martha' – tells a simple story: on the eve of their wedding, a young nineteenth-century couple contemplate their future; they then set up house in the American wilderness, encountering an itinerant preacher and a wise, sympathetic older pioneer woman. Between Copland's music and Graham's dance, the inner lives of all four characters are revealed, somehow transcending the simplicity of their particular story into a parable about Americans conquering a new land. Premiered on this day in 1944 at the Library of Congress in Washington, DC, it won Copland the Pulitzer Prize the following year.

The title came late to the project, on Graham's suggestion, and is a phrase from a poem by Hart Crane, 'The Dance':

> *O Appalachian Spring! I gained the ledge;*
> *Steep, inaccessible smile that eastward bends*
> *And northward reaches in that violet wedge*
> *Of Adirondacks! . . .*

(Copland later admitted that, having composed the music without knowing what the ballet would eventually be called, he was sheepishly amused when people told him he captured so perfectly the beauty of the Appalachians in his music.)

31 October

Missa Papae Marcelli
1. Kyrie
by Giovanni Pierluigi da Palestrina (1525–1594)

I considered suggesting spooky music for Halloween today, but decided the anniversary of an obscure Augustinian monk nailing ninety-five complaints against the Roman Catholic church to the castle church at Wittenburg was of marginally more significance to music history.

So there was Martin Luther, on this day in 1517, single-handedly kicking off the Protestant Reformation – and radically destabilizing the iron grip of Catholicism on Europe. In 1545, the leaders of the Catholic Church met in northern Italy for a twenty-year conference known as the Council of Trent and thus began the Counter-Reformation. This would have an impact on all aspects of religious and cultural life – including, as we saw with Thomas Tallis (7 August), music.

Church clergy had actually been pushing for a reform of the musical liturgy since as long ago as 1322, but it was during the Counter-Reformation that we hit what I shall term 'peak polyphony crisis', when the question of textual intelligibility was most vexed. The legend goes that the Council was threatening to outlaw polyphony altogether – unfathomable, given its sonic glories – until Roman church musician and choirmaster Palestrina heroically stepped in. He wanted to prove that a polyphonic composition could set text in such a way that the words could be clearly understood *and* still be complex and beautiful to the ear. His Mass for Pope Marcellus was duly performed before the Council, and met with such rapture that delegates swiftly changed their minds and allowed polyphony to remain. Hurrah!

Some details may or may not be apocryphal, but the legend endures: ever since, Palestrina has been hailed as the 'saviour' of church polyphony. And don't we love him for it.

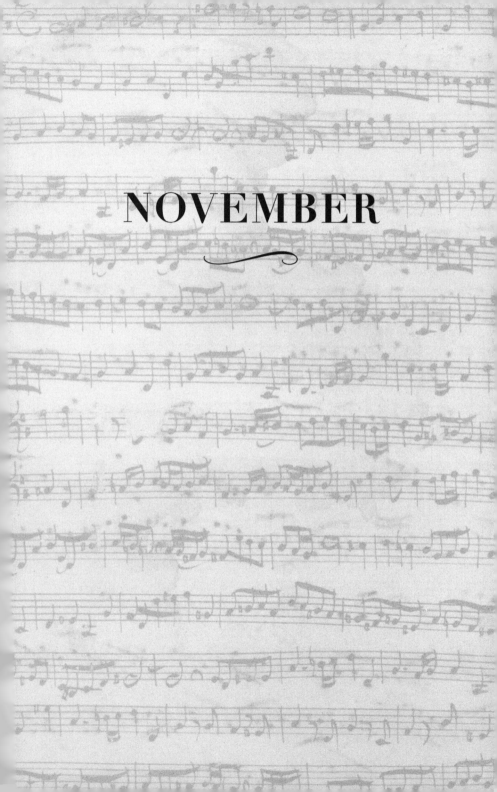

NOVEMBER

1 November

Symphony no. 9 in D minor ('Choral'), op. 125
4: Presto
by Ludwig van Beethoven (1770–1827)

It was on this day in 1993 that the Maastricht Treaty came into effect, marking the founding of the European Union (EU). A fitting day, then, to hear the iconic music on which the EU's official anthem is based.

The anthem gets played at all major occasions held by the EU and Council of Europe. Its objective, officially, is *'to celebrate the values [member states] share and their unity in diversity. It expresses the ideals of a united Europe: freedom, peace, and solidarity'.*

Beethoven was a fervent believer in Enlightenment values, and in this climactic fourth movement sets text from Friedrich Schiller's poem 'An die Freude' ('To Joy'), written in 1785 as a *'celebration of the brotherhood of man'.*

Deine Zauber binden wieder	*Your magic reunites*
Was die Mode streng geteilt;	*All that has customarily been*
Alle Menschen werden Brüder,	* strictly divided,*
Wo dein sanfter Flügel weilt.	*All men will become brothers,*
	Wherever your gentle wing rests . . .

The reach of this piece has been inestimable, heard everywhere from Japanese prisoner-of-war camps to Tiananmen Square, from the Beatles to Stanley Kubrick, from *Sister Act 2* to Fifa World Cup qualifiers. A spokesman for the German Chancellor Angela Merkel recently described it as *'a hymn to humanity, peace and international understanding'.* In other words:

Seid umschlungen, Millionen!	*. . . Be embraced, you millions!*
Diesen Kuß der ganzen Welt!	*This kiss is for the entire world.*

2 November

Parce mihi Domine
by Cristóbal de Morales (c. 1500–1553)

Time to meet the first Spanish composer to achieve international renown. Hugely prolific, well travelled and famous in his day, the music of Cristóbal de Morales was considered by certain critics of the time to be among the most perfect ever created. He wrote more than twenty masses and a hundred motets, many of which were distributed widely around Europe and even made it as far as Peru and Mexico. The earliest printed polyphony in the New World was, in fact, a book of Morales' masses from 1544, which can still be seen in the cathedral of Pueblo, Mexico.

This pacifying, purifying choral work sets text from Job. It comes from Morales' *Officium defunctorum* (the Office of the Dead): a prayer cycle said for the repose of the soul on All Souls' Day, which is today:

Parce mihi Domine,	*Spare me, O Lord,*
nihil enim sunt dies mei.	*for my days are nothing.*

3 November

For Now I am Winter
by Ólafur Arnalds (b. 1986)

If the November gloom is getting you down, spare a thought for our friends in Iceland, who live with only four to six hours of daily sunlight at this time of year. And on that note, a very happy birthday to the wonderful Icelandic musician Ólafur Arnalds, whom we met earlier this year paying homage, in his distinctive way, to his beloved Frédéric Chopin (9 August).

For many years, Arnalds felt compelled to keep his love for classical music on the down-low as he forged a much hipper path in hardcore, punk and electronica. Now, he's out and proud, as it were – and celebrated as one of the most dynamic and interesting voices on the contemporary classical scene. Hugely prolific and working across multiple genres, including film and television scores as well as concert-hall commissions, he's frank about one challenge facing millennial composers that their predecessors never had to deal with: how to eke out time to compose in an age of near-constant digital distraction. *'It's a matter of me deciding I'm going to sit down now and make music'*, he says. *'I turn off my phone and I turn off my computer. I sit there until something comes out.'*

For the album on which this track appears, Arnalds teamed up with another lavishly gifted thirty-something, Nico Muhly (26 August), for the orchestrations. It's a golden combination. This is intelligent, thoughtful, affecting music. I find the pristine vocal textures of this atmospheric choral work particularly nourishing, offering a gleam of sonic salvation.

'I've continued dealing with the idea of hope', Arnalds says. *'No matter how bad things seem, there is always light at the end of the tunnel . . .* For Now I am Winter *is asserting that the winter is never for ever. There's spring after winter.'* Praise be.

4 November

Piano Concerto in A minor, op. 16
2: Adagio
by Edvard Grieg (1843–1907)

Speaking of wintry northern climes, it was whilst on a holiday away from his native Norway that a twenty-four-year-old Edvard Grieg composed his magnificent piano concerto.

Grieg, who died on this day, had been much inspired by hearing Clara Schumann give a performance of her husband Robert's piano concerto (also in A minor, as it happens) around 1858. It would be another ten years before he put pen to paper on his, but it still bears the imprint of Schumann's influence – as well as the effects of Grieg's perennial preoccupation with evoking the sounds, traditions and melodic contours of his beloved homeland. (*'I am sure my music has a taste of codfish'*, he once joked.)

The concerto, whose first moment has one of the most famous openings in all of music, is characterized by a tremendous vitality throughout; this bittersweet but emotionally lustrous second movement seems to overflow with feeling. Like many pieces that are much loved today, the concerto was critically mauled at its premiere (see e.g. 24 April, 9 July, 20 September), but from the outset it found fans and admirers in leading musical figures such as Franz Liszt and Grieg's dear friend, Percy Grainger, who made it a cornerstone of his performance repertoire.

A little factoid for any tech geeks like me out there: this was the first ever piano concerto to be recorded – by pianist Wilhelm Backhaus, two years after Grieg's death. Due to the limits of technology at the time, it was edited down to a snappy six minutes.

5 November

Music for the Royal Fireworks, HWV 351
4: 'La Réjouissance': Allegro
by George Frideric Handel (1685–1759)

Handel's *Music for the Royal Fireworks* has nothing to do with today's tradition of Guy Fawkes' Night and bonfires in Britain, but as pyrotechnical music goes, it's hard to beat.

The piece was actually written to accompany a huge fireworks display in London's Green Park in 1749 to celebrate the end of the War of the Austrian Succession and the signing of the Treaty of Aix-la-Chapelle, seen as a major success for Britain. Before the grand ceremony took place in central London, near the royal residence of St James's Palace, a full public rehearsal was staged at the Vauxhall Pleasure Gardens, south of the river. Astonishingly, more than twelve thousand people rocked up, each paying two shillings and sixpence. The unexpected turnout caused a solid three-hour traffic jam of carriages on London Bridge – at the time the only way to cross the Thames around that stretch of the river.

This boggles my mind: I'm trying to think of pop stars, let alone classical composers, that could today command a paying audience of over twelve thousand people for a *rehearsal*. It just goes to show how central this music used to be to audiences of all backgrounds; and how the label of 'classical' or 'popular' is so nonsensical, so restricting, so pointlessly alienating. Popular music, surely, is *just stuff people like to listen to*; back in the day, everyone liked listening to this.

6 November

Density 21.5
by Edgard Varèse (1883–1965)

Remember earlier in the year when we heard that Frank Zappa was obsessed with the music of a relatively obscure Frenchman called Edgard Varèse (21 August)? Well here he is, a composer who had a particular focus on exploring the possibilities of timbre and rhythm, and who was ruthless in forging his own musical aesthetic, irrespective of the bafflement with which audiences sometimes greeted it. '*To stubbornly conditioned ears, anything new in music has always been called noise*', he once pointed out, adding: '*What is music but organized noises?*'

Indeed Varèse, who died on this day, tended to describe his work as 'organized sound' rather than 'music'; his ideas, as well as his pioneering adventures in electronics, would go on to have a profound influence on many composers of the post-war avant-garde, including John Cage (12 August).

Varèse moved to Manhattan and in 1927 took US citizenship, but he maintained close ties with his native Europe. This piece was composed at the request of French flautist Georges Barrère, for the premiere of his platinum flute – the density of platinum being around 21.5 grams per cubic centimetre. There are obvious limitations that arise when writing for any unaccompanied melodic instrument, even for the likes of Bach and Ysaÿe (see 16, 17 August). But Varèse pulls it off, teasing out the unique character of the flute and showing off its unexpectedly dramatic range: from its husky, sensual lower register to its pure and bird-like highest.

7 November

'La Nuit et l'amour' – 'Night and Love'
Interlude from *Ludus pro patria*
by Augusta Holmès (1847–1903)

We've already encountered the talented Irish-French pianist and composer Augusta Holmès in a roundabout way: it's said that César
Franck wrote the spectacular violin sonata we heard earlier in the year
(18 June) whilst in the throes of love for her. (An unfortunate situation
as he was married; and as we'll soon see, his wife did not take too
kindly to Franck's coded musical declarations of passion.)

Holmès's own romantic life was in any case complicated: she was
also beloved of Liszt, Saint-Saëns, Rimsky-Korsakov, Wagner and the
poet Catulle Mendès, with whom she had five children. Setting all that
aside, she's most interesting for her music. Holmès started composing at the age of twelve, began putting out music under a male
pseudonym, Hermann Zenta, and went on to write at least four
operas, a symphony, twelve symphonic poems and over 120 songs – for
which she also supplied her own poetry.

When her father died, Holmès, who never married, became the heir
to his fortune. Now independently wealthy and unattached, she was
able to publish under her own name and spend her money on whatever
she pleased. In her case, that was music lessons: she began studying
with Franck and produced some major works in this period. Unlike
some female composers who were constrained to stay within the supposedly 'respectable' confines of chamber music and art-song, she
favoured dramatic, epic, mythological subjects and had no qualms
about tackling gigantic canvases: for her *Triumphal Ode*, for example,
written in 1900 for the Paris World Exhibition, she called for no fewer
than nine hundred singers and a three-hundred-piece orchestra.

8 November

Piano Quintet in F minor, M. 7
1: Molto moderato quasi lento – Allegro
by César Franck (1822–1890)

Officially, this piece was dedicated to Franck's friend, the composer and pianist Saint-Saëns. *Unofficially*, Franck's mind was full of his student Augusta Holmès while he wrote it. Holmès, admitted Franck, *'arouses me in the most unspiritual desires'*. Unfortunately she had a similar effect on Saint-Saëns. *'This beautiful pythoness . . . caused [art] to flourish all about her,'* he remarked. *'As Venus fecundated the world when she knotted her tresses, so Augusta Holmès shook over us her reddish locks, and when she was prodigal with the lightning of her eyes and the brilliance of her voice, we ran to our pens, our brushes; and works were born.'* He'd proposed to Holmès a number of times and always been gently rebuked. (Pythoness!)

Saint-Saëns first played the quintet at the 1880 Paris premiere. Eyewitnesses describe him as becoming increasingly flustered and enraged, apparently reading some covert message into the music. At the end, he refused to shake hands with Franck and stormed offstage, leaving the score open at the piano – a gesture of explicit disdain.

The details may have been embellished, and it is possible Saint-Saëns simply disliked the music, but this emotionally charged piece certainly caused ructions in Parisian musical circles. Saint-Saëns discouraged further performances of the work, and Mrs Franck publicly condemned her husband and his *'impure and seductive student'*.

Humans, eh? Whatever the truth, it's an astonishing depiction of a heart and mind shredded by passion and conflict. For what it's worth, the relationship between Franck and Holmès remained close. He died on this day; Holmès commissioned a bronze medallion from Auguste Rodin for his tomb.

9 November

Cello Suite no. 2 in D minor, BWV 1008
4: Sarabande
by Johann Sebastian Bach (1685–1750)

On this morning in 1989, the celebrated cellist Mstislav Rostropovich was at home with his family in Paris when he heard radio reports of the Berlin Wall coming down. Born in Soviet Azerbaijan, raised in Baku and Moscow, Rostropovich had been a student of the persecuted Shostakovich. He and his wife had suffered under the Soviets for supporting the dissident writer Alexander Solzhenitsyn; expelled in 1974, Rostropovich was stripped of his citizenship. Exiled to the west, he knew all too well the spiritual deprivations of communism and the crushing effects of an oppressive regime.

And now this. *'The Berlin Wall was a symbol of a separation of humankind for him',* his daughter Olga recalled. *'So it was out of this world, surreal, we could not believe it. My father was overwhelmed with emotion. After a while he said, "I have to be there" – and then he disappeared.'*

With all commercial flights to Berlin booked, Rostropovich called a friend with a private plane. They arrived at Checkpoint Charlie the next day. Small problem: no chair. Cellists can't really play standing up. A chair procured, he sat down; took out his instrument; and as crowds of East and West Berliners gathered, began to play.

You can see footage online of the impromptu recital (remarkably, given the pre-smartphone age). There he is, in a jacket and tie, looking for all the world like somebody's kindly granddad, sitting in a rickety chair, in front of that wretched wall, his face etched with feeling, playing Bach, his whole soul pouring into those eternal, universal notes.

It became one of the iconic, enduring images from that momentous time.

10 November

Pieces for keyboard, Book 4, ord. 21e, no. 3
'La Couperin'
by François Couperin (1668–1733)

In September we encountered 'Couperin the Great' through the prism of his modern-day fanboy, Thomas Adès. On the anniversary of Couperin's birth, here he is writing three years previously: a keyboard solo of quietly meditative grace. It comes from Book 4 of the set of dozens of pieces that Couperin wrote for harpsichord and organized into 'orders' based on key signatures – in this case, E minor.

The clarity and surface simplicity of this work belies the technical revolutions being quietly wreaked by its brilliant composer – not least the use of a pianist's thumbs. Seriously: before Couperin, players used only eight fingers, which seems mad to us now, but there you go!

11 November

Brittany, op. 21 no. 1
by Ernest Farrar (1885–1918)

On Armistice Day, a moment to reflect on the lives of the many composers, from all sides, lost in the utter senselessness of the Great War. Britain was robbed of such talents as George Butterworth, Cecil Coles and William Denis Browne; Germany of the brilliant young Rudi Stephan; France of Albéric Magnard; Spain of Enrique Granados; Australia of Frederick Kelly. And so on, and so on. It's devastating to contemplate. Many of the brightest musical lights of the early twentieth century went out; other composers who were lucky enough to survive the conflict physically were nevertheless irrevocably affected by its horrors – Ravel, Vaughan Williams, Elgar, Alban Berg and innumerable others would be marked by their personal experiences of service or otherwise between 1914 and 1918.

I've chosen a lovely song from 1914 by Ernest Farrar, the much-loved teacher of Gerald Finzi (29 June, 27 September). Farrar enlisted in the Grenadier Guards in 1915 and in February 1918 was commissioned as Second Lieutenant, 3rd Battalion Devonshire Regiment. On his second day at the Western Front, Farrar was killed at the Battle of Epehy.

The war would end, on this day, just a few weeks later.

12 November

Three Pieces for two violins and piano
1: Praeludium
by Dmitri Shostakovich (1906–1975)

Nobody seems to know when or why Shostakovich wrote these Austrian-style salon vignettes for violin duet and piano accompaniment. In their easy charm and simplicity, they are, shall we say, somewhat uncharacteristic of his output – which in turn gets some critics all flustered. Was Shostakovich, a composer of such searing musical intellect, a victim of the horrors of Soviet artistic repression, making some kind of *satirical* comment? Are they *political*? What do they really *mean*?

To which I say: just press play and relax. The fact that among his many politically scarred, wracked and epic masterpieces Shostakovich also produced the odd bit of chamber music that is fleeting, expressive, poignant, unburdened by ideology and politics is okay: the world is not going to fall in. Sometimes, we all need a couple of minutes of music like this in our lives. They are among the first duets I ever played as a kid and I've loved them with all my heart ever since.

Anyway, it'll be back to business as usual next month: just wait until you hear Shostakovich's Tenth Symphony. Don't say I didn't warn you . . .

13 November

Forgotten Memories, First Cycle
'Sonata Reminiscenza' in A minor, op. 38. no. 1
by Nikolai Medtner (1880–1951)

Today we meet the man whom Sergei Rachmaninov considered *'the most talented of all contemporary composers ... One of those rare people – as a musician and a human being – who grow in stature the closer you get to them'*.

Not everyone would have agreed with his rhapsodic assessment of the Russian-born, Paris-based pianist and composer Nikolai Medtner, who died on this day. The views Medtner held about music could not have been less fashionable at the time. Insisting on the primacy of lyric melody, tonality and form, he had no truck with any aspect of the musical trends destabilizing everything around him, from Schoenberg's serialism to Stravinsky's neoclassicism. In this sense, Medtner was a man catastrophically out of place, out of time.

Given his preoccupations as a writer of piano music, it was Beethoven, perhaps unsurprisingly, who was his ultimate hero: *'The greatest representative of [the piano sonata], Beethoven conceived his sonatas as one song'*, he noted, *'which by the simplicity of its theme and its vertical correlation, from the beginning to the end of each of his works, illumined to us the whole complexity of his architectonic construction and of his horizontal correlation.'*

Such highfalutin statements were considered so outdated by the time Medtner was peddling his brand of musical conservatism around modernist Europe that he was ignored at best, ridiculed at worst. Largely unknown to the general public, he spent most of his life in abject poverty and even now his name tends to be heard only in the most niche piano circles. But I was knocked sideways when I first heard this sonata, jam-packed as it is with ideas, with lyrical melodies and rich, surprising, satisfying harmonies. Hey, if it's good enough for Rachmaninov ...

14 November

Fantasia in G minor
by Fanny Mendelssohn (1805–1847)

Perhaps it's because it's November, but I seem to be drawn inexorably to minor keys this month; bear with me though, because while Fanny Mendelssohn opens her *Fantasia* for cello and piano with a somewhat melancholic and brooding tonal palette, she soon ups both mood and tempo, throwing open the shades to let in light and lyricism in abundance.

As ever with Fanny's music, I'm so struck by her musical imagination, her great sensitivity and the sheer directness with which she seems to want to communicate with us. Remember, this is the woman who was so desperate to express herself in this way that she wrote over 450 pieces, despite the lack of support from even those closest to her and the fact there was little hope of them ever being published.

Remember, too, how virtuosic Fanny was as a pianist: how she could play practically anything she turned her attention to, how Felix himself admitted she was far superior a pianist to him? Yet Fanny, who was born on this day, made just one public appearance, as the soloist in her brother's first piano concerto at a benefit concert. What must it have been like to have to sit on her hands like that, as it were? Almost nothing of Fanny's music was published in her lifetime; lots of it today remains in private collections. Perhaps that means that many more pieces that have been attributed for centuries to Felix may yet turn out to be by his sister. Who knows? We've seen a growing critical interest in Fanny's work in recent years; I sincerely hope this is just the beginning . . .

15 November

Symphony no. 2 in C minor ('Resurrection')
4: 'Urlicht' – primeval light
by Gustav Mahler (1860–1911)

Rather than being drawn to write youthful music in his, well, youth, Mahler spent his twenties trying to solve the riddles of the universe, treating the symphony as a vehicle in which he could pose the thorniest questions of life and try to figure out his complex and wracked belief system. *'The symphony'*, he once told Jean Sibelius, *'must be like the world; it must embrace everything.'*

Mahler was around twenty-seven when he began work on this particular all-encompassing embrace. He initially devised a 'programme' for it: the first movement, he explained, represents a funeral and explores questions such as *'Is there life after death?'* (no biggie); the second looks back to happier times; the third tackles the futility of life; the fourth longs for a release from the meaningless woes of worldly being; and the fifth revisits previous doubts and questions to make a final, transcendent stretch for everlasting renewal. All pretty casual stuff, then. Although Mahler later withdrew the programme, it gives us a revealing insight into his mindset at the time.

For some listeners, this is all too much: Mahler's symphonies are just too big, too ripe, too unwieldy. For others, the symphonies represent the zenith of human artistic endeavour. For me, they're pretty much the noblest musical attempts I can think of, except perhaps Bach's Passions or Bruckner's Ninth, to 'eff the ineffable' (for want of a better way of putting it). I'm not alone. A recent Proms performance of the 'Resurrection' symphony reportedly received the longest-ever ovation of anything performed there. And in 2016, the original handwritten score was sold at Sotheby's for £4.5 million, so far the highest ever price for a musical manuscript sold at auction.

16 November

Beata viscera
by Pérotin (*fl.* 1160–1225)

This music might seem mind-spinningly ancient and other-worldy to us, composed as it was around 1220, but in writing this monophonic 'conductus', which celebrates the 'blessed flesh' of the Virgin Mary, the medieval French composer known as Pérotin was actually writing at the height of fashion. A 'conductus' meant creating a brand-new melody rather than calling upon an existing chant: it was pretty radical.

Elsewhere, Pérotin is believed to have been responsible for introducing four-part polyphony into Western music – for which we can all mightily thank him – but beyond that, and the fact he probably worked at the Cathedral of Notre Dame in Paris, we know almost nothing about him. Still – 1220! What a thought.

17 November

Bachianas brasileiras, no. 5
1. Aria (Cantilena)
by Heitor Villa-Lobos (1887–1959)

Yesterday's twelfth-century monophonic chant segues beautifully, I think, into today's similarly unusual piece featuring a single, soaring vocal line. It's like a sonic wink across time and space, whether intentional or not.

As we saw back in September, Villa-Lobos, who died on this day, was preoccupied with finding a musically compelling way to combine his interest in European music with the sounds, themes and feelings of his native Brazil. His set of nine suites of so-called *Bachianas brasileiras* are perhaps the most perfect expression of this, reflecting as they do his twin passions for Bach and Brazil.

It's not that they exactly fuse local folk tropes with high German Baroque; rather that Villa-Lobos ingeniously and lovingly adapts and applies Bachian harmonic or contrapuntal procedures to Brazilian music – to unusual, unforgettable effect.

This fifth, composed between 1938 and 1945, is particularly dreamy, with a solo soprano over an accompaniment of eight cellos. Opening with an expansive, adagio aria, as Bach himself might have done (see 17 September), the piece soon progresses to a spirited Latin-inflected *danza*. This, explained the composer, '*represents a persistent and characteristic rhythm much like the emboladas, those strange melodies of the Brazilian hinterland*'. The melody, he adds, '*suggests the birds of Brazil*'.

Tarde, uma nuvem rósea, lenta e transparente.	*Afternoon, a rosy, slow and transparent cloud in the air, dreamy and beautiful!*
Sobre o espaço, sonhadora e bela!	
Surge no infinito a lua docemente,	*The Moon sweetly emerges into infinity,*
Enfeitando a tarde . . .	*Decorating the afternoon like a gentle maiden.*

359

18 November

Musica ricercata no. 7 in B flat major
by György Ligeti (1923–2006)

Along with the likes of Pierre Boulez (26 March) and John Cage (12 August), the Hungarian composer György Ligeti has to be one of the most vital and progressive figures of the post-war avant-garde in music. Beyond the niche confines of the contemporary classical scene, his music has also reached wide mainstream audiences thanks to superfan director Stanley Kubrick using it in films such as *2001: A Space Odyssey* (1968) and *The Shining* (1980).

The composer Thomas Adès (24 September) says he hears in Ligeti's music what he described to my BBC Radio 3 colleague Tom Service as *'the heat-death of the universe'*. (Is *that* all?) Even taking a less extreme view, this frenetic piano piece, which was premiered on this day, does always strike me as a fine musical metaphor for modern life: on the surface, I give you the right hand, with its smooth, serene, high notes; underneath, meanwhile, witness relentless chaos bubbling away. (Or is that just my life?)

That roiling left hand certainly injects the piece with a restless, antsy momentum, so if you have somewhere to get to in a hurry, I find this to be terrifically energizing music. Go go go!

19 November

~~~~~~~~~~~

Ground after the Scotch Humour
by Nicola Matteis (*fl.* 1670–1713)

On this day in 1674, the great British diarist (and contemporary of Samuel Pepys) John Evelyn had been out and about in London, catching one of the hot tickets of the time. In his diary that night, he noted the following:

> *I heard that stupendious violinist Signor Nicola (with other rare Musitians) whom certainly never mortal man Exceeded on that instrument, he had a stroak so sweete, & made it speake like the Voice of a man; & when he pleased, like a Consort of severall Instruments: he did wonders upon a Note: was an excellent Composer also. Nothing approch'd the violin in Nicola's hand: he seem'd to be spiritato'd & plaied such ravishing things on a Ground as astonishd us all.*

We don't know if that piece by Matteis, a travelling Neapolitan fiddler and composer of many a ground, was this one – but it certainly fits the bill: *stupendious* and *spiritato'd* indeed . . .

20 November

White Light Chorale
by Param Vir (b. 1952)

The Delhi-born composer Param Vir grew up in a sonorous household: his mother was a singer of classical north Indian music. Aged nine, he started the piano, and as a teenager became captivated by Western music alongside the traditional Indian forms he was absorbing all around him. ('*Ragas, talas, plainsong, Palestrina, Strauss and 12-tone rows all meeting in the mind of a teenager in post-colonial Delhi?*' he recalls. '*This was surely a fortuitous conjunction of influences!*') In 1983, Vir met Peter Maxwell Davies (5 May) who encouraged him to move to Britain, where he studied at the Guildhall School of Music and Drama and won a raft of composition prizes.

Vir draws his inspiration from a wide pool, including mythology, folklore art, poetry, literature and sculpture; especially that of his countryman Anish Kapoor. He writes across multiple genres: chamber music, symphonic works, opera and theatre; he's relentlessly curious, and resistant to labels. '*The world today is an extraordinary meeting-point for divergent identities, cultures, languages, thought forms, and ideologies all jostling together in some amazing dance*', he says, adding: '*I'm interested in the culture of the whole world.*'

One of Vir's preoccupations is colour and its effect on perception. Given the culture from which he hails, when he talks about this stuff it feels less wacky than it might otherwise. '*I am interested in qualities of colour embodied in the chakra spectrum of energy*', he explains. '*We now know that we respond to certain colours because they have a very specific resonance with our energy structure, and different colours have very different therapeutic or healing or energizing properties.*'

For this solo piano chorale, written in 2000, he evokes white light and the effect is luminous.

21 November

~~~

'When I am laid in earth'
from *Dido and Aeneas*
by Henry Purcell (1659–1695)

On the anniversary of Henry Purcell's death today, the ultimate lament.

There are all sorts of technical reasons this emotionally eviscerating piece has had such a seemingly universal impact – *passus duriusculus*, anyone? – but they don't need to be understood to be felt. Put simply(ish), Purcell takes a five-bar 'ground bass' – a repeating bass-line; what we would these days call a 'loop' – with its notes descending inexorably in despair. Then, he decides not to fit the tune going over the top into a matching five-bar unit, which we might expect, but instead stretches it over a *nine*-bar phrase, with that loop going on underneath all the time. So we're already a little messed-up and wrong-footed by that, even before this yearning, wrenching melodic line with its heartstring-tugging leans and swerves (technically called grace notes or 'appogiaturas') hits us.

And then, boy, it *really* hits us. '*Remember me!*' Dido pleads, initially on a single repeated note before swooning upwards in a final, beyond-desperate imperative: '*Remember me!*'

It's so damn simple; so damn heartbreaking. Has there ever been a more human, more mortal utterance?

> *When I am laid, am laid in earth, May my wrongs create*
> *No trouble, no trouble in thy breast;*
> *Remember me, remember me, but ah! forget my fate.*
> *Remember me, but ah! forget my fate.*

22 November

Hymn to St Cecilia
by Benjamin Britten (1913–1976)

Britten's birthday, on this day, happily coincides with St Cecilia's day. She was the patron saint of music, and the composer had long imagined writing something to celebrate their joint day. His friend W. H. Auden wrote him a beautiful poem, which Britten would go on to set in a playful and beguiling chorus.

Ardent pacifists, Britten and his partner, the tenor Peter Pears, travelled to the USA in April 1939. When war broke out, they were advised to stay in the US as 'cultural ambassadors'. Within three years they were compelled to return home. But on the day they travelled, US customs inspectors confiscated the musical manuscripts from Britten's luggage, suspecting them of being some sort of code. Among the stash was the *Hymn to St Cecilia*.

Incredibly, Britten managed to recreate the whole thing from scratch while he and Pears sailed to London on the MS *Axel Johnson*. It was first broadcast by the BBC on Britten's twenty-ninth birthday/St Cecilia's day, 1942.

> *In a garden shady this holy lady*
> *With reverent cadence and subtle psalm,*
> *Like a black swan as death came on*
> *Poured forth her song in perfect calm . . .*
>
> *. . . Blessed Cecilia, appear in visions*
> *To all musicians, appear and inspire:*
> *Translated Daughter, come down and startle*
> *Composing mortals with immortal fire.*

23 November

Siete canciones populares españolas
4. Jota
by Manuel de Falla (1876–1946)
arr. Paul Kochanski (1887–1934)

We celebrate another musical birthday today: that of the leading Spanish composer Manuel de Falla.

By the time he wrote this suite in 1914, Falla had been living in Paris for seven years, where he'd fallen in with a fashionable musical crowd that included Debussy, Ravel and Stravinsky. You can hear strains of their signature impressionism and neoclassicism infusing his work from this period, but, like his fellow Spaniards Isaac Albéniz and Enrique Granados, Falla never loses sight of his roots. *'The harmonic effects that our guitarists produce,'* he once observed, *'unconsciously represent one of the wonders of natural art.'* Falla remained captivated by the traditional musical material of his native land and within a year of writing this had returned to Madrid.

Originally written for voice and piano, this suite is basically a sheaf of love letters to various regions of his beloved Spain, from Asturias in the north to Andalusia in the south. They are, as you might expect, brimful of smashing dance rhythms – such as this Aragonese jota – and catchy melodies, although at times Falla also references the darker colours of the gypsy flamenco tradition. The suite has subsequently been arranged for all sorts of combinations: such is its vivacity and appeal that the music seems to work any which way. I'm particularly taken by a version for violin and piano, by turns deliciously spiky and sensual.

24 November

Three Sacred Hymns
1. 'Hail Mary, full of grace, mother of God'
by Alfred Schnittke (1934–1998)

'*The goal of my life*', Alfred Schnittke once revealed, '*is to unify serious music and light music, even if I break my neck in doing so.*' The neck remained intact: Schnittke didn't quite achieve his goal. I'd say we still have some way to go on that front. But at least he gave it a noble shot.

Soviet-Jewish by background, Schnittke was much influenced in his early composing career by Dmitri Shostakovich; and then by serialists such as Arnold Schoenberg. Later, he became disenchanted with what he referred to, sidelong, as the '*puberty rites of serial self-denial*'. As he put it: '*Having arrived at the final station, I decided to get off the already overcrowded train. Since then I have tried to proceed on foot.*'

That ambulant and individualistic spirit took Schnittke into a mode dubbed 'polystylism': as the name suggests, he mixed and matched a multiplicity of styles from both past and present, according to the whims – sometimes eccentric, sometimes brooding – of his vast creative imagination. His biographer writes that Schnittke, who was born on this day, '*fell in love with music which is part of life, part of history and culture, part of the past which is still alive*' – a grand way of putting it.

Schnittke himself talked of the importance, as human beings, of '*holding on to the feeling that the mystery is truly limitless*'. You can hear his faith in that principle in the spare and mysterious vocal textures of this lofty setting of the Ave Maria.

25 November

___

Adagio for Strings
by Samuel Barber (1910–1981)

It was on this day in 1963 that Jacqueline Kennedy convened the National Symphony Orchestra in Washington, DC, for the state funeral of her husband, John F. Kennedy, who had been assassinated in Dallas, Texas, three days earlier. Broadcasting on the radio to millions, the orchestra performed Samuel Barber's *Adagio for Strings*.

The *Adagio*, adapted from the slow movement of Barber's 1936 string quartet, was said to be the slain president's favourite piece of music. It has also been used at the funerals of Albert Einstein, Princess Grace, and at official memorials for Diana, Princess of Wales, and the victims of the 9/11 terrorist attacks.

The piece has become a shorthand for unutterable sorrow.

Barber was twenty-six when he wrote it.

I'll let the music speak for itself.

26 November

Music for Pieces of Wood
by Steve Reich (b. 1936)

A terrific example, today, of music that does what it says on the tin: this indeed is music for pieces of wood, no more, no less. Written in 1995 for five players, the idea grew, says Reich, *'out of a desire to make music with the simplest possible instruments'*. Each player has a pair of wooden claves, the sorts of cylindrical pieces of hard wood you might find in a toddler's toy box, here selected for their particular pitches and resonant timbre.

The piece is modelled on Reich's signature 'phasing' technique, where a single rhythmic figure is *'offset and overlapped with itself in a constantly evolving composite texture'*. Its scintillating, addictive rhythmic structure is based on the process of rhythmic 'buildups' or the substitution of beats for rests, and plays out in three sections of ever-decreasing pattern length – 6/4, 4/4, 3/4 – until eventually the whole thing expires, spent.

Whether you're aware of those mathematical patterns or not, the overall effect is mesmerizing. I'll never forget the first time I ever heard this: years later, it has lost none of its capacity to thrill.

27 November

'Hymn to the Dawn'
from *Choral Hymns from the Rig Veda*
by Gustav Holst (1874–1934)

The chances are you've probably heard music by Gustav Holst, whether you knew it or not: his suite *The Planets* is ubiquitous, 'Mars' and 'Jupiter' in particular being regularly called into service by all sorts – advertisers, film composers, Led Zeppelin, and so on.

But many years before Holst immortalized his place in musical history with those celestial bodies, this most English of composers (who elsewhere busied himself collecting rural Somerset folk songs and teaching at a private girls' secondary school) was finding his compositional voice through a deep fascination with ancient Indian culture. In 1907, amid a sudden craze in artistic circles for all things Eastern, Holst bought a copy of the three-thousand-year-old collection of Vedic hymns known as the *Rig Veda*. Between 1908 and 1912, having learned Sanskrit in order to translate the poetry himself, Holst then set a selection of them to music – and it marked a significant moment in his development.

This eerie and unusual hymn to the dawn is scored for the haunting combination of women's voices and harp. It confects an atmosphere and mood that is quite unlike anything else in Holst's output – or that I've heard anywhere else, in fact.

> *Hear our hymn, O Goddess,*
> *Rich in wealth and wisdom,*
> *Ever young yet ancient,*
> *True to Law Eternal . . .*

28 November

Nocturne no. 8 in D flat major, op. 27 no. 2
by Frédéric Chopin (1810–1849)

We've heard many different nocturnes over the course of the year – from John Field, eighteenth-century godfather of the form (17 March) and twenty-first-century reinventor Dobrinka Tabakova (17 July) to Chopin's Polish predecessor Maria Szymanowska (25 July) and that haunting contemporary Icelandic take from Ólafur Arnalds and Alice Sara Ott (9 August).

In a way they've all been leading up to this, because more than anyone, Chopin takes the raw material of a nocturne – a liquid, free-wheeling bel canto-style melody in the right hand; dramatic broken rhythms in the left – and alchemizes it with his singular musical genius into miniatures that contain multitudes. Lyrically sumptuous and hyperromantic on the surface; you'll find, nonetheless, that there's darkness in them there depths. *'Guns buried in flowers'* is how Robert Schumann memorably put it.

There are twenty-one of the beauties to choose from. I've suggested one of my all-time favourites (with a metaphorical, editorial gun to my head), but if you're in need of a bit of soul maintenance you could do much worse than finding an album of the complete Chopin *Nocturnes* and letting them all, every single one, work their individual magic on you.

29 November

'Pur ti miro' – 'I gaze at you'
from *The Coronation of Poppea*
by Claudio Monteverdi (1567–1643)

In March, we encountered Monteverdi the maverick madrigalist: here he is, on the anniversary of his death, proving why he was also such a revolutionary force for the development of opera: the first composer to recognize the dramatic and emotional potential of throwing music, words, action and stagecraft together in a single heady mix.

It sounds obvious now, but before Monteverdi, no composer had put the concerns of actual humans front and centre of the musical experience. According to music writer Jan Swafford, Monteverdi was the first to '*create opera out of characters who live, breathe, love and hate*'.

The ones in *The Coronation of Poppea* (1643) certainly do a whole lot of loving and hating. The setting is ancient Rome, AD65. Nero, the Roman emperor, is married to Octavia but in love with Poppea, who is engaged to Otho, who is in turn beloved of Drusilla. Basing his opera on historical events and real people, Monteverdi weaves gripping drama out of the morally ambiguous story of how adulterous Poppea achieves her ambition and is crowned empress.

As we'll hear in this ravishing duet, Monteverdi also prefigured the modern song, eschewing the polyphony that was everywhere in the Renaissance, in which all vocal elements are equal, and instead exploring the futuristic possibility that words and feelings could be more directly conveyed through a single melodic line over accompaniment:

Pur ti miro,	*I gaze at you,*
Pur ti stringo,	*I embrace you,*
Pur ti godo	*I desire you*

30 November

Miserere
by James MacMillan (b. 1959)

On St Andrew's Day, music from a towering presence in British cul-tural life: the Ayrshire-born Sir James MacMillan.

A devout Catholic and a smart, engaged presence on social media, MacMillan embraces matters of spirituality and politics head-on, where many others would play it safe. (Imagine: he does God *and* poli-tics!) 'Jimmy', as he introduces himself, is cheering proof that you can be a classical composer of transcendent order yet not lock yourself away in the proverbial ivory tower. As a composer he is invariably in dialogue with his God but he uses his giant brain, he engages his heart, he gets his hands dirty with the stuff of human life; he's one of us.

And then, the music. *The music.* The first time I encountered it, I was at university and happened to be walking along a street near one of the college chapels out of which was pouring this sublime noise. Hypnotized, I followed the sound and found myself watching a choir rehearsing for a concert that evening. Immobilized by beauty, I felt the music wash over me, into me, transport me onto a different plane of being. Spiritually high, when the rehearsal finished I asked someone what had just happened. *'James MacMillan'*, came the reply. *'Seven Last Words from the Cross.'* I cancelled my plans for that evening, went to the concert, bought the CD, and have been addicted ever since.

His punchy and gut-wrenching *Miserere* setting gives a nod to Allegri (7 February) in its plainsong and harmonies, but does some-thing altogether different. MacMillan unleashes these big expressive outbursts, juxtaposed with moments of virtual silence, then resolves everything into a catharsis of pure and exquisite E major. This is a profoundly personal setting, but universal, I think, in its directness.

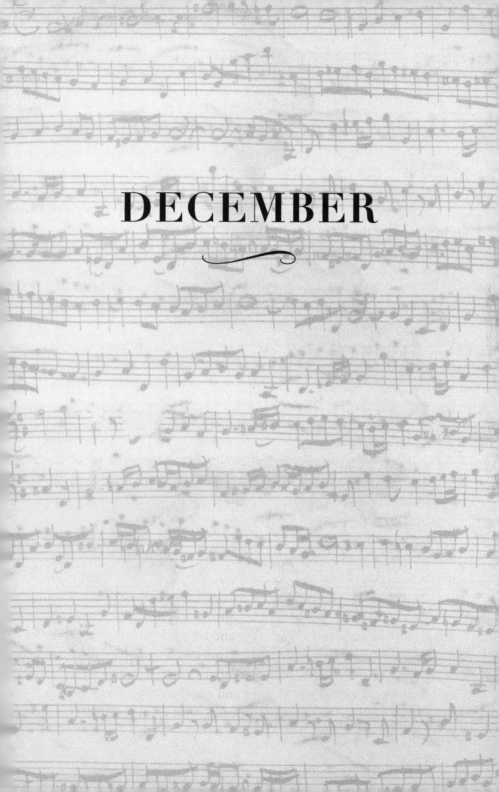

DECEMBER

1 December

~~~~~~~~

O Magnum Mysterium
by Morten Lauridsen (b. 1943)

Well, hello December. The last month of our musical year. I promise we're not about to embark on an entire month of Christmas music. I still have so much non-festive music to share with you (and by now you're probably hearing carols everywhere you go anyway).

But just to set the tone for the festive season, I wanted to start December with one of the most beautiful nativity settings I have ever heard. This was composed in 1994 by the American composer, Morten Lauridsen, whom we first met all the way back in January and who joins the ranks of composers with unusual day jobs (Philip Glass the taxi driver/plumber; Borodin the groundbreaking chemist; Delius the orange-picker, and so on). A son of America's Pacific Northwest, before he went to study composition in California, Lauridsen worked as a firefighter for the Forest Service and was a lookout on an isolated tower near Mount St Helens.

These days, the US National Medal of Arts-winner divides his time between Los Angeles and an island in the San Juan Archipelago, in his native Washington State, which he calls his 'composing refuge'. I think you can hear that sense of space, of scope, of awe-inspiring natural perspective infusing his music. O great mystery indeed . . .

O magnum mysterium,	*O great mystery,*
et admirabile sacramentum,	*and wonderful sacrament,*
ut animalia viderent Dominum	*that animals should see the*
natum,	*Lord born,*
iacentem in praesepio!	*lying in a manger!*

2 December

'Mon coeur s'ouvre à ta voix' – 'My heart opens itself up to
your voice' from *Samson and Delilah*
by Camille Saint-Saëns (1835–1921)

If you were a young and ambitious French composer in the mid-
nineteenth century, the chances are you'd really want to be taken
seriously by writing a successful opera. Opera was still the most
highly regarded musical form, so although Saint-Saëns had produced
many other acclaimed works by the late 1870s, his lack of recognition
in the operatic world so far was a source of frustration.

All that was to change with his take on the story of Samson and
Delilah, which was premiered on this day in 1877. Not that it was
immediately smooth sailing for the project: its biblical subject matter
raised eyebrows in his native France, and the Paris Opéra refused to
stage it. Only after the wrangling of Saint-Saëns' friend Franz Liszt,
who had until recently been music director in Weimar, was it given a
staging at all – in Germany, in a German translation. Saint-Saëns had
to wait until 1892 to supervise a production at his beloved Paris Opéra,
by which time it was an avowed hit: that same year it was produced
everywhere from Monaco to Florence to New Orleans.

This incredibly beautiful aria comes from Act 2, as Delilah attempts
to lure Samson into revealing the secret of his strength.

Mon cœur s'ouvre à ta voix,	*My heart opens itself up to your*
comme s'ouvrent les fleurs	*voice*
aux baisers de l'aurore!	*Like the flowers open themselves up*
	To the kisses of the dawn!

What an image! What a song!

3 December

Fandango
by Antonio Soler (1729–1783)

A funky little foot-tapper today from a radical-thinking priest who also happened to be one of the great Spanish composers of the late eighteenth century. Padre Soler, who was baptized on this day, studied with Domenico Scarlatti (26 October), took holy orders at the age of twenty-three and became organist at the magnificent Hyeronimite monastery El Escorial, near Madrid, built during the Spanish Renaissance.

Soler was a brilliant musician and became the go-to keyboard teacher for the Spanish royal family. As a composer, his music encompasses keyboard writings, church cantatas, chamber works for unusual combinations, instrumental concertos and incidental music for a play by Calderón, the Spanish Golden Age's answer to Shakespeare. In his music you can hear the mind of a curious and ambitious maverick at work: Soler dabbles in unexpected harmonic progressions, complex canons and even musical microtones (which in turn required him to invent a whole new keyboard instrument, the *afinador*). In 1762 he collected some of his ideas into a book on musical theory, *The Key to Modulation*, which caused something of a controversy among harmonic traditionalists.

I particularly love this box-fresh fandango. Truly, Soler's approach to dropping the bass could teach a modern DJ a thing or two.

4 December

Violin Concerto in D major, op. 35
1. Allegro moderato
by Pyotr Ilyich Tchaikovsky (1840–1893)

Summer probably seems a distant memory by now, but you may remember back in June we heard Tchaikovsky's melancholy 'Barcarolle' from *The Seasons* and I mentioned that his sham marriage to a student triggered, in the closeted gay composer, a disastrous spell of depression, attempted suicide and writer's block.

It was to a resort in Switzerland that Tchaikovsky went to try and put himself back together. At first, things did not go so well. Struggling to compose a new piano sonata, he wrote to his brother: '*I worked unsuccessfully, with little progress . . . I'm again having to force myself to work, without much enthusiasm . . . I'm having to squeeze out of myself weak and feeble ideas, and ruminate over each bar. But I keep at it, and hope that inspiration will suddenly strike.*'

It did. Before long, Tchaikovsky's muse quite literally returned in the form of another of his students, the violinist Iosif Kotek. It's long been understood by music historians that the two were lovers; whatever the nature of their relationship, we know that they made a lot of music together and Tchaikovsky was soon sufficiently recovered to put pen to paper on one of the finest pieces ever written for the violin – the Concerto in D major, which was premiered on this day in 1881. Kotek gave the composer invaluable advice from a soloist's perspective. '*How lovingly he busies himself with my concerto!*' Tchaikovsky told his brother. '*It goes without saying that I would have been able to do nothing without him. He plays it marvellously!*'

Tchaikovsky initially dedicated the concerto to Kotek but then changed his mind, telling his publisher he was wary of the gossip this would engender. Kotek never forgave him.

5 December

Symphonie fantastique, op. 14
2: 'Un bal'
by Hector Berlioz (1803–1869)

If yesterday's piece was (probably) inspired by illicit love, today's was (definitely) inspired by the unrequited sort.

Berlioz is one of music's great romantics, prone to weeping over works by his heroes Virgil, Shakespeare and Beethoven. 'Awe-inspired' by the latter, he also adored the music of Christoph Willibald Gluck (5 October) and went on to influence many later Romantics, including Wagner, Liszt, Strauss and Mahler.

In early 1829, the composer revealed to a friend: *'For some time I have had a descriptive symphony . . . in my brain. When I have released it, I mean to stagger the musical world.'* And stagger it he did. Finished when Berlioz was twenty-six and premiered on this day in 1830, *Symphonie fantastique* is subtitled 'An Episode in the Life of an Artist'. The condition Berlioz was seeking to 'describe' was his overpowering infatuation for an Irish actress called Harriet Smithson, whom he had first seen in an 1829 production of *Hamlet* at Paris's Odéon theatre.

He'd obsessively tried to win her heart ever since, to no avail. *'Can you tell me what it is'*, he wrote to another friend, *'this capacity for emotion, this force of suffering that is wearing me out? . . . Oh my friend, I am indeed wretched – inexpressibly! . . . Today it is a year since I saw HER for the last time . . . Unhappy woman, how I loved you! I shudder as I write it – how I love you!'*

But never let it be said that music is not a powerful thing: *Symphonie fantastique* eventually won Smithson over and in October 1833 they were married. (The union was sadly not to last.)

6 December

Lux Aurumque
by Eric Whitacre (b. 1970)

Another nod towards Christmas today in this luminous work for mixed chorus by the Grammy-winning American composer Eric Whitacre.

He is a terrific example of a contemporary composer who's had a wide reach beyond the confines of the classical world. He has addressed the UN Speaker's Programme and the World Economic Forum; appeared at the iTunes Festival; and given two main stage TED talks based on his Virtual Choir project, which ingeniously brought together singers from at least 110 countries all over the globe in a digital 'performance' of this work, which was uploaded onto YouTube in 2011. (It has since been viewed well over five million times: not bad for a piece of contemporary classical choral music.)

Although it's sung in Latin, the inspiration for the piece came from a poem in English, 'Light and Gold', by Whitacre's contemporary Edward Esch – whose *'genuine, elegant simplicity'*, he says, immediately appealed. Whitacre explains: *'A simple approach was essential to the success of the work, and I waited patiently for the tight harmonies to shimmer and glow.'*

They do exactly that.

7 December

In the Mists
1: Andante
by Leoš Janáček (1854–1928)

Leoš Janáček didn't write a lot of piano music, but what he did is wonderfully distinctive. Rather than peddling the sort of technical pyrotechnics many composers feel compelled to conjure on a keyboard (thanks to the example set by Liszt & co.), he instead goes for maximum atmosphere. I love the brooding, evocative opening for example of his last work for piano, the cycle *In the Mists*, whose first public performance took place on this day in 1913.

This is wintry mood music that could not be further in feel from the brassy, brilliant Sinfonietta by Janáček that we heard earlier in the year (26 June). It reflects a more introspective aspect of this fascinating composer's musical temperament, in that he had just emerged from a difficult period both personally – his daughter, Olga, had died in 1903 – and professionally – he was becoming increasingly vexed by the failure of his operas to find a place in the repertoire.

Although Janáček did go on to have some success with operas, especially *The Cunning Little Vixen* (1921–1923), in the meantime piano and chamber music seemed a safer bet for actually getting his music published and performed. In January 1912, he heard a concert featuring Debussy's 'Doctor Gradus ad Parnassum' (1 May), which may well have inspired him to write this cycle. Certainly it bears the imprint of Debussy-esque impressionism – although, as ever with Janáček, the language is uniquely his own.

8 December

Ave verum
by Philip Stopford (b. 1977)

As we've seen, sacred choral music is having a golden moment of the kind not seen since the Renaissance – an unlikely state of affairs that gives me much joy. Today's gem was written by the British composer Philip Stopford whilst he was based at St Anne's Cathedral, Belfast.

The piece was commissioned as a gift from the Protestant community at St Anne's to the Catholic community at St Peter's, the Catholic cathedral a mile away. With the history of violence that had riven Belfast for so long, it was a powerful gesture, says the composer, to bring people together through music. *'The motet is about the body and blood of Christ, which is a central aspect of both faiths'*, he points out. *'When we did it for the first time in 2007, the choir of St Anne's performed it at St Peter's; then it was the other way around; and in the third performance the two communities came together and sang it as one.'*

The delightfully unpretentious Stopford very much sees himself as a *'jobbing church musician'* in the centuries-old tradition of, say, Thomas Tallis. *'You write for the forces at your disposal: this is living music, people are singing this here and now.'* Inspired by the likes of Walton, Stanford and Gibbons, of this beautifully simple and uncluttered setting he says: *'You look at the words, you take the meaning, you see what others have done and you put your own take on it. I'm not exactly stepping out of the box tonally, it's not so ambitious in that respect, but I want lots of people to be able to sing it. Music has to be practical for people to be able to do it.'*

The approach is working: Stopford, who is now based at a choir in upstate New York, has sold over a million dollars' worth of sheet music; his works are lovingly embraced by choirs around the world. I'm not surprised.

9 December

Improvisation on 'Winter' from *The Four Seasons*
by Gabriela Montero (b. 1970)
after Antonio Vivaldi (1678–1741)

Earlier in the year, we heard that dazzling contemporary interpretation of Vivaldi's timeless *Four Seasons* by Max Richter (22 March). Here's another one, albeit in a very different vein, from the brilliant Venezuelan pianist, composer and improviser Gabriela Montero.

When I describe Montero as improviser, I really mean it. Where jazz artists are invariably expected to be able to newly mint wonders out of a single bar or phrase, it's extremely rare to find a classical artist who can comfortably do this. The Caracas-born Montero bucks the trend. And it's magic to behold. She sits at the piano, picks out a few notes, and away she goes – sweeping us up in a magical mystery tour that might take in tango, impressionism and the blues, but always yields up the original melody in a way that makes us hear it anew.

Early on in her career, Montero says she feared that classical purists might not take her seriously for her ability to do this, but these days, thanks to the support of some starry colleagues, she celebrates it, even taking requests from audiences at the end of her concert programmes. I'll never forget watching her riff on Bach live at the Proms and the collective gasp that went around the Royal Albert Hall as we realized what was happening.

Montero is not just a superb, multifaceted musician but a politically engaged human being. Driven by an unswerving belief that music can inspire empathy, she has become an increasingly passionate and vociferous advocate for human rights through music and public discourse, in her native Venezuela and beyond. She was even named by Amnesty International as its first Honorary Consul.

10 December

Ave Maria
attributed to Giulio Caccini (c. 1551–1618)

Earlier this year, we encountered Giulio Caccini's talented and pioneering daughter Francesca Caccini, who is generally regarded as being the first woman in history to compose an opera (see 3 February). No doubt she was much inspired by her father, Giulio, a musician at the court of the Medici family in Florence, who wrote three of the earliest operas in existence. (Two of these, by the way, were based on the Orpheus myth which would go on to inspire so many others featured on these pages, including Monteverdi, Gluck, Telemann, Milhaud and Birtwistle.)

Caccini was buried on this day in the church of Santissima Annunziata in Florence. This dramatic and deeply moving setting of the Ave Maria only came to light in the twentieth century thanks to a relatively obscure Russian musician named Vladimir Vavilov; its compositional background is shrouded in mystery and there are still some unanswered questions over its authorship. But it's generally attributed to Caccini – and in any case, upon listening, most other concerns dissolve in the work's sheer beauty. Whoever wrote the setting, it's something else.

11 December

Piano Concerto no. 18 in B flat major, K. 456
1: Allegro vivace
by Wolfgang Amadeus Mozart (1756–1791)

Selecting a Mozart piano concerto was a sort of torment. How, how to choose? He wrote more than twenty of them: the first aged eleven, the last just a year before he died. They are each in their own way masterpieces. Taken as a whole, they also provide an overview of musical development between the late Baroque and early Classical periods, with the final few looking ahead still further to what Beethoven and other great Romantics would do with the piano concerto.

It was back in 1711 that the Italian craftsman Bartolomeo Cristofori had created a prototype of what would become the piano, although it was years before the instrument as we know it became widespread. While Haydn had tried his hand at a concerto for the new keyboard, it was Mozart who really showed what wonders could be weaved, especially when combined with full orchestral accompaniment.

These concertos are among my closest musical friends, each one offering a different aspect of companionship, contemplation or consolation. I was eleven myself when I first fell in love (with no. 23, as it happens), after finding a cassette tape lying around during a summer holiday. I cannot imagine my life without them. They've accompanied me on myriad adventures, been a soundtrack to love affairs and broken hearts and endless loads of washing done, dinners cooked, exams revised for, articles written, flights flown, tube journeys taken. They've been there whenever (and for whatever) I need them: as dependable as they are life-enhancing.

In the end I could not in good faith recommend one over another, so I've cheated and gone for the concerto Mozart likely wrote for Maria-Theresia von Paradis (25 June). Please consider this a diving-off point and explore them all!

385

12 December

Jesus Christ the Apple Tree
by Elizabeth Poston (1905–1987)

With under a fortnight to go until Christmas, we can surely permit ourselves another carol. The intriguing Englishwoman Elizabeth Poston – who, as well as being a talented composer was a pioneering BBC broadcaster, had a penchant for naked horse riding, and may or may not have doubled as a secret agent during the Second World War – described herself rather brilliantly as a *'littlemonger'*. In general that meant she preferred working on small-scale miniatures rather than tackling large-scale orchestral canvases.

The littles she mongered are delightful. As a student at the Royal College of Music, Poston studied with the great folk-song collector Ralph Vaughan Williams (14 June), so it's perhaps no surprise that she too was often drawn to folk material for musical inspiration. The words of this anonymous eighteenth-century Christmas carol first appeared in the collection *Divine Hymns, or Spiritual Songs* compiled by the Baptist minister Joshua Smith in New Hampshire in 1784. Her exquisitely simple setting is a breath of festive fresh air.

> *The tree of life my soul hath seen,*
> *Laden with fruit and always green:*
> *The trees of nature fruitless be*
> *Compared with Christ the apple tree.*

13 December

Concerto Grosso in G minor ('Christmas Concerto'), op. 6 no. 8
2. Adagio – Allegro – Adagio
by Arcangelo Corelli (1653–1713)

Sticking with the festive mood, I thought today would be a good day to hear a piece by Arcangelo Corelli known as the 'Christmas Concerto' because its manuscript bears the inscription *'Fatto per la notte di Natale'* – 'Made for the night of Christmas'.

Corelli, as we saw back in January, was a vital figure in the development of the Baroque concerto form. As a man, he was modest: less the flash fiddler, more the team player. As a result, his writing tends to be relatively uncomplicated – though no less charming to the ear – which may be one of the reasons he became one of the most popular composers of the era, and has remained so among string players. Whether in the seventeenth, eighteenth, nineteenth, twentieth or twenty-first century, his concerti grossi remain terrifically fun to play as part of a gang of friends – collegial music-making at its most democratic and enjoyable.

As I was listening to this piece again, I couldn't help thinking that, although it very much comes from the Italianate tradition, you can hear in its alluring pastoral mood shades of the quintessentially English string music that would emerge from later composers such as Elgar, Finzi, Goodall and Tippett (see e.g. 2 June, 15 August, 27, 29 September). Consider it an early Christmas gift.

14 December

Nesciens mater Virgo virum
by Jean Mouton (before 1459–1522)

These days, the French Renaissance composer Jean Mouton is largely unknown outside niche choral circles, and I must confess that I'd never come across his music before a friends' wedding in 2014 brought it to my attention. The groom, a former choirboy, had included in their ceremony this sublime setting of an anonymous antiphon for Christmastide. It was so beautiful, I could hardly believe my ears.

Technically speaking, the power of the setting comes primarily from the way Mouton formulates an extraordinarily complex canonical structure, passed between eight voice parts. But, as ever, I don't believe you need to understand the mathematics to instinctively feel the effect. As the conductor and composer Graham Ross says, it is *'a masterpiece, but a humble one: the amazing thing about it is that the technical brilliance disappears when you listen to it, and that in itself is part of its genius. You become so transfixed by this sublime, slow moving music that unfolds itself so beautifully, you're unaware of the technical mastery behind it.'*

Nesciens mater Virgo virum,
peperit sine dolore Salvatorem
   saeculorum,
ipsum Regem angelorum;
sola Virgo lactabat, ubere de caelo
   pleno.

Not knowing a man, the Virgin
   Mother
Brought forth without sorrow the
   Saviour of the ages,
Him the King of angels;
Alone, the Virgin suckled him,
   filled with the milk of heaven.

15 December

Lágrima
by Francisco Tárrega (1852–1909)

Sometimes music falls into your life in the most serendipitous and unlikely of ways. It was on a miserable tube journey at rush hour in London that I first encountered this piece, which has gone on to be one of my favourite works for classical guitar. Squashed into a carriage, everyone sodden and cross from the pouring rain outside, I was shoved up so close to the passengers around me that I couldn't move my arms to retrieve my book from my bag. Yet I had a perfect view over a fellow passenger's shoulder to the pages of the novel she had open. So I'm afraid, instinctively, I did that annoying thing of reading over her shoulder; I couldn't help myself.

I still to this day do not know the title of the book, as I only read a few pages before she alighted, but my interest had been sufficiently piqued by the mention, in the text, of a piece of music called *Lágrima*. As soon as I too got off the tube and had free use of my arms again, I searched online on my phone and within seconds Tárrega's delicate, sensuous music was flooding my ears on the rain-lashed walk home. (Technology can be a wonderful thing.)

I later discovered, thanks to the Montenegrin guitarist Miloš Karadaglić, that there was a pleasing coincidence in the way I had chanced upon it. Tárrega, who died on this day, apparently wrote it on his one and only trip to London around 1880. '*It was raining all the time and he was very depressed and homesick*', Miloš says, '*and he wrote this simple piece, Lágrima, which means teardrop, and every note is like a tear. It's such a delicate little piece, and there's so much more to it than what's on the page.*'

16 December

Es ist nun aus mit meinem Leben – Now my life is ended
by Johann Christoph Bach (1642–1703)

Speaking of music arriving in unexpected ways: this piece was introduced to me by a friend at a Christmas party a few years ago, pressed into my hands like some illicit substance. I'd never heard it; knew almost nothing about this particular Bach (an older cousin, once removed, of J. S.). But having been, so often, the one madly peddling classical music to unconvinced friends, I was sufficiently charmed to press play as soon as I could.

My friend had promised it would change my life – and it does. Quietly, but convincingly. It changes my life in the way that only the most beautiful music can. I hope it does yours, too.

17 December

Symphony no. 10 in E minor, op. 93
2: Allegro
by Dmitri Shostakovich (1906–1975)

Joseph Stalin died in March 1953. Nine months later, on 17 December, Shostakovich unveiled his new symphony. It was the first he had written since he was denounced in 1948, and it's hard not to get the impression that he was pouring into this astonishing work something of his emotions, repressed for so long during Stalin's brutal and seemingly inexhaustible reign of terror (see e.g. 22 January). The British conductor Mark Wigglesworth suggests that, emotionally, this symphony exudes a *'tired and drained quality'* that reflects the poet Anna Akhmatova's words from 'The Return':

> *The souls of all my dears have flown to the stars*
> *Thank God there's no one left for me to lose so I can cry.*

Through this music, we feel the exhaustion, Wigglesworth says, of all who lived and died through that quarter century of tyranny. And nowhere is that more apparent than this breathtaking second movement, which begins fortissimo (very loud) and is followed by no fewer than fifty crescendos (getting louder all the time). There are only two diminuendos, where the music gets quieter. *'The effect'*, says Wigglesworth, *'is self-explanatory. The emotion is not so much a depiction of Stalin himself, but an anger that he ever existed. In fact, such was his hold over the people, that the hysteria greeting his funeral cortège was so great that hundreds of people were crushed to death by tanks trying to keep order and protect the coffin. It is typical of Stalin that he should have continued to be responsible for people's deaths even from beyond the grave.'*

18 December

The Lamb
by John Tavener (1944–2013)

John Tavener, whom we first encountered back in May, occupies a special place in British music. A man of profound spirituality and quiet generosity, his music has provided consolation and a sort of sonic refuge to millions of listeners – from his Mercury Prize-nominated *The Protecting Veil* to the *Song for Athene*, heard in 1997 at the funeral of Diana, Princess of Wales, as her cortège departed from Westminster Abbey.

There is, of course, much more to Tavener's music than what feels like permission to retreat from the modern world for a few minutes, but for mainstream audiences that aesthetic is perhaps what makes him so cherished. Perhaps best loved of all is his crystalline setting of William Blake's poem 'The Lamb', which Tavener based on just seven notes.

Looking back, the composer later explained that he had written this over a single, divinely inspired afternoon in 1982 for his then three-year-old nephew, Simon. Reflecting on the way the piece had captured hearts around the globe, Tavener referred back to the original Blake poem. *'Blake's child-like vision'*, he said, *'perhaps explains* The Lamb's *great popularity in a world that is starved of this precious and sacred dimension in almost every aspect of life.'*

Ain't *that* the truth?

> *Little Lamb who made thee*
> *. . . Gave thee such a tender voice,*
> *Making all the vales rejoice!*
> *. . . Little Lamb who made thee*
> *. . . Dost thou know who made thee . . .*

19 December

~~~~~

Theme from *A Clockwork Orange*
by Wendy Carlos (b. 1939)

We've heard from quite a few pioneers in the field of electronic classical music – Rautavaara, Boulez, Reich, Richter and so on. Today we meet the godmother of the synthesizer, Wendy Carlos.

After studying music and physics, Carlos worked as a tape editor in New York and became friends with Robert Moog, inventor of a groundbreaking synthesizer. Carlos helped refine the machine to give it more dynamic range and sensitivity, and in her visionary 1968 project *Switched-on Bach*, proved that it could be considered a musical instrument like any other. Giving Bach's six Brandenburg Concertos a uniquely twentieth-century treatment, she smashed the barriers between acoustic and synthesized sounds. That triple-Grammy-winning record became the first platinum-selling classical album, and remains the most influential electronic classical recording of all time. *'Wendy has built up lyrical sounds nobody ever heard coming out of a digital synthesizer before'*, Moog said. *'Nobody is in her league.'*

Carlos has always been ambitious in her desires for electronic music; namely, *'that it share the same musical values of the best of acoustic music performance: nuanced, rubato, expressive, plastic, and ever-changing, ever-shifting'*. She's taken that aesthetic onto many a musical platform, including film scores such as Stanley Kubrick's *The Shining* (1980) and *A Clockwork Orange* (1971), which deliberately riffed on music from Berlioz's *Symphonie fantastique* (see 5 December) and was released on this day.

Born Walter, Carlos was a pioneer in other respects too. In 1968 she began transitioning and finally came out as a transgender woman in a 1979 *Playboy* interview, announcing, *'I'm anxious to liberate myself.'*

393

20 December

Cradle Song
by Michael Berkeley (b. 1948)

Inching closer to Christmas, it's time for another carol: this one by my multi-talented and multi-award-winning Radio 3 colleague, the composer, author and broadcaster Michael Berkeley. Previously a member of a rock group, this godson of Benjamin Britten (13 June, 22 November) writes opera, ballet and instrumental music, and as a former chorister, is steeped in the glories of Britain's long and illustrious choral tradition.

Berkeley has described his music as having '*a strong emotional content which audiences react to*'. This short carol setting for treble voice is a touching example. Berkeley says he was very attracted by the '*devotional simplicity*' of the words (from 'Balulalow', first published in 1567 as a translation of a Martin Luther Christmas carol by the sixteenth-century Scottish brothers John, Robert and James Wedderburn). The effect, Berkeley says, is that of a 'gentle lullaby'.

He wrote it in 1976, and it's dedicated to his brother Julian.

> *O my deir hert, young Jesus sweit,*
> *Prepare thy creddill in my spreit,*
> *And I sall rocke thee in my hert,*
> *And neuer mair from thee depart.*

21 December

Overture from Nutcracker Suite
by Duke Ellington (1899–1974)
after Pyotr Ilyich Tchaikovsky (1840–1893)

*Duke Ellington and Peter Ilich Tchaikovsky met in Las Vegas
while Duke's band was setting attendance records at the Riviera
Hotel. For the first time in Ellington history, Duke had decided to
devote an entire album to arrangements of another composer's
works instead of his own, and Tchaikovsky was the natural choice.*

*Because the suite is a favorite form for Ellington composition, the
Nutcracker was the obvious Tchaikovsky work to choose. Duke and
Billy Strayhorn needed some reassurance that nobody, including the
famous Russian composer, would mind if the Suite was translated
into the Ellington style, but once those fears were banished, they
attacked the Sugar-Plum Fairy and the Waltz of the Flowers as if
they were no more sacred than [legendary Ellington song] Perdido.*

So began the sleeve notes by copywriter Irving Townsend for the
1960 Columbia Records release of Duke Ellington's genius take on
Tchaikovsky's seasonal favourite, *The Nutcracker.* It was tongue-in-
cheek, obviously: Tchaikovsky had been dead six years when Ellington
was born; it would be another six before the railroad town of Las Vegas
was even established. But what a delicious thought, eh? Tchaikovsky
and Ellington hanging out in Sin City, swapping musical ideas, comparing notes on their shared love of the suite form, collaborating on
this glorious festive treat.

We've seen how seriously the jazz legend Ellington was taken by
his counterparts in the classical world – but the affection was definitely mutual. As Ellington said of Tchaikovsky: *'That cat was it.'*

22 December

What sweeter music?
by John Rutter (b. 1945)

British composer John Rutter is the undisputed King of Christmas: a master technician who manages to conceal his infrastructural workings to produce gorgeous choral music of seemingly great simplicity, especially for this time of year.

This exceedingly touching carol was written in 1998 for the Choir of King's College, Cambridge, with whom Rutter has long been closely associated. It was commissioned as part of the choir's famous annual ceremony of Nine Lessons and Carols, which is broadcast every year all around the globe.

Rutter admits that he particularly enjoyed *'the opportunity to write for the slot in the service immediately after the reading about the journey of the Wise Men'* because it gave him the chance to *'highlight in the text the idea of the gifts that we can bring'.* He bases the piece on a seventeenth-century Christmas carol by Robert Herrick (1591–1674), which was originally *'Sung to the King in the Presence at White-Hall'* – the monarch in question being King Charles I.

It is, indeed, hard to think of a sweeter musical gift:

> *What sweeter music can we bring*
> *Than a carol, for to sing*
> *The birth of this our heavenly King?*
> *Awake the voice! Awake the string!*

23 December

'Evening Prayer'
from *Hansel and Gretel*
by Engelbert Humperdinck (1854–1921)

Not to be confused with the pop singer who has sold over 150 million records (he of 'Please Release Me' fame) *this* Englebert Humperdinck is best known for his opera *Hansel and Gretel*. Based on a fairy tale by the Brothers Grimm, it was first performed in Weimar on this day in 1893 and conducted by Richard Strauss, who considered it a masterpiece.

The origins of the project were rather more humble: Humperdinck originally composed music for four songs about Hansel and Gretel that his sister Adelheid had written as a puppet show for her young daughters. Brother and sister then collaborated on the full-length opera, and it was an instant success.

It's been much loved by audiences young and old ever since. In 1923, it was chosen by the Royal Opera House as their first ever radio broadcast, and in 1931 became the first opera to be transmitted by New York's Metropolitan Opera. It continues to be programmed by major opera houses around the world, often at Christmas time.

This contemplative evening prayer takes place after they are lost in the woods and have been visited by the Sandman, who makes them very sleepy. Before they close their eyes, Hansel and Gretel sing this hymn for protection:

Abends, will ich schlafen gehn,   *When at night I go to sleep*
Vierzehn Engel um mich stehn   *Fourteen angels watch do keep*

24 December

Siegfried Idyll
by Richard Wagner (1813–1883)

Just imagine, if you will, Cosima Wagner, Richard's wife (and Liszt's daughter), lying in her bed on Christmas morning, December 1870, and gradually coming round to consciousness with the strains of this utterly heavenly music – which sounds as though it itself is waking – floating upwards towards her.

It was being played by a small group of local orchestral players on the stairs of their villa at Tribschen in Switzerland. It seems to have been intended by Wagner as both a birthday present for Cosima – they had married in August; she was born on this day – and a celebration of their family: she had given birth to their first son Siegfried (or 'Fidi') the previous year. Certainly Wagner filled his score with the tenderest of musical references, and its official title is: *'Tribschen Idyll with Fidi's birdsong and the orange sunrise, as symphonic birthday greeting. Presented to his Cosima by her Richard.'*

'As I awoke', Cosima later recalled in her diary, *'my ear caught a sound, which swelled fuller and fuller; no longer could I imagine myself to be dreaming: music was sounding, and such music! When it died away, Richard came into my room with the children and offered me the score of the symphonic birthday poem. I was in tears, but so were all the rest of the household. Richard had arranged his orchestra on the staircase, and thus was our Tribschen consecrated for ever.'*

Intimate as it was, Wagner intended for it to remain a private piece of music, just for them, but for financial reasons he was forced – to Cosima's chagrin – to sell it to a publisher. Six years later, he incorporated it into his opera *Siegfried* – and the name has stuck.

25 December

Christmas Oratorio, BWV 248
1: Chorus: 'Jauchzet, frohlocket, auf, preiset die Tage' –
'Celebrate, rejoice, rise up and praise these days'
by Johann Sebastian Bach (1685–1750)

So many things we could have heard on Christmas Day, but you probably won't be surprised that I've chosen Bach, and his mighty and magnificent cantata for the festive season. The so-called *Christmas Oratorio* comprises six parts, and, as he often does, Bach breezily recycles music from earlier compositions in pulling it together.

This rousing opening chorus, for example, first appeared in a secular cantata, no. 214, composed in 1733 to celebrate the birthday of the Queen of Poland. The original chorus calls forth drums, trumpets and strings to fill the air, and in this festive version for Christmas Day Bach ramps up the drama still further, in a dizzyingly joyous call to 'Celebrate, rejoice, rise up and praise these days!' As well as a bevy of exultant human voices, his colourful and vivid orchestration features trumpets, timpani, flutes, oboes, oboes d'amore, violins, viola and bass. It's a fantastic combination.

The first ever performance of this movement took place at St Nicholas's Church in Leipzig on this day in 1734. Exactly two hundred and seventy years later, on Christmas Day, 2004, I had the joy of playing it for the very first time. I was in Jerusalem for the Palestine Bach Festival. We were an orchestra composed of young Israeli and Palestinian musicians, as well as a handful of Brits. Christians, Muslims, Jews. Humans. Playing Bach – playing together. I'll never forget it as long as I live. Merry Christmas!

26 December

Stabat mater
by Giovanni Battista Pergolesi (1710–1736)

After those ravishing treatments by Vivaldi (18 April) and Alissa Firsova (24 July), we come to our third and final *Stabat mater* setting of the year. Giovanni Battista Pergolesi, who was felled by tuberculosis at twenty-six, managed to be something of a sensation in his short life: he composed in many musical forms, including opera and instrumental concertos, and although his music sounds quite ancient to us now, he was regarded in his day as the architect of a new and radically direct style. *'Pergolesi was born'*, raved one French composer from the next generation, *'and truth was known!'*

For all those other works, it is his heartrending account of the thirteenth-century Catholic hymn which has secured Pergolesi's place in musical history. The emotionally searing and occasionally dissonant duet between soprano and alto evokes Mary's vigil at the foot of the Cross in music that is at times sweetly touching; at others quite agonizing. It captivated audiences from the outset, becoming the most frequently printed musical work of the eighteenth century. And its fame soon spread around Europe, where it was put to other uses, including as a setting for poetry by Alexander Pope in England and Friedrich Gottlieb Klopstock in Germany. Bach, meanwhile, was sufficiently dazzled that he directly based his setting of Psalm 51 (BWV 1083) on Pergolesi's music – an expression of his utmost admiration.

27 December

O Gaúcho (Corta-jaca)
by Francisca Edwiges Neves 'Chiquinha' Gonzaga
(1847–1935)

The illegitimate daughter of a mixed-race mother and white father, Chiquinha Gonzaga overcame some pretty spectacular odds to become one of Brazil's greatest musical pioneers. Defying her family and the husband she'd been forced to marry, she forged an impressive independent career as a pianist and composer; wowed audiences on tour in Germany, Belgium, Spain, Portugal, Italy, France, England and Scotland; and went on to become her country's first ever female conductor. She was also an ardent suffragist, campaigned against slavery, and helped to found a performers' rights collecting society. She was still writing operas in 1934, the year before she died.

In 1895 Gonzaga had one of her greatest successes in the form of incidental music to an operetta, *Zizinha maxixe* (1895), from which this *corta-jaca* comes. It is a super-spirited take on the traditional Brazilian tango or *maxixe* that emerged in Rio in the 1860s, and blends elements of Afro-Brazilian dances such as the *lundu* with European ones such as the polka – not unlike what her compatriot Villa-Lobos (7 September, 17 November), born forty years later, would do.

The title literally means 'cut the jackfruit' and, I'm told, is laced with innuendo – perhaps fitting for a fiercely independent woman who ran away from various husbands and partners and ended up falling in love with a man thirty-six years her junior. (Devoted to the end, he was still by her side when she died, aged eighty-eight.)

28 December

~⌒~

Piano Sonata in C major, Hob. XVI no. 50
1: Allegro
by Joseph Haydn (1732–1809)

Just in case you've fallen into the post-Christmas stupor that I invariably find myself in at this time of year, this crisp and fizzy little keyboard number from Haydn should do the trick.

As we heard earlier this month, Haydn was, like his contemporary Mozart, one of the great pioneers of the early piano repertoire (see 11 December). He wrote around sixty sonatas for the new instrument, not every one particularly well known but all offering terrific opportunities for a soloist to show off everything from precise and virtuosic technique to a more lyrical sensibility.

It's unthinkable to imagine the later development of the piano sonata in the hands of composers such as Beethoven and Liszt without acknowledging their debt to Haydn. I find this one in C the perfect musical antidote to yet another leftover turkey sandwich and the dregs of the Quality Street tin.

29 December

Agnus Dei
by Wojciech Kilar (1932–2013)

A change of mood today from the Polish composer Wojciech Kilar, who died on this day. Kilar was a hugely respected film composer, scoring over a hundred movies and collaborating with many of his country's greatest filmmakers, including Roman Polanski (*The Pianist*, 2002), as well as with international directors such as Francis Ford Coppola (*Bram Stoker's Dracula*, 1993).

Along with composers such as Henryk Górecki (4 April), Kilar was also one of the leading lights of the Polish avant-garde classical music scene, known as the New Polish School. In this classical realm he wrote symphonic music, chamber works, instrumental pieces and works for large chorus. His music had a profound impact on the next generation of Polish composers, as we have already heard (see 19 September).

Kilar once said, intriguingly, that he believed he had '*discovered the philosopher's stone*', and that '*there was nothing more beautiful than the solitary sound or concord that lasted eternally, that this was the deepest wisdom, nothing like our tricks with sonata allegros, fugues, and harmonics*'.

I think you can hear the composer striving for something like eternal concord in his haunting setting of the Agnus Dei, which seems to pull off the curious musical trick of both echoing back and looking forwards in time.

Something to ponder as another year draws almost to its close . . .

30 December

The long day closes
by Arthur Sullivan (1842–1900)

The name Arthur Sullivan may not perhaps ring bells, but the chances are you'll have heard of Gilbert and Sullivan, a British brand almost as iconic as Marks and Spencer or fish and chips.

Before he was one half of that legendary operetta-producing machine, Sullivan was a talented and prolific composer of 'part-songs', that is, pieces written for several vocal parts. These were all the rage in Victorian England, where amateur choral societies were springing up around the land and groups of families and friends were revelling in the sheer delight of coming together to sing songs.

I find this one, with its plaintive harmonies and touching sentiment, particularly lovely. Setting words by the arts critic, writer, editor, poet (and professional gossip) Henry Fothergill Chorley, it conjures a pensive mood for the penultimate day of the year.

> *No star is o'er the lake,*
> *Its pale watch keeping,*
> *The moon is half awake,*
> *Through gray mist creeping,*
> *The last red leaves fall round*
> *The porch of roses,*
> *The clock hath ceased to sound,*
> *The long day closes . . .*

31 December

Champagne Polka
by Johann Strauss II (1825–1899)

Pop the champagne, it's New Year's Eve!

Johann Strauss II was part of a family of composers – no relation to Richard and Franz – who defined a certain sound of nineteenth-century Vienna. He composed over five hundred waltzes and other forms of dance music, hence his nickname the 'Waltz King'. Apparently, he specifically had in mind the sound of champagne corks popping when he wrote this effervescent polka: they make their appearance around one minute in – the perfect musical prelude to tonight's festivities.

It seemed fitting to close our musical year with a celebration. I hope you've enjoyed these twelve months of sonic adventure as much as I have, and that this will be the springboard for many more years of musical wonder to come.

Thanks for joining me for the ride, and happy New Year!

Acknowledgements

O ver the course of more than three decades of making, thinking, writing and communicating about music I have accrued a multitude of debts – musical, emotional, intellectual, practical, professional, personal – to many remarkable people. Those who have helped to bring *Year of Wonder* to life are too many to name, but my most heartfelt thanks to some particular people in no particular order:

My violin teachers, Helen Brunner and Rodney Friend. My inspirational colleagues at the BBC and in particular at Radio 3. Special thanks to my fellow broadcasters, above all Tom Service, from whom I have learned so much, and whose generosity extended to reading parts of the book before publication. Elsewhere in the world of arts broadcasting, thank you to everyone at the Royal Opera House, and, in New York, WQXR's Matt Abramovitz and Graham Parker.

In the world of print journalism, I've been fortunate to have a number of editors who've given me invaluable opportunities along the way: thanks especially to Sarah Sands and Matthew D'Ancona for taking such an early punt; and to Emma Duncan and Fiammetta Rocco at the *Economist/1843*; Tim de Lisle; Alice Fishburn at *FT Weekend*; Matthew Anderson at the *New York Times;* Rebecca Laurence at BBC Culture and Oliver Condy at *BBC Music Magazine*.

Endless gratitude to my musical hero, Daniel Barenboim, and members of his West-Eastern Divan Orchestra; also to John Harte, Michael Stevens, Nicholas Collon and everyone involved in the Choir of London – thank you for the ultimate musical education.

Peter Florence, you have given me the world through your wondrous imaginings. Thank you. Love also to Elizabeth Day, Sam West,

Eddie Redmayne, Amber Sainsbury, Andrew Staples, James Rhodes, Alison Balsom, Tara Hacking, Rowan Lawton, Lisa Dwan, Lucinda Nicholson, Simon Walker, Graham Hodge, Simon Schama, Revel Guest, Rob and Corisande Albert and family. For making it physically possible for me to write, thanks beyond thanks to Rohan Silva and his team at Second Home; to Nick Jones and everyone at Soho House; and to Tim Botteril at Spotify.

It has been an absolute delight to work with Lindsey Evans, Kate Miles, Georgina Moore, Sarah Hulbert, Viviane Bassett, Siobhan Hooper, Louise Rothwell, Frances Doyle, Robert Chilver, Katie Day, Vicky Abbott and everyone at Headline Home: thank you for your enthusiasm, perspicacity and support, and for embracing *Year of Wonder* so whole-heartedly; enormous thanks too to Katie Green for intelligent and fastidious copy-editing. Rosemary Scoular, you are the agent of dreams – my sincerest gratitude to you and everyone at United, especially Aoife Rice, Meg Townend and Dallas Smith.

Delving deeper into the world of music-streaming technology has been a thrill to this tech geek. Thanks to Denzyl Feigelson, Jonathan Gruber and all at Apple Music; to Alison Bonny at Spotify; and to Yonca Brunini and Paul Lotherington at Google.

I am grateful to Emily Ezust of the invaluable Lieder Net Archive for granting her permission for me to quote various song translations. Many thanks also to Zadie Smith for graciously allowing me to quote from *On Beauty;* to the Reverend Dr James Hawkey for assuring me that it's okay to respond rhapsodically to sacred music without having the faith to back it up; and to Nico Muhly, Lucy Parham, Mark Wigglesworth, Philip Stopford, Graham Ross and Alissa Firsova for various notes on the music.

On the home front, all the love to my family: Perry, Lisa, Elodie, Carys, Elliot, Katey, Jagger, Hunter, Noah and Stacia. To my parents-in-law Eli and Lawrie Geller, thanks yet again for providing refuge, hospitality and dinner in the face of imminent deadlines. The saintly

Bianke Ohle arrived in our lives in the nick of time; writing this book would simply have been impossible without her.

I didn't grow up with my father, Humphrey, so we will never know what musical adventures might have been had we had the chance to get to know each other sooner, but when it comes to incurable curiosity and a hunger for living life we are peas in a pod. I am beyond grateful for his eagle eye and encyclopedic musical knowledge.

Tom, you are my daily wonder. Bobby, I miss you every day.

This book would have been inconceivable without my mother, Gillian, who took seriously the freakish demands of a toddler who wanted to play the violin, figured out a way for me to do it, against the odds, and has supported me every day, every hour, every minute, ever since. Mum, this is all you.

Well – almost all. This book definitely would not exist were it not for James, who got the measure of me so quickly he actually suggested we went to listen to Duruflé on our first date; and has been, ever since, my very best thing. Thank you.

Notes on Sources

January

4. Robert Schumann on Beethoven's late quartets as quoted in Robert Alexander Schumann, *Music and Musicians, Essays and Criticisms*, translated and edited by F. R. Ritter (Oxford University Press, 1877), p. 391: archive.org/stream/ musicmusicianseooschu#page/390/mode/2up/search/Beethoven+late+quartet

6. Max Bruch quoted in *Encyclopaedia Britannica*: www.britannica.com/topic/ Violin-Concerto-No-1-in-G-Minor-Op-26

7. Poulenc to Roland Gelatt as quoted on NPR Music Deceptive Cadence: www.npr. org/sections/deceptivecadence/2013/01/30/170662245/a-little-part-of-poulenc-in-all-of-us

   'menace of the occupation . . .' Poulenc in a letter to Nora Auric, 1 January 1941, as quoted by Graham Johnson in liner notes for Hyperion Records: www.hyperion-records.co.uk/tw.asp?w=W4319

9. Edgar Krasa as quoted in Gail Wein, 'A Life Profile' on The Defiant Requiem Foundation website: www.defiantrequiem.org/survivor-stories/edgar-krasa/

   Raphael Schächter as quoted by survivors including Edgar Krasa in Denis D. Gray, 'We will sing to the Nazis what we cannot say', ibid.

11. Duruflé as quoted in Russell Platt, 'Elegant Theft: Maurice Duruflé's Requiem', the *New Yorker*, 8 March 2012: www.newyorker.com/culture/culture-desk/elegant-theft-maurice-durufls-requiem

    'Where charity and love are . . .' translated from the Latin by CBH.

12. Mendelssohn quoted in *Encyclopaedia Britannica*: www.britannica.com/topic/ Octet-for-Strings-in-E-Flat-Major-Op-20

13. Clara Schumann's diary, 10 June 1853, quoted in Berthold Litzmann, *Clara Schumann: An Artist's Life Based on Material Found in Diaries and Letters*, vol. 2. Anonymous critic quoted in Nancy B. Reich, 'Clara Schumann', in *Women Making Music: The Western Art Tradition, 1150–1950*, edited by Jane Bowers and Judith Tick (University of Illinois Press 1986), p. 249.

14. Italian libretto by Giuseppe Giacosa and Luigi Illica; English translation by CBH.

15. Audience member as quoted in Rebecca Rischin, *For the End of Time: The Story of the Messiaen Quartet* (Cornell University Press, 2006), p. 69.

18. 'Roses climb his life . . .' from the chapter 'Lifeleading' in William H. Gass, *Reading Rilke: Reflections on the Problems of Translation* (Knopf Doubleday 2013). Lauridsen as quoted by Byron Adams in liner notes for Hyperion Records: www. hyperion-records.co.uk/dw.asp?dc=W9207_67580

20. German text by Franz Schober; English translation by CBH.

22. Shostakovich as quoted in *A Shostakovich Casebook*, edited by Malcolm Hamrick Brown (Indiana University Press, 2005), p. 74.
'Muddle Not Music' from *Pravda*, 28 January 1936, as quoted in 'Muddle Not Music – Pravda's review of Shostakovich's opera Lady Macbeth' on the website History in an Hour: www.historyinanhour.com/2013/09/25/muddle-not-music-pravdas-review-of-shostakovichs-opera-lady-macbeth/

25. 'O my Luve's like a red, red rose . . .' by Robert Burns: www.scottishpoetrylibrary.org.uk/poetry/poems/red-red-rose

26. 'the laziest student . . .' as quoted in Mary E. Davis, *Erik Satie* (Reaktion Books, 2007), p. 19.

28. French text by Paul Verlaine; English translation by Grant A. Lewis.

30. Fauré and Saint-Saëns both quoted in John Henken's programme notes for the LA Philharmonic: www.laphil.com/philpedia/music/sonata-no-1-major-op-13-gabriel-faure

31. 'music with repetitive structures' as quoted in Tom Service, 'A guide to Philip Glass's music', *Guardian*, 3 December 2012: www.theguardian.com/music/tomservice-blog/2012/dec/03/contemporary-music-guide-philip-glass
Composer's note taken from his website: philipglass.com/compositions/echorus/

February

1. Italian text by Giuseppe Giacosa and Luigi Illica; English translation by CBH.

7. Translation of the Latin text taken from the 1662 Book of Common Prayer, as in Ivor Atkins's English edition of the *Miserere* (Novello, 1979).

8. Translated from the Italian by CBH.

9. Schoenberg as quoted in Arnold Schoenberg, *Style and Idea: Selected Writings*, edited by Leonard Stein and translated by Leo Black (California University Press, 1984), p. 218.

10. Composer's words taken from her website: charlottebray.co.uk/works/choral/agnus-dei/

13. Leonard Bernstein's diary as quoted in Susan Kay's programme notes for the LA Philharmonic: www.hollywoodbowl.com/philpedia/music/symphonic-dances-from-west-side-story-leonard-bernstein

15. 'music for the eyes' as quoted in Alice M. Caldwell, 'Moravian Sacred Vocal Music' in *The Music of the Moravian Church in America*, edited by Nola Reed Knouse (University of Rochester Press, 2008), p. 90.
Mozart as quoted in Otto Jahn, *The Life of Mozart*, vol. 2 (Cambridge University Press, 2013), p. 442.

16. Schumann's diary as quoted in John Daverio, *Robert Schumann, Herald of a 'New Poetic Age'* (Oxford University Press, 1997), p. 242.

19. Composer's words taken from his website: olagjeilo.com/sheet-music/choral-satb-a-cappella/northern-lights/

21. Words from the Roman Catholic liturgy translated by CBH.
    'Blessed are they that mourn . . .' from Matthew v, 4 (the second verse of the Sermon on the Mount, and the second of what is known as the Beatitudes).

25. Letter from Camille Saint-Saëns to Durand, 9 February 1886, as quoted in Sabina Teller Ratner, *Camille Saint-Saëns, 1835–1921: A Thematic Catalogue of His Complete Works*, vol. 1 (Oxford University Press, 2002), p. 191.

26. From Max Richter, 'Millions of us knew the Iraq war would be a catastrophe. Why didn't Tony Blair?' in *Guardian*, 8 July 2016: www.theguardian.com/commentis-free/2016/jul/08/iraq-war-tony-blair-creativity-chilcot-inquiry

27. Elsa and Albert Einstein as widely quoted, e.g. in Mitch Waldrop, 'Inside Einstein's Love Affair With "Lina" – His Cherished Violin', *National Geographic* magazine, 3 February 2017: news.nationalgeographic.com/2017/02/einstein-genius-violin-music-physics-science

28. *'passionate pilgrimage of the soul'* as quoted in Diana McVeagh, 'Elgar, Sir Edward', Grove Music Online, Oxford Music Online.
    Elgar in rehearsal as quoted in Bernard Shore, *Sixteen Symphonies* (Longmans, Green, 1949), p. 275.
    From 'Song: Rarely, rarely, comest thou' by Percy Bysshe Shelley.
    Elgar in a letter to Alice Stuart-Wortley as quoted in Michael Kennedy, *The Life of Elgar* (Cambridge University Press, 2004), p. 133.

29. *'give me the laundress' bill . . .'* as quoted in Indro Montanelli, *L'Italia giacobina e carbonara (1789–1831)* (Rizzoli, 1972), p. 612; translated by CBH.
    Beethoven as quoted in Burton D. Fisher, *The Barber of Seville* (Opera Journeys Publishing, 2000), p. 24.
    Rossini's note on the manuscript as quoted in John Quinn's review for Musicweb: www.musicweb-international.com/classrev/2013/Apr13/Rossini_mass_4167422.htm

March

8. 'irrefutably badass' from Alex Ross, 'Prince of Darkness: the murders and madrigals of Don Carlo Gesualdo' in the *New Yorker*, 19 and 26 December 2011: www.newyorker.com/magazine/2011/12/19/prince-of-darkness
   Stravinsky as quoted in Ivan Hewett, 'Ivan Hewett's Classic 50 No 33: Carlo Gesualdo – Asciugate i Begli Occhi', the *Telegraph*, 8 August 2013: www.telegraph.co.uk/culture/music/classical-music-guide/10225158/Ivan-Hewetts-Classic-50-No-33-Carlo-Gesualdo-Asciugate-i-Begli-Occhi.html

10. *'used with the composer's kind permission'* as quoted in Peter Jost, 'Filched Melodies – Sarasate's "Zigeunerweisen" (Gypsy Airs) under suspicion of plagiarism', on publisher G. Henle Verlag's website, 19 August 2013: www.henle.de/blog/

en/2013/08/19/filchedmelodies___sarasate's-'zigeunerweisen'-gypsy-aires-under-suspicion-of-plagiarism

14. Samuel Pepys diary as quoted in Stephen Johnson, 'What is . . . Tarantella?' on the *BBC Music Magazine* website, 10 June 2016: www.classical-music.com/article/what-istarantella

15. Italian text by *Nicola Francesco Haym*; English translation by CBH.

16. Schubert as quoted in *Franz Schubert's Letters and Other Writings*, edited by Otto Erich Deutsch and translated by Venetia Savile (Greenwood Press, 1928).

17. Freidrich Kalkbrenner quoted in Patrick Piggott, *The Life and Music of John Field, 1782–1837, Creator of the Nocturne* (University of California Press, 1973), p. 100. Franz Liszt's preface to his edition of John Field's *Nocturnes* (J. Schuberth & Co., 1859).

20. Italian text by Ottavio Rinuccini; translation by Amber Sainsbury.

21. Schumann as quoted by Robert Philip in liner notes for Hyperion Records: www.hyperion-records.co.uk/dw.asp?dc=W2721_67485

22. Composer quoted in conversation with Tom Service, 'Max Richter spring-cleans Vivaldi's The Four Seasons', *Guardian*, 21 October 2012: www.theguardian.com/music/2012/oct/21/max-richter-vivaldi-four-seasons

25. From Béla Bartók, 'The Influence of Peasant Music on Modern Music' (1931) in *Béla Bartók: Essays*, selected and edited by Benjamin Suchoff (St Martin's Press, 1976), p. 341.

26. Pierre Boulez as quoted in Peter Culshaw, 'Pierre Boulez: "I was a bully, I'm not ashamed"', the *Telegraph*, 10 December 2008: www.telegraph.co.uk/culture/music/classicalmusic/3702982/Pierre-Boulez-I-was-a-bully-Im-not-ashamed.html

27. Messiaen as quoted in Roger Nichols, 'Pierre Boulez obituary', *Guardian*, 6 January 2016: www.theguardian.com/music/2016/jan/06/pierre-boulez
Mozart entered the words *'true opera'* in his thematic catalogue, p. 30, viewable on the British Library website: www.bl.uk/turning-the-pages/?id=0d3ac4d1-793c-4021-b178-9c666c90f2bc&type=book

28. Takemitsu as quoted by Alex Ross in 'Toward Silence: The intense repose of Toru Takemitsu', *New Yorker*, 5 February 2007: www.newyorker.com/magazine/2007/02/05/toward-silence

29. Frahm quoted in Tristan Bath, 'The Listener Is The Key: Nils Frahm Interviewed', The Quietus, 30 October 2013: thequietus.com/articles/13703-nils-frahm-interview

April

1. Letter to Nadezhda von Meck, 21 January/2 February 1878, as quoted in *The Life and Letters of Peter Ilich Tchaikovsky*, edited by Modeste Tchaikovsky and translated by Rosa Newmarch (Minerva Group, 2004), p. 165.
Dick Rowe quoted by George Harrison, as referenced e.g. by Brian Viner in 'The man who rejected the Beatles', the *Independent*, 12 February 2012: www.independent.co.uk/arts-entertainment/music/news/the-man-who-rejected-the-beatles-6782008.html

3. Brahms writing *'for himself alone'* as quoted in Jan Swafford, *Johannes Brahms: A Biography* (Alfred A. Knopf, 1997), p. 578.
   Brahms writing to Clara Schumann as quoted in Jan Swafford, 'Bittersweet symphonies' in the *Guardian*, 26 April 2003: www.theguardian.com/music/2003/apr/26/classicalmusicandopera.artsfeatures2

4. *'If you can live without . . .'* as quoted in the composer's obituary by Maev Kennedy, 'Polish composer Henryk Górecki dies, aged 76', *Guardian*, 12 November 2010: www.theguardian.com/music/2010/nov/12/polish-composer-henryk-gorecki-dies
   'You know how it is . . .' Composer quoted in Bernard Jacobson, *A Polish Renaissance* (Phaidon, 1995), p. 174.

5. 'the Dean of American composers': term in familiar use; see e.g. John Rockwell, 'Copland, Dean of American Music, Dies at 80', *New York Times*, 3 December 1990: nytimes.com/books/99/03/14/specials/copland-obit.html
   'It was wonderful . . .' as quoted in Aaron Copland and Vivian Perlis, *Copland: 1900 Through 1942* (St Martin's/Marek, 1984), p. 64.
   Wallace as quoted by Alan Brinkley in *The American Century in Europe*, edited by R. Laurence Moore, Maurizio Vaudagna (Cornell University Press, 2003), p. 12.
   Goosens as quoted in Elizabeth B. Crist, *Music for the Common Man: Aaron Copland during the Depression and War* (Oxford University Press 2009), p. 183.

6. *Morning Chronicle* critic as quoted in H. C. Robbins Landon, *Haydn: Chronicle and Works*, vol. 4 (Indiana University Press, 1976), p. 241.

7. Ravel as widely quoted, referenced e.g. on Carnegie Hall blog, 'When Ravel met Gershwin', 9 April 2012: www.carnegiehall.org/BlogPost.aspx?id=4294985697

8. Milhaud to Burt Bacharach as quoted in Mihai Cucos, 'A Few Points about Burt Bacharach . . .', *Perspectives of New Music* 43, no. 1 (Winter 2005), p. 205.

11. 'objective nationalism': www.newworldencyclopedia.org/entry/Alberto_Ginastera

13. *'consummate drama'* as quoted in Stephen Johnson, *Wagner: His Life and Music* (Naxos Music Books, 2007), p. 145.

14. German text from verse 2 of 'Frühlingslaube' by Johann Ludwig Uhland; English translation by David Gordon, quoted with permission.

15. Chopin as quoted by Herbert Glass in his programme notes for the LA Philharmonic: www.laphil.com/philpedia/music/piano-concerto-no-2-frederic-chopin

16. Mary Pendarves as quoted in Edward Blakeman, *The Faber Pocket Guide to Handel* (Faber and Faber, 2011), p. 277.

17. Composer as quoted in Ezgi Ustundag, 'Meredith Monk brings Ellis Island to Life' on the Duke University website Duke Today (29 October 2012): today.duke.edu/2012/10/monkresidency

18. Lines from the *Stabat mater* translated from the Latin by CBH.

20. Lines from John Dryden, *Oedipus* (1679).
    Dryden as quoted in 'The Epistle Dedicatory' from *Amphitryon: Or, the Two Sosia's. A Comedy. As it is Acted at the Theatre* (George Grierson, 1723).

23. Berlioz as quoted in Gary Taylor and Terri Bourus, 'Why Read Shakespeare's Complete Works?' in *The New Oxford Shakespeare*, edited by Gary Taylor, John Jowett, Terri Bourus and Gabriel Egan (Oxford University Press, 2016), p. 5. *'How sweet the moonlight . . .'* from *The Merchant of Venice*, by William Shakespeare – Lorenzo: Act 5, scene 1, lines 54–57.

26. *'dedicati agli Artisti'* is part of the autograph manuscript; see e.g. chase.leeds.ac.uk/article/paganini-24-capricci-per-il-violino-solo-dedicati-agli-artisti-op-1-robin-stowell/

28. 'Lay a garland . . .' Pearsall's text based on lines from Beaumont and Fletcher's *The Maid's Tragedy* (1619) – Aspasia's Song.

30. Mendelssohn writing to Ferdinand David, 30 July 1838, as quoted in *Letters of Felix Mendelssohn Bartholdy from 1833 to 1847 edited by Paul Mendelssohn Bartholdy and Dr Carl Mendelssohn Bartholdy with a Catalogue of All His Musical Compositions compiled by Dr Julius Rietz*, translated by Lady Wallace (Longman Green, 1863), p. 91.

May

2. Tavener quotes taken from liner notes by Robin Griffith-Jones and John Taverner: www.stephenlayton.com/sites/default/files/server_files/user/vottbooklet.pdf and from the composer's website: johntavener.com/inspiration/the-veils/the-veil-of-the-temple/

5. Maxwell Davies quoted in Tom Service, 'Peter Maxwell Davies at 80: "The music knows things that I don't"', in *Guardian*, 19 August 2014: www.theguardian.com/music/2014/aug/19/peter-maxwell-davies-at-80-interview

7. Schumann quoted in John Rink, 'The Vocal and the Symphonic' in *The Cambridge Companion to Brahms*, edited by Michael Musgrave (Cambridge University Press, 1999), p. 81.

8. Speech given by Prime Minister Winston Churchill to the House of Commons, 20 August 1940: www.churchill-society-london.org.uk/thefew.html
Britten on Walton quoted in Philip Brett, 'Auden's Britten' in *Music and Sexuality in Britten: Selected Essays*, edited by George E. Haggerty (University of California Press, 2006), p. 199.

9. Composer quoted in David Brown, *Tchaikovsky: The Man and his Music* (Faber and Faber, 2010), p. 153.

10. As quoted in David Fanning's liner notes for Hyperion Records (2003): www.hyperion-records.co.uk/dc.asp?dc=D_CDA67425

11. As quoted in Rudi Blesh, *They All Played Ragtime: The True Story of an American Music* (Alfred A. Knopf, 1950, reprinted by Read Books Ltd, 2013), p. 204.

12. Letter from Doctors Calmeil and Ricord to Andrea Donizetti, 31 January 1846, quoted in Herbert Weinstock, *Donizetti and the World of Opera in Italy, Paris and Vienna in the First Half of the Nineteenth Century* (Random House, 1963), p. 247.

15. French text by Jean Racine, translated by CBH.

17. Grieg as quoted in John Bird, *Percy Grainger* (Elek Books, 1976), p. 117.

18. Mahler as quoted on the Gustav Mahler website: www.gustav-mahler.eu/index. php/werken/98-das-lied-von-der-erde-1908/316-introduction
Words by the eighth-century Chinese poet Li T'ai Po, translated by Hans Bethge, in *Die chinesische Flöte*; English translation © Emily Ezust, courtesy of the Lieder Net Archive.
21. Italian text by Ruggero Leoncavallo; English translation by CBH.
26. 'Waitin' text by Arnold Weinstein, *Cabaret Songs*, set 1 (1977–1978).
27. Saint-Saëns as quoted in Tom Service, 'Symphony guide: Saint-Saëns's Third (the Organ symphony), *Guardian*, 25 February 2014: www.theguardian.com/music/ tomserviceblog/2014/feb/25/symphony-guide-saint-Saëns-organ-tom-service
29. Debussy and Saint-Saëns as widely reported, e.g. in Stephen Walsh, *Stravinsky: A Creative Spring: Russia and France, 1882–1934* (University of California Press, 2003), p. 211, and in Lucy Moore, *Nijinsky: A Life* (Profile Books, 2013). Stravinisky as widely quoted, e.g. in Stephen Walsh, *Stravinsky: The Second Exile: France and America, 1934–71* (Jonathan Cape, 2006), p. 478.

June

1. *'laziest student . . .'* as quoted in *Erik Satie: Music, Art and Literature*, edited by Caroline Potter (Routledge, 2013), p. 90.
'untalented' as referenced in Edward Lockspeiser, *Debussy: Volume 1, 1862–1902: His Life and Mind* (Cambridge University Press archive, 1979), p. 145.
'Queen of the Slow Waltz' as referenced in Robert Orledge, *Satie the Composer* (Cambridge University Press, 1990), p. 113.
5. Danish String Quartet as quoted on the website of publisher Edition.S: www. edition-s.dk/composer/the-danish-string-quartet
6. *'Rubens of Russian Music'* as referenced on BBC Radio 3, Composer of the Week: www.bbc.co.uk/programmes/p029s6vw
10. *'Life and death . . .'* as quoted in Lydia Goehr, 'The Curse and Promise of the Absolutely Musical: *Tristan und Isolde* and *Don Giovanni'* in *The Don Giovanni Moment: Essays on the Legacy of an Opera*, edited by Lydia Goehr and Daniel Herwitz (Columbia University Press, 2006), p. 143.
11. German text by John Henry Mackay; English translation© Emily Ezust, courtesy of the Lieder Net Archive.
12. Quoted in Sir Henry Wood, *My Life of Music* (Gollancz, 1938), pp. 147–148.
13. W. B. Yeats, 'Down by the Salley Gardens' quoted in *The Norton Anthology of English Literature*, vol. 2, edited by M. H. Abrams and Stephen Greenblatt (W. W. Norton, 2005), p. 2,024.
14. Excerpts from George Meredith, 'The Lark Ascending', selected by Ralph Vaughan Williams and included as a preface to his original score.
Times critic as quoted in Douglas Lee, *Masterworks of 20th-Century Music: The Modern Repertory of the Symphony Orchestra* (Psychology Press, 2002).

15. 'transcendental as described in the full title of the études.
    Debussy's warning as reported in Dr ToniMarie Marchioni's programme notes for
    the Carnegie Hall: www.carnegiehall.org/ch/popups/programnotes.aspx?id=10737
    418576&pn=10737418575

16. Richard Barnfield, *The Passionate Pilgrim*, sonnet 8, lines 5–6, as quoted in Christopher
    R. Wilson and Michela Calore, *Music in Shakespeare: A Dictionary* (A & C Black, 2005).

17. Composer's words taken from the programme note on his website: davidlangmusic.
    com/music/i-lie
    Yiddish text by Joseph Rolnick; translated by Kristina Boerger.

18. *'ideal interpreter'* as quoted by Steven Isserlis in his programme notes for Hyperion
    Records: www.hyperion-records.co.uk/tw.asp?w=W3653

19. Wagner writing to Liszt, quoted in Edwin Hughes, 'Liszt as Lieder Composer' in
    The Musical Quarterly, vol. 3, no. 3 (Oxford University Press, July 1917), p. 390.

20. Busoni's quote about *'sonorous air'* referenced in Erinn E. Knyt, *Ferruccio Busoni
    and His Legacy* (Indiana University Press, 2017), p. 213.

21. Quote from Shakespeare's *The Merchant of Venice*, Act 4, scene 1, lines 184–189.

23. *'wearying, maddening depression'* Tchaikovsky writing to Nadezhda von Meck, 6
    November 1877, as quoted in *The Life and Letters of Peter Ilich Tchaikovsky*, edited
    by Modeste Tchaikovsky and translated by Rosa Newmarch (Minerva Group,
    2004), p. 229.
    Letter to Modeste, 1876, quoted in Gail Saltz, *Anatomy of a Secret Life: The
    Psychology of Living a Lie* (Morgan Road Books, 2006).
    'Life is beautiful in spite of everything . . .' letter from spring 1870 as quoted in *The
    Life and Letters of Peter Ilich Tchaikovsky*, edited by Modeste Tchaikovsky and
    translated by Rosa Newmarch (Minerva Group, 2004), p. 116.

24. Glenn Gould quoted in *The Glenn Gould Reader*, edited by Glenn Gould and Tim
    Page (Alfred A. Knopf, 1984), p. 438.
    Text attributed to Orlando Gibbons; first published in Gibbons's *First Set of
    Madrigals and Motets of 5 Parts* (1612).

26. *'strong mind in a sound body'* principle referenced in Wikipedia: en.wikipedia.org/
    wiki/Sokol
    Janáček as quoted in James Porter, 'Bartók's *Concerto for Orchestra* (1943) and
    Janáček's *Sinfonietta* (1926): Conceptual and Motivic Parallels' in *Bartók Perspec-
    tives: Man, Composer and Ethnomusicologist*, edited by Elliott Antokoletz, Victoria
    Fischer and Benjamin Suchoff, Oxford University Press (2000), p. 158.

27. John Donne, 'Our Last Awakening' from *A Sermon Preached at White-hall,
    February 29, 1628*, revised and edited by Eric Milner-White (1963).

30. Lines from Wilfred Owen, *The War Poems*, edited by Jon Stallworthy (Chatto and
    Windus, 1994), p. 117.

'*freedom, light and love*' quoted in Tom Service, 'Jonathan Harvey: Touching the Void' in the *Guardian*, 26 January 2012: www.theguardian.com/music/2012/jan/26/jonathan-harvey-not-very-british

July

1. Quoted in Jean-Jaques Rousseau *Dictionnaire de Musique* (Duchesne, 1775), vol.1, p. 376.
   Satie coined the term '*musique d'ameublement*' in 1917 and it was in wide use after 1920; see e.g. Robert Orledge, *Satie the Composer* (Cambridge University Press, 1990), p. 222.

3. Rachmaninov as widely quoted, e.g. in Michael Steinberg, *The Concerto: A Listener's Guide* (Oxford University Press, 1998), p. 369.

7. Musical directions from the score: '*espressivo*' ('expressive'), '*seelenvoll*' ('soulful') and '*mit innigster Empfindung*' ('with the most heartfelt sentiment') – translations CBH. Mengelberg's 'Love! A Smile enters his life' as quoted in Michael Markham, *The New Mythologies: Deep Bach, Saint Mahler and the Death Chaconne, LA Review of Books* 26 October 2013: lareviewofbooks.org/article/the-new-mythologies-deep-bach-saint-mahler-and-the-death-chaconne/

8. Joplin quoted in Philip Clark, 'Scott Joplin's ragtime gets its dues' in *Guardian*, 22 January 2014: www.theguardian.com/music/musicblog/2014/jan/22/scott-joplin-ragtime-josh-rifkin-the-sting

10. Mendelssohn letter quoted in Wolfgang Dinglinger, 'Programme of the Reformation Symphony' as quoted in *The Mendelssohns: Their Music in History* edited by John Michael Cooper and Julie D. Prandi (Oxford University Press, 2002), p 130.

11. Gershwin quoted in 'Gershwin explains why his Porgy and Bess is called "folk opera"' in *The New York Times*, 2 November 1935.

12. Wagner quoted in Michael Sternberg, *The Concerto: A Listener's Guide* (Oxford University Press, 2000), p. 454.

16. All quotes about the dance from Julia Sutton, 'Canary' in *International Encyclopedia of Dance*, edited by Selma Jeanne Cohen (New York: Oxford University Press, 1998), vol. 2, p. 50.

17. Composer in conversation with *The Arts Desk*, 9 March 2015: www.theartsdesk.com/classical-music/10-questions-composer-dobrinka-tabakova

18. *On Beauty* by Zadie Smith (Hamish Hamilton, 2005), p. 69. Copyright © Zadie Smith, 2005. Reproduced by permission of Penguin Books Ltd.

19. Ellington as quoted in *Visions of Jazz: The First Century by Gary Giddins* (Oxford University Press, 2000), p. 103.
    Richard Nixon quoted in Matthew C. Whitaker, *Icons of Black America: Breaking Barriers and Crossing Boundaries* vol.1 (ABC-CLIO, 2011), p. 269.

20. Chopin as quoted by Ates Orga in Hyperion liner notes: www.hyperion-records.co.uk/dc.asp?dc=D_CDH55180

Constantia Gladowska as quoted in 'Au Revoir, Poland' in Michel Steen, *The Lives and Times of the Great Composers* (Icon Books, 2011).

21. Dvořák as quoted in Milan Slavicky, 'String quartet in F major Op. 96, "American"', sleeve notes to *Dvořák: String Quartets (complete)*, Stamitz Quartet. Brilliant Classics No. 99949 (2002).

23. As widely referenced, e.g. in Rory Mulholland, 'The black Mozart', *Guardian*, 12 February 2002: www.theguardian.com/culture/2002/feb/12/artsfeatures.arts
   Alexandre Picard as referenced in Gabriel Banat, *The Chevalier de Saint-Georges: Virtuoso of the Sword and the Bow* (Pendragon Press, 2006), pp. 68–70.

24. In conversation with the author, March 2017.

26. Martin Luther as quoted in 'Defining the Master of the Notes' by Jeffrey Dean in the *Times Literary Supplement*, 7 September 2001: www.the-tls.co.uk/articles/private/defining-the-master-of-the-notes

27. Brahms in a letter to Clara Schumann, June 1877, as quoted in *Letters of Clara Schumann and Johannes Brahms, 1853–1896*, 2 vols, edited by Berthold Litzmann (Hyperion Press, 1979).

31. Clara Schumann as quoted in Grant Hiroshima, LA Philharmonic programme note: www.laphil.com/philpedia/music/sonata-b-minor-franz-liszt-0
   Eduard Hanslick as quoted in Leo Carey 'My Liszt Obsession', *The New Yorker*, 23 October 2013: www.newyorker.com/culture/culture-desk/my-liszt-obsession

August

2. *'outburst of the soul'* quoted in Michael Whorf, *American Popular Song Composers: Oral Histories, 1920s–1950s* (McFarland, 2012), Introduction, p. 9.
   'It is only that which cannot be expressed' from composer's article 'At the Crossroads' in *The Sackbut* (September, 1920), as quoted in *Oxford Treasury of Sayings and Quotations* edited by Susan Ratcliffe (Oxford University Press, 2011), p. 305.

3. As printed in Wolfgang Boettcher, Weiner Urtext Edition of the score, p. vii.

4. German text by Hermann Hesse; English translation © Emily Ezust, courtesy of the Lieder Net Archive.

5. Saint-Saëns as quoted in Brian Rees, *Saint-Saëns: A Life* (Chatto and Windus, 1999), p. 11.

6. Composer in conversation with *BBC Music Magazine*, 2 September 2015: www.classical-music.com/article/eleanor-alberga
   Robert Irvine in conversation and traditional Jamaican lyrics as quoted in the *Herald*, 14 September 2016: www.heraldscotland.com/arts_ents/14740675.Forget_personal_glory__Robert_Irvine_wants_his_music_to_be_useful_/

7. As referenced in Ryan Turner, Emmanuel Music programme note: emmanuel-music.org/notes_translations/notes_motets/n_tallis_if_ye_love_me.htm

8. Composer quoted on score (Boosey & Hawkes, 1995): www.boosey.com/cr/music/Steve-Reich-Duet/4730

Composer in interview with Joshua Klein, Pitchfork, 22 November 2006: pitchfork.com/features/interview/6490-steve-reich/

9. Composer quoted in 'The Chopin Project' by Jonathan Frahm, Popmatters, 2 April 2015: www.popmatters.com/review/191703-lafur-arnalds-alice-sara-ott-the-choping-project/

12. John Cage in 'Defense of Satie' (1948) as quoted in 'The Intent of the Musical Moment' in *Writings through John Cage's Music, Poetry, and Art*, edited by David W. Bernstein and Christopher Hatch (University of Chicago, 2010), p. 105.
'I wanted to mean it' as quoted in John Cage, 'The Roaring Silence' in *A Life by David Revill* (Skyhorse, 2012), chapter 12, part 2.
'purposeless play' as quoted in John Cage, *Silence: Lectures and Writings* (Wesleyan University Press, 1973; first edition 1961), chapter 11.

13. Mengelberg's *'Love! A Smile enters his life'* as quoted in Michael Markham, *The New Mythologies: Deep Bach, Saint Mahler and the Death Chaconne*, LA Review of Books, 26 October 2013: lareviewofbooks.org/article/the-new-mythologies-deep-bach-saint-mahler-and-the-death-chaconne

14. As quoted in Maurice Hinson *Music for More than One Piano: An Annotated Guide* (Indiana University Press, 2001), p. 73.

17. *'consciously* postmodern *idiom'* as quoted by Michael Jameson on the website AllMusic: www.allmusic.com/composition/sonata-for-violin-solo-no-2-in-a-minor-obsession-op-27-2-mc0002407719

19. Casals as quoted in Yale School of Music online resources: music.yale.edu/tag/enescu/
Enescu as quoted in Dominic Saunders, 'The Mozart we Missed', *Guardian*, 25 October 2002: www.theguardian.com/music/2002/oct/25/classicalmusicandopera.artsfeatures
Menuhin in conversation with the author, December 1996.

20. Scene from *The Seven Year Itch*, directed by Billy Wilder, written by George Axelrod and Billy Wilder, produced by Billy Wilder, Charles K. Feldman and Doane Harrison (1955), as referenced in Ellen Tremper, *I'm No Angel: The Blonde in Fiction and Film* (University of Virginia Press, 2006), p. 212.

21. Composer as quoted in Jack Sullivan, *New World Symphonies: How American Culture Changed European Music* (Yale University Press, 1999), p. 149.

22. French text by Henri Meilhac and Ludovic Halévy; English translation by CBH.

23. Listener George Moore to Maud Cunard, 1916, as quoted by Alex Ross in the blogpost 'In praise of Debussy' on his website, 28 April 2011: www.therestisnoise.com/2011/04/in-praise-of-debussy.html
'imbecilic' as referenced by Nigel Simeone, 'Debussy and expression' in *The Cambridge Companion to Debussy*, edited by Simon Trezise (Cambridge University Press, 2003), p. 102.

26. Nico Muhly as quoted in Alex Ross, 'The Long Haul', *The New Yorker*, 28 November 2011: www.newyorker.com/magazine/2011/11/28/the-long-haul
'*slow food*', Nico Muhly in the *New York Times*, 1 April 2017: www.nytimes.com/2017/04/01/arts/music/nico-muhly-andrew-gant.html
'*hypnotically calm*', composer in conversation with the author, 2017.

27. Elgar as quoted in Jack Sullivan, *New World Symphonies: How American Culture Changed European Music* (Yale University Press, 1999), p. 55.
Coleridge-Taylor as quoted in 'Pan-Africanism, race and the USA' on Samuel Coleridge-Taylor in 'Black Europeans', British Library Online Gallery: www.bl.uk/black-europeans/articles/samuel-coleridge-taylor

28. Savall's words taken from his sleeve notes to *The Routes of Slavery* for Hespèrion XXI: Alia Vox AVSA9920

30. Dvořák as quoted in Peter Laki, programme note, 16 March 2015: www.purdue.edu/convocations/program-notes-academy-of-st-martin-in-the-fields-with-jeremy-denk-piano/

31. Granados letter, 31 August 1910, as quoted in Ates Orga, Hyperion liner note: www.hyperion-records.co.uk/dc.asp?dc=D_SIGCD146
'*gorgeous treat*' Ernest Newman, quoted in Orrin Howard, LA Philharmonic programme note: www.laphil.com/philpedia/music/goyescas-h64-no-1-los-requiebros-enrique-granados

September

1. Mary Coleridge (1861–1907), 'L'Oiseau bleu', *Poems*, no. 52 (1907).

3. Lines from Virgil, *The Aeneid*, translated by John Dryden (1697).
John Cage quoted in Michael Nyman, *Experimental Music: Cage and Beyond* (Cambridge University Press, 1999), p. 35.

5. Mozart letter quoted in Herbert Glass's programme note for the LA Philharmonic: www.laphil.com/philpedia/music/clarinet-quintet-major-k-581-wolfgang-amadeus-mozart

6. Sebastién de Brossard as quoted in 'Women Composers in Italy' in *Women Making Music: The Western Art Tradition, 1150–1950*, edited by Jane M. Bowers and Judith Tick (University of Illinois, 1987) p. 141.

7. '*map of Brazil*' widely quoted e.g. in Eero Tarasti, *Heitor Villa-Lobos: The Life and Works, 1887–1959* (McFarland, 1995), p. 39.

8. Simrock as quoted on the official Dvořák website: www.antonin-dvorak.cz/en/piano-quartet2
Dvořák letter as quoted in James Keller, *Chamber Music: A Listener's Guide* (Oxford University Press, 2010), p. 176.

9. Italian text by Aurelio Aureli. English translation by CBH.

10. Pejačević letter as quoted in the Maud Powell Society newsletter: www.maudpowell.org/signature/Portals/0/pdfs/New%20Articles/Dora%20Pejacevic%20for%20Signature.pdf

11. Composer as quoted on WQXR website: www.wqxr.org/story/154627-robert-moran-trinity-requiem/

12. Schumann as quoted in Eric Frederick Jensen, *Schumann* (Oxford University Press, 2012), p. 34.

13. Schoenberg as quoted on the official Arnold Schoenberg Centre website: www.schoenberg.at/index.php/en/the-news-2/scherzo-f-dur-fuer-streichquartett

15. Webern as quoted in Richard Dettmer on the website AllMusic: www.allmusic.com/composition/langsamer-satz-slow-movement-for-string-quartet-mc0002369041
    'cultural Bolshevism' as referenced in Lucy Miller Murray, *Chamber Music: An Extensive Guide for Listeners* (Rowman & Littlefield, 2015), p. 414.
    'degenerate art' as referenced in Frank Northern Magill, *Dictionary of World Biography: The 20th Century, O–Z* (Routledge, 1999), p. 3, 916.

17. Bach's note from the title page of the first edition of the 'Goldberg' Variations, published by Schmid, 1714, as sourced in Ralph Kirkpatrick's edition of this work (G. Schirmer, 1938).
    'prepared for the soul's delight' as quoted in Peter Williams, *Bach: The Goldberg Variations* (Cambridge University Press, 2001), p. 3.

18. Translated from the Italian by CBH.

20. Composer as quoted in Erik Tawaststjerna, *Sibelius: 1865–1905* (University of California Press, 1976), vol. 1, p. 20.

23. Verdi as quoted in Carolyn Abbate and Roger Parker, *A History of Opera: The Last Four Hundred Years* (Penguin, 2012).
    Italian text by Felice Romani; English translation by CBH.

24. Thomas Adès as quoted in Howard Posner, LA Philharmonic programme notes: www.laphil.com/tickets/baroque-ades-amp-couperin/2008-05-21
    'Couperin the Great' as referenced in Encyclopaedia Britannica: www.britannica.com/biography/Francois-Couperin-French-composer-1668-1733

25. *'fundamental law'* as noted in e.g. Graham Sadler (ed.), *The New Grove French Baroque Masters* (Grove/Macmillan, 1988), p. 278.
    'the Isaac Newton of music' as referenced in 'Rousseau: Music, Language and Politics' by Tracy B. Strong in *Speaking of Music: Addressing the Sonorous*, edited by Keith Chapin and Andrew H. Clark (Fordham University Press, 2013), p. 88.
    Alexis Piron quoted in Jean Malignon, *Rameau* (Seuil, 1960), p. 16.

26. Schubert as quoted in Jack Adler, *Soulmates from the Pages of History: From Mythical to Contemporary, 75 Examples of the Power of Friendship* (Algora, 2013), p. 135.
    German text by Friedrich Rückert; English translation by Lynn Thompson.

27. *'very shy, but full of poetry'* as quoted in Diana McVeagh, *Gerald Finzi: His Life and Music* (Boydell and Brewer, 2010), p. 9.

29. Composer quoted on Howard Goodall website: www.howardgoodall.co.uk/works/other-works/and-the-bridge-is-love

Thornton Wilder, *The Bridge of San Luis Rey* (Boni & Liveright, 1927).

30. French libretto by Michel Carré and Eugène Cormon; translated by CBH.

October

1. '*little Mozart*', '*Bourgeois girls . . .*' and '*Women have not been considered . . .*' as quoted in Thea Dark *I Care If You Listen* online magazine, 1 October 2012 www. icareifyoulisten.com/2012/10/french-composers-names-cecile-chaminade Ambroise Thomas quoted in Hyperion liner notes by Nigel Simeone, 2017 www.hyperion-records.co.uk/c.asp?c=C122

2. Max Bruch as quoted in *All These Vows: Kol Nidre*, edited by Lawrence A. Hoffman (Jewish Lights Publishing, 2011), p. 61.

3. '*I appear at times merry*', Hugo Wolf as quoted in Kay Redfield Jamison, *Touched with Fire* (Simon and Schuster, 1996), p. 21.
   '*objective lyricist*', '*duty to the poet*' and '*true content*' quoted in Amanda Glauert, *BBC Music Magazine* website www.classical-music.com/topic/hugo-wolf
   German text by Eduard Mörike; English translation © Emily Ezust, courtesy of the Lieder Net Archive.

4. Nicholas Cords quoted in Carnegie Hall programme note: www.carnegiehall.org/ ch/popups/programnotes.aspx?id=1728&pn=1726

6. '*knocked sideways*' as quoted in John Bridcut, *Essential Britten: A Pocket Guide for the Britten Centenary* (Faber and Faber, 2012).
   Percy Bysshe Shelley (1792–1822), 'Autumn: A Dirge', appears in *Posthumous Poems* (1824).

9. Rautavaara quoted in Jonathan Buckley, *The Rough Guide to Classical Music* (Dorling Kindersley, 2010), p. 440.

11. Bruckner as quoted by Eric Levi in Hyperion liner notes, 2015: www.hyperion-records.co.uk/dc.asp?dc=D_SIGCD431
   '*farewell to life*' as referenced in *The Cambridge Companion to Bruckner*, edited by John Williamson (Cambridge University Press, 2004) p. 115.

12. Pola Beytelman, *Isaac Albeniz: Chronological list and thematic catalog of his piano works* (Harmonic Para Press, 1993).

14. Puccini as quoted in David R. B. Kimbell, *Italian Opera* (Cambridge University Press, 2004), p. 586.

15. 'Love (III)' by George Herbert (1593–1633) www.musicsalesclassical.com/ composer/work/1689/2741

18. '*asparagus*' as quoted in Sergei Bertensson, Jay Leyda and Sophie Satin, *Sergei Rachmaninoff: A Lifetime in Music* (Indiana University Press, 2001), p. 191.
   '*I started work on it . . .*' as quoted by Ivan Moody in Hyperion liner notes, 1994: www.hyperion-records.co.uk/dc.asp?dc=D_CDH55318

19. '*she watched the* Watership Down *footage*' Sarah Wooley quoted in article by Adam Sherwin, *Independent*, 28 November 2015 www.independent.co.uk/arts-

entertainment/tv/news/1977-story-of-transgender-pioneer-angela-morley-to-be-broadcast-on-bbc-radio-4-a6752956.html

20. As quoted on composer's website: www.cherylfranceshoad.co.uk/bio

22. 'Mademoiselle' a nickname widely known, see e.g. Mademoiselle – Conversations with Nadia Boulanger by Bruno Monsaingeon, Carcanet (1985).
'advice' as quoted in 'Boulanger as Teacher' in Ned Rorem, 'The Composer and the Music Teacher', *New York Times*, 23 May 1982: nytimes.com/1982/05/23/books/the-composer-and-the-music-teacher.html
'your music' as widely quoted, e.g. in DeNeen Brown, 'When Quincy Jones teaches, he starts with the classics', *Washington Post*, 14 November 2010: www.washingtonpost.com/wp-dyn/content/article/2010/11/12/AR2010111200154.html

24. As quoted in Cecilia Bartoli, 'Genius, Scandal and Death: Maria – Singer and Diva' in *Maria*, Decca Music Group CD/DVD (2007).

25. Sally Beamish as quoted in 'How the theft of my viola turned me into a composer', *Guardian*, 25 August 2016: www.theguardian.com/music/2016/aug/25/viola-theft-composer-sally-beamish-proms-merula-perpetua
'expression of our grief' taken from the composer's website: www.sallybeamish.com/pid/771/info.html

28. As quoted in Herbert Glass, LA Philharmonic programme notes: www.laphil.com/philpedia/music/moldau-bedrich-smetana

29. Koussevitsky as quoted in *BBC Music Magazine*: www.classical-music.com/topic/george-gershwin-0
Gershwin as quoted in 'George Gershwin and Jazz' in *The Gershwin Style: New Looks at the Music of George Gershwin* edited by Wayne Joseph Schneider (Oxford University Press, 1999), p. 185.

30. 'The Dance', from *The Complete Poems of Hart Crane* by Hart Crane, edited by Marc Simon. Copyright 1933, 1958, 1966 by Liveright Publishing Corporation. Copyright © 1986 Marc Simon. Used by permission of Liveright Publishing Corporation.

November

1. Anthem objective as quoted on European Union website: europa.eu/european-union/about-eu/symbols/anthem_en Schiller
'celebration of the brotherhood of man' widely quoted e.g. in *Anthems and the Making of Nation States: Identity and Nationalism in the Balkans*, edited by Aleksandar Pavkovi and Christopher Kelen, (I.B. Tauris, 2015).
Merkel aide as quoted by Bryony Jones on CNN.com, 7 July 2017: edition.cnn.com/2017/07/07/europe/ode-to-joy-beethoven-g20-merkel-trump/index.html
German text by Friedrich Schiller; English translation by CBH.

2. Job vii, 16; English translation by CBH.

3. Composer as quoted in interview with Erin Lyndal Martin, *Popmatters*, 21 April 2013: www.popmatters.com/feature/170322-really-wanted-break-peoples-expectations-interview-olafur-arnalds/

4. *'codfish'* widely quoted e.g. in John Lloyd and John Mitchinson, *QI: Advanced Banter* (Faber and Faber, 2008).

6. Composer as quoted in 'The Liberation of Sound', by Edgard Varèse, and Wen-chung Chou, *Perspectives of New Music 5*, no. 1 (Autumn–Winter 1966), pp. 11–19.

8. Franck, *'arouses me in'* from R. J. Stove, 'Franck after Franck: The Composer's Posthumous Fortunes', *Musical Times*, Spring 2011.
   Saint-Saëns, *'This beautiful pythoness'*, from *New York Times*, 1 February 1903, p.14.
   'Quintet of Discontent: César Franck and Augusta Holmès on the website Interlude: www.interlude.hk/front/quintet-of-discontent

9. Olga Rostropovich interviewed by the BBC World Service, twenty-five years after the fall of the Berlin Wall: soundcloud.com/bbc-world-service/rostropovich-and-the-berlin-wall-25-years-on

13. Rachmaninov widely quoted, e.g. in The Schubert Club programme, April 13–June 2, 2014: issuu.com/schubertclub/docs/an_die_musik_apr13-june2
    Medtner on Beethoven as quoted in Charles William Keller, *The Piano Sonatas of Nicolas Medtner* (PhD dissertation, Ohio State University, 1971), pp. 5–6.

15. Mahler as quoted in Stephen E. Hefling, *Song of the Earth* (Cambridge University Press, 2000), Preface, p. x.
    Mahler's programme as quoted on Philharmonia website: www.philharmonia.co.uk/explore/repertoire/252/mahler-symphonyno_2-resurrection

17. Villa Lobos as quoted on the website AllMusic: www.allmusic.com/composition/bachianas-brasileiras-no-5-for-voice-8-cellos-a-389-mc0002433953
    Portuguese text by Ruth Valadares Corrêa; English translation by Laura Claycomb, courtesy of Lieder Net Archive.

18. Composer quoted in Thomas Adès and Tom Service, *Thomas Adès: Full of Noises: Conversations with Tom Service* (Faber and Faber, 2012).

19. John Evelyn as quoted in Margaret Campbell, *The Great Violinists* (Faber and Faber, 2011).

20. Composer quoted in conversation about childhood influences and divergent identities with Huw Rhys James (1999) on his website: www.paramvir.net/about/interview-with-huw-rhys-james-1999/
    Composer in conversation about chakras and colour with Jonathan Reekie (2000): www.paramvir.net/about/interview-with-jonathan-reekie-2000

22. Boosey & Hawkes score www.boosey.com/cr/music/Benjamin-Britten-Hymn-to-St-Cecilia-choral-version/4822&langid=1

23. Manuel de Falla as widely quoted, e.g. in Nelson R. Orringer, *Lorca in Tune with Falla: Literacy and Musical Interludes* (University of Toronto Press, 2014), p. 66.

24. Composer as quoted in Alfred Schnittke, *A Schnittke Reader* (Indiana University Press, 2002), Introduction, p. xiv.
    'puberty rites of serial self-denial' as widely quoted e.g. in *Gramophone* magazine, 2008.

'*fell in love with music*' as quoted in Alexander Ivashkin, *Alfred Schnittke* (Phaidon Press, 1996), p. 32.

'*mystery is* truly *limitless*' as quoted in Alfred Schnittke, *A Schnittke Reader* (Indiana University Press, 2002), p. 8.

26. Composer quoted on publisher's website: www.boosey.com/cr/music/Steve-Reich-Music-for-Pieces-of-Wood/102362

    Description as per Jeremy Grimshaw on the website AllMusic: www.allmusic.com/composition/music-for-pieces-of-wood-for-5-pairs-of-tuned-claves-mc0002370366

27. English text by Gustav Holst, published as part of his translations to Choral Hymns from the Rig Veda Group 3, H. 99, p. 26, no. 3.

28. Schumann as quoted in Maurice Hinson, *Guide to the Pianist's Repertoire*, 3rd ed. (Indiana University Press, 2001), p. 195.

29. Jan Swafford as quoted on NPR's *Milestones of the Millennium*, part of the Performance Today series: www.npr.org/programs/specials/milestones/990519.motm.monteverdi.html

    Italian text by Giovanni Francesco Busenello; English translation by Amber Sainsbury.

December

1. '*composing refuge*' quoted from the composer's website: www.mortenlauridsen.net/WaldronIsland.html

   Latin translation of *O Magnum Mysterium* by Lucinda Nicholson.

2. French text by Ferdinand Lemaire; English translation by CBH.

4. '*I worked unsuccessfully*' Tchaikovsky in a letter to Anatolii Tchaikovsky, 2/14–4/16 March 1878 (Letter 776), quoted in Modeste Tchaikovsky, *The Life and Letters of Tchaikovsky*, p. 116.

   '*How lovingly*' quoted in David Brown, *Tchaikovsky: The Crisis Years, 1874–1878* (New York: W. W. Norton and Company, 1983), p. 261.

5. Berlioz quoted by David Cairns in *Berlioz: Volume One: The Making of an Artist, 1803–1832* (University of California Press, 2003).

   Michael Rose, *Berlioz Remembered* (Faber and Faber, 2001).

6. Composer's words taken from his website: www.ericwhitacre.com/music-catalog/satb-choral/lux-aurumque

8. Private interview with author, July 2017.

12. Composer as quoted in article by Christopher Lambton, *Daily Telegraph*, 15 March 1997: www.telegraph.co.uk/culture/4707901/Playing-for-victory.html

    Lyrics from *Divine Hymns, or Spiritual Songs*, compiled by Joshua Smith (New Hampshire, 1784).

14. Graham Ross quoted from private interview with author.

    www.sjcchoir.co.uk/listen/sjc-live/mouton-j-nesciens-mater-virgo-virum

    English translation by Jamie Hawkey.

15. Miloš Karadaglić as quoted in Adam Sweeting, 'Miloš Karadaglić a guitar lesson from the classical maestro', *Telegraph*, 13 June 2012: www.telegraph.co.uk/culture/music/classicalmusic/9330165/Milos-Karadaglic-a-guitar-lesson-from-the-classical-maestro.html

17. Lines from 'The Return' by Anna Akhmatova (1944); English translation by Stanley Kunitz and Max Hayward.
Mark Wigglesworth's words taken from his website: www.markwigglesworth.com/notes/marks-notes-on-shostakovich-symphony-nos-5-6-10/

18. Composer's words taken from his programme note (2004), as quoted on the website Music Sales Classical: www.musicsalesclassical.com/composer/work/11167
'The Lamb', *The Complete Poetry and Prose of William Blake*, edited by David E. Erdman (Anchor Books, 1988).

19. Carlos quoted from composer's own website: www.wendycarlos.com/
'Moog' referenced in Natasha Macdonald-Dupuis, 'Wendy Carlos: Godmother of Electronic Muisc and Badass Trans Woman', 11 August 2015: thump.vice.com/en_au/article/53agdb/wendy-carlos-godmother-of-electronic-music-and-badass-trans-woman

20. Composer as referenced in David Lister, *Independent*, 29 March 1998: www.independent.co.uk/voices/an-artist-in-the-garden-michael-berkeley-profile-1153074.html

21. From the original sleeve notes by Irving Townsend for Columbia Records, 1960.

22. Composer as quoted in Andrew Green, Hyperion liner notes, 2001: www.hyperion-records.co.uk/dw.asp?dc=W4109_GBAJY0124505
John Rutter's text, based on a seventeenth-century Christmas carol by Robert Herrick.

23. German text by Adelheid Wette.

24. Cosima's diaries as quoted in 'Happy Christmas dear Cosima' in *Gramophone* magazine: www.gramophone.co.uk/editorial/happy-christmas-dear-cosima

25. English translation © Pamela Dellal, courtesy Emmanuel Music Inc.

26. French composer André Grétry quoted in Barry S. Brook, 'Pergolesi: Research, publication and performance' in *Pergolesi Studies*, vol. 1, edited by Francesco Degrada (Pendragon, 1986), p. 3.

29. Composer as quoted in official Polish Culture website: culture.pl/en/artist/wojciech-kilar

30. Lines by H. F. Chorley from 'The Long Day Closes' taken from The Gilbert and Sullivan Archive: www.gsarchive.net/sullivan/part_songs/long_day.html

Index